IMAGES
of America

WHITING AND ROBERTSDALE

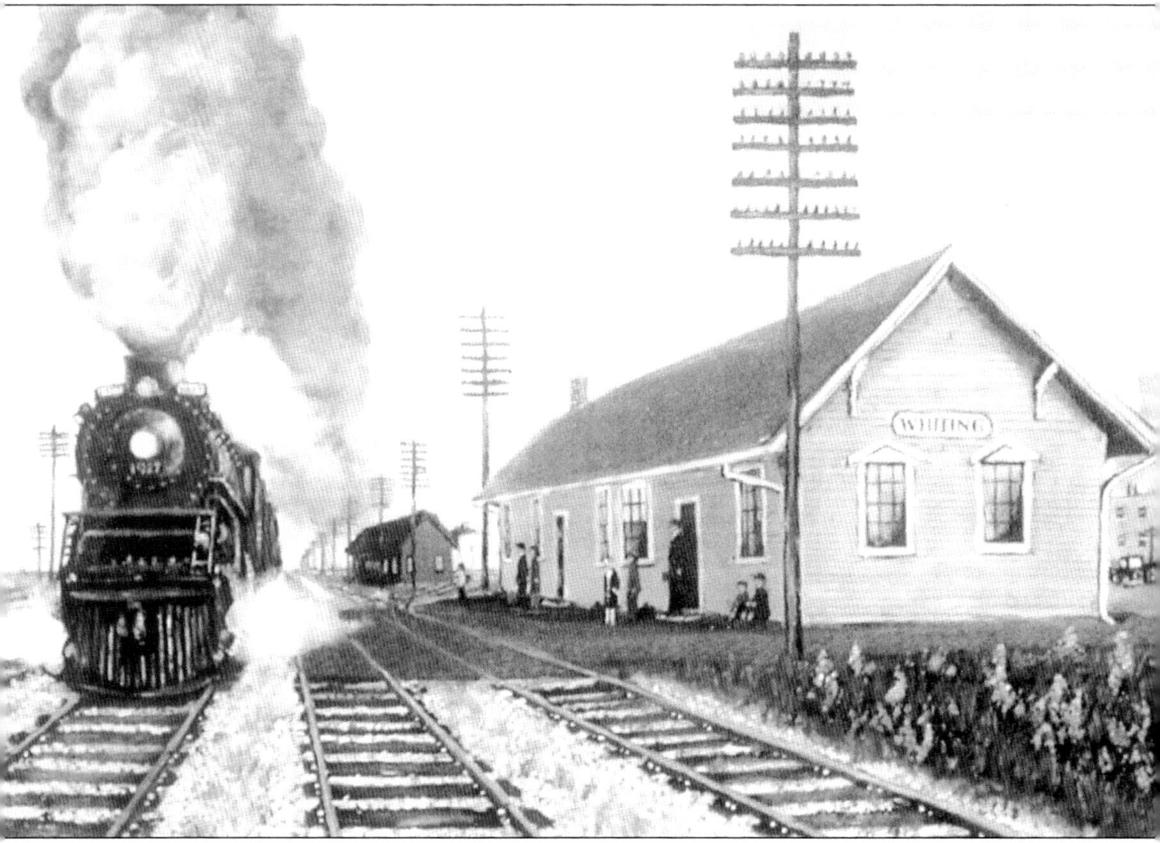

In this artistic rendering, Whiting resident Al Odlivak memorializes a train depot where many immigrants arrived in Whiting with few belongings, a fear of the unknown, and a great deal of hope for the future. Odlivak, often referred to as "Whiting's own Norman Rockwell," was masterful at evoking emotion and nostalgia that cannot be explained with mere words. (Odlivak family.)

ON THE COVER: One of the most popular and long-standing traditions in Whiting-Robertsdale is the annual Fourth of July parade. On the cover is a patriotic float entered by Whiting's American Legion Post No. 80 in the 1940s as it passes in front of the crowd gathered along 119th Street. The storefront in the background is Indiana Plumbing and Supply Company, which was owned by Max Sherman and located at the corner of 119th Street and Central Avenue. (Whiting Historical Society.)

IMAGES
of America

WHITING AND ROBERTSDALE

Kimberly Eck and Jennifer Linko

ARCADIA
PUBLISHING

ISBN 978-0-7385-9861-1

Published by Arcadia Publishing
Charleston, South Carolina

Printed in the United States of America

Library of Congress Control Number: 2012955336

For all general information, please contact Arcadia Publishing:
Telephone 843-853-2070
Fax 843-853-0044
E-mail sales@arcadiapublishing.com
For customer service and orders:
Toll-Free 1-888-313-2665

Visit us on the Internet at www.arcadiapublishing.com

This book is dedicated to the memory of our beloved ancestors who toiled and sacrificed to build a place for us to call home.

Contents

ACKNOWLEDGMENTS

The creation of this book has been a wonderful journey that has allowed us to reminisce with family, reconnect with old friends, and establish new relationships. The common bond we all share is a love and appreciation of Whiting and Robertsdale, and it has been a pleasure learning more about the community through their memories and photographs.

We would like to thank the following members of the Whiting community who were particularly helpful to us as we searched for photographs and information to tell the best stories about Whiting: Gayle Faulkner Kosalko, Jim and Carole Vrabel, Carol Jacobson, and Jim Sandrick.

New friends we met along the way who provided wonderful photographs and stories include Joe Coates, Joe Macak, Milan Matuska, Peggy Koval, Anthony Borgo, Elaine Gehring, Dolores Paunicka Callahan, Kathy Winsberg, Bill Harbour, Bill and Judy Sunderman, Robert Fasiang, Al Odlivak, Marie Jean Mulholland, Cynthia Jackson, and Karen Holmes.

These longtime friends were also a wonderful source of information for us and provided the encouragement that kept us going: David Mores, Gerri and Farmer Householder, Suzy Culbertson, Ben and Joann Saliga, Karen and Victor Garcia, Donald Poppen, and Barbara Boncela Devitt.

We would also like to thank Arcadia Publishing for accepting our proposal for this book and Sandy Shalton, our acquisitions editor, who was tremendously encouraging and understanding throughout the entire project.

Lastly, we would like to thank our families who provided the inspiration for this book, starting with our grandparents John and Anna Tkach and our parents—Gerald and Nancy Tatarek and Edward and Rosemary Domasica. Additionally, we would like to thank Greg Domasica, Ruth Tkach, Mike Domasica, Barbara Detloff, Fran and Gloria Lentvorsky, Lori Lentvorsky, Paul and Anna Baran, and John and Mickey Tkach for their contributions to this project.

And, of course, we would like to thank our immediate family members, especially Mike Eck and Luke Linko, for all of their support and encouragement during this project. Without their assistance, patience, and understanding, this project would not have been possible.

Introduction

The communities of Whiting and Robertsdale are part of what is known as the Calumet Region in the northwestern corner of Indiana. Located just a few miles east of Chicago across the Indiana-Illinois state line, it is considered part of the greater Chicagoland area, and much of its history can be attributed to its proximity to Chicago. The Calumet Region consists of the northern portions of Lake and Porter Counties in Indiana and includes the cities of Whiting, Hammond, East Chicago, and Gary. The Grand Calumet and the Little Calumet Rivers flow through the region and are part of the inland waterway system connected to Lake Michigan.

With all of the industry that now dominates the Calumet Region, it is hard to imagine that it was once home to rolling sand dunes and thick marshes that provided shelter to many types of flora and fauna along the shores of Lake Michigan and its shallow inland lakes.

Pheasants, ducks, turkeys, foxes, minks, frogs, and fish were abundant along the lakeshore, and by the 1830s, the area had become a popular hunting and fishing destination, attracting many Chicago residents looking for a retreat from the city. As interest in the area began to increase, inns and hunting lodges began to spring up. One of the earliest lodges in the Whiting area was opened by Hannah Berry near Berry Lake in 1834, and one of the most magnificent was the Berry Lake Lodge, built by Henry Eggers.

Travel along the sand dunes and through the waterways was difficult, but early settlers found ways to overcome the challenges and took advantage of the natural resources the land provided. They harvested ice from the inland lakes, sand from the dunes, and logs from the forested areas and shipped their products to the Chicago marketplace. The local woods also produced an abundance of several types of berries that were packed in barrels and sold in Chicago as well.

In the early 1850s, the area was still sparsely populated—fewer than 100 people lived north of the Little Calumet River in Lake County—and swampland in the area was being sold for $1.25 an acre. The relatively low price appealed to several enterprising immigrants and prosperous land investors, who began to buy up all of the available land. These early land purchasers eventually became common household names in the Whiting-Robertsdale community: Roberts, Forsythe, Schrage, Eggers, Vater, Atchison, and Reese, to name a few.

The problem of transportation through the swamplands was solved when the railroads began building their tracks to Chicago during the 1850s. The need for railroad workers attracted German and Irish immigrants, who were able to purchase plots of land at reasonable prices and began establishing small family settlements.

The railroads became the catalyst that would transform the land of thick marshes and sand dunes into one of the largest industrial areas in the world. They were also the source of the names for both Whiting and Robertsdale.

When George Roberts, the largest landowner in the area, donated a right-of-way through his land to the Pennsylvania Railroad, the railroad gave the name Robertsdale to the station it built there in his honor. In 1869, an engineer in charge of a freight train ditched the train near what is now Whiting Park in an attempt to avoid an accident with an oncoming passenger train. Following the incident, the railroad built a sidetrack at the site to avoid future collisions and named it Whiting's Siding after the engineer, Herbert L. "Pop" Whiting.

Until 1889, the Whiting community was a quiet little settlement. Residents relied either on the natural resources of the land or worked on the railroads. Children received a rudimentary education in a tiny schoolhouse in Robertsdale. Everything changed dramatically, however, when the Standard Oil Company arrived to begin construction on an oil refinery on land it had been secretly purchasing for months beforehand.

Construction of the refinery began in May 1889, and the Standard Oil Company of Indiana was incorporated a month later. Experienced construction workers were brought to the area from other Standard Oil refineries to supervise the 1,500 laborers who went to work building it.

Because much of the initial planning and land purchases had been done in secrecy, the local townspeople were surprised when the heavy construction began. Some soon found employment at the refinery, while others opened various businesses to serve the needs and wants of the growing population. Property values soared, and some people sold portions of their land at a substantial profit. Others chose to build rental properties to house the newcomers.

As Whiting began to grow, it took on the atmosphere of a frontier town, complete with several saloons, wooden sidewalks, small stores, and multiple boardinghouses.

The initial construction of the refinery was completed in the summer of 1890, and in September, fires were started under the stills. On Thanksgiving Day, the first shipment of kerosene left the Whiting refinery for the marketplace.

Before construction of the refinery began, Whiting was too small to be incorporated as a town, so it credits its founding date to the arrival of Standard Oil Company in 1889, and anniversary celebrations are based on that year. Whiting was officially incorporated as a town in 1893 and as a city in 1903.

The thin strip of land between Whiting and the Illinois state line known as Robertsdale became home to the overflow of people who had come to work at the refinery. Even though it was annexed by Hammond in 1897, Robertsdale became inextricably connected to Whiting, sharing schools, churches, a zip code, and eventually, a chamber of commerce.

In the extreme northwestern corner of Indiana, near the Illinois state line, was a small area known as Roby, named for Edward H. Roby, who had purchased the land from Caroline Forsythe in 1873. The area had become infamous for its exciting, and often illegal, activities, which attracted large numbers of thrill-seekers from Illinois and Indiana. Gambling, horse racing, and prizefighting were among the activities that took place there until around 1905. Roby was also annexed by Hammond in 1897 and has since been absorbed by Robertsdale.

Whiting-Robertsdale experienced rapid growth in the early years after its founding. In 1880, the Census Bureau recorded a population of 115 for Whiting; by 1900, the population had reached nearly 4,000. Despite the many challenges presented by the rapid growth, Whiting-Robertsdale grew to become a close-knit community rich in traditions and varied ethnic backgrounds.

This book pays tribute to all those who contributed to the development of the community and who taught future generations about work ethic, commitment, faith, hospitality, generosity, and perseverance, all of which continue to thrive in Whiting-Robertsdale to this day. The photographs in the following pages are intended to illustrate the daily activities of the people—how they worked, how they raised their families, what they did for enjoyment, and how they celebrated their accomplishments—and to highlight the wonderful melting pot that is the result.

One

Making History

The initial construction and operation of the Whiting oil refinery created thousands of new jobs. Many workers came from Standard Oil companies already established in Ohio and Pennsylvania, and many more were immigrants new to the United States in search of promising opportunities.

The thousands of new residents who arrived to fill the jobs created a huge demand for housing as well as other goods and services. Some of the earliest settlers already established in the area were positioned to meet those needs, and many opened stores and businesses that were instrumental in building the community.

While Standard Oil had quickly built one of the largest refineries in the world, it faced challenges early on with the quality of its products. Chemists and researchers were brought to Whiting to solve the problems, and some of the most important discoveries in the oil industry took place at the Whiting refinery.

Initially, kerosene was the dominant product of the Whiting refinery, and gasoline was considered a waste product. The earliest challenge with refinery production was to eliminate the sour sulphur smell from the crude oil that was being piped in from Lima, Ohio. Dr. William Burton went to work to solve that problem in the 1890s. The next challenge was to find a way to increase the yield of gasoline from crude oil. In 1909, at a still in Whiting, Dr. Robert E. Humphreys revolutionized the petroleum industry when he developed the thermal cracking process.

Realizing the need to build a comfortable and productive community for its employees, Standard Oil sponsored community events, provided land for schools and libraries, and presented Whiting with the gift of a community center that provided recreational facilities and activities.

The strong work ethic of the immigrant workers partnered well with the ambitious goals and objectives of the Whiting refinery. This partnership resulted in a refinery that contributed much to the world and created an environment where people had stable employment, saved money, built homes, and raised their families with a sense of security. The company, the community, and the citizens prospered.

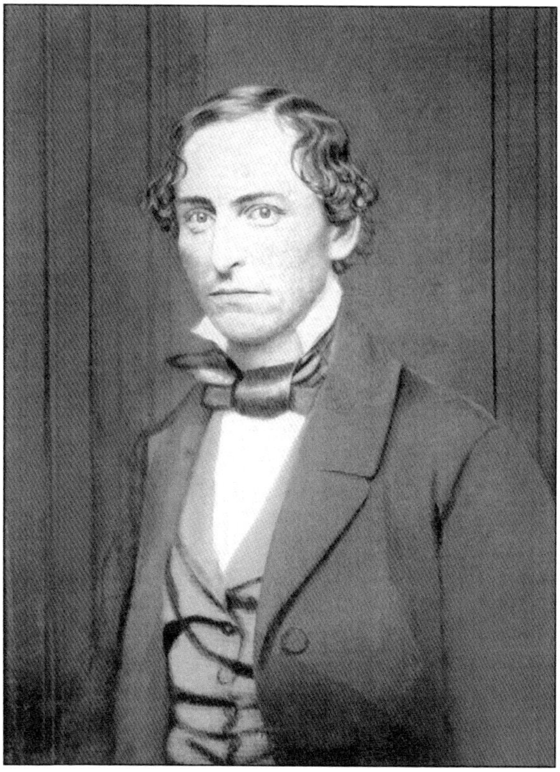

Herbert "Pop" Whiting was a railroad engineer who ditched his freight train to avoid an accident with a fast-moving passenger train in 1869 near what is now Whiting Park. Soon afterward, the railroad put in a sidetrack at the site and named it Whiting's Siding. The Standard Oil Company eventually shortened the station name to Whiting when it decided to build its refinery there. (Whiting Public Library.)

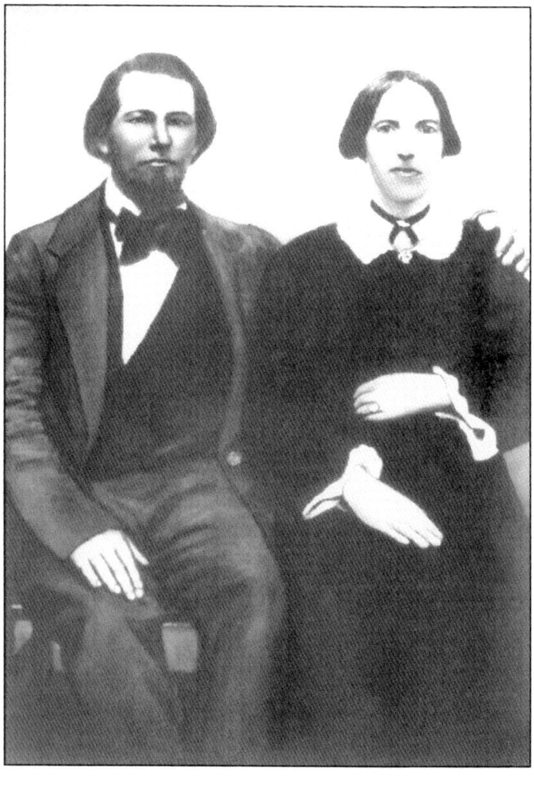

The Vater and Eggers families were among the earliest settlers in the Whiting area and established one of the area's first industries, harvesting ice from Berry Lake. In addition to their business ventures, the families were joined by the marriage of John Friedrich Karl Vater and Georgina Augusta Eggers, seen here. To further forge the family relationship, Georgina's brother, Heinrich Eggers, married Vater's sister, Amelia. (Judy Vater Sunderman.)

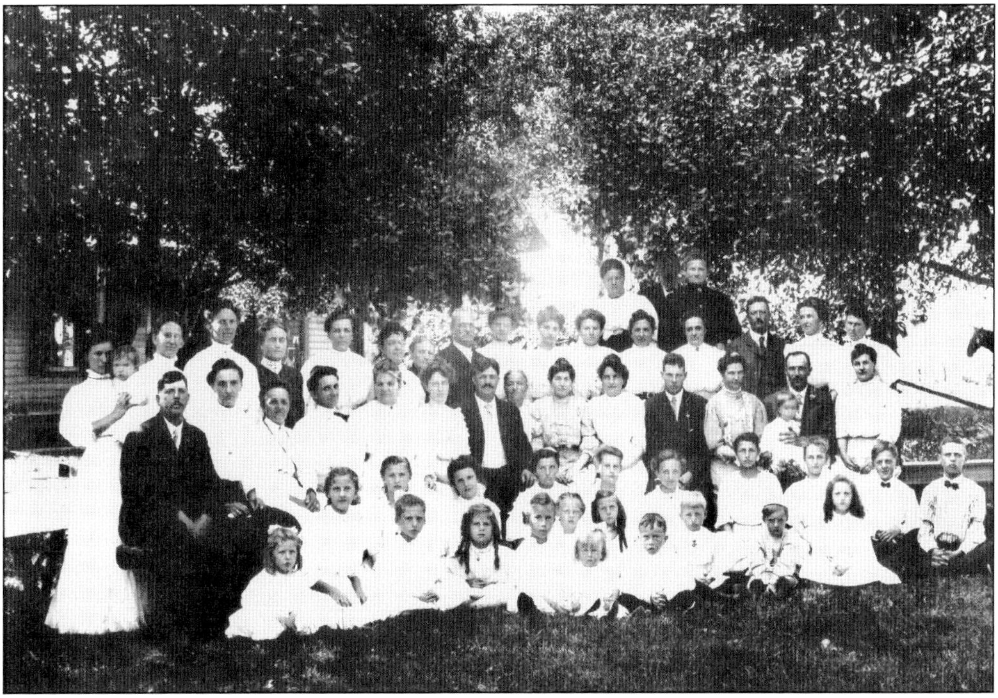

John and Georgina Vater lived in Chicago for several years before deciding to move their growing family to a more suitable location near Berry Lake in 1867. They had 12 children, three of whom died at a young age. In 1905, the family house was moved to the growing city of Whiting. The Vater family is seen here at a reunion in 1907. (Suzanne Vater Culbertson.)

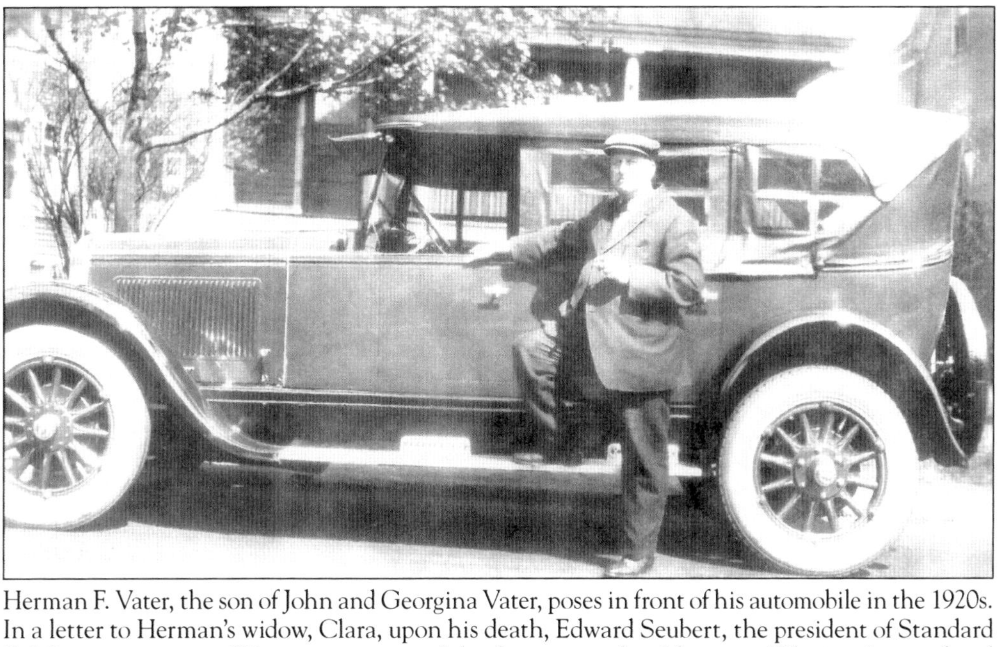

Herman F. Vater, the son of John and Georgina Vater, poses in front of his automobile in the 1920s. In a letter to Herman's widow, Clara, upon his death, Edward Seubert, the president of Standard Oil Company, wrote, "Herman was one of the finest men that I knew at Whiting. I considered him one of my life-long friends and always had kindly recollections of our old association and comradeship." (Judy Vater Sunderman.)

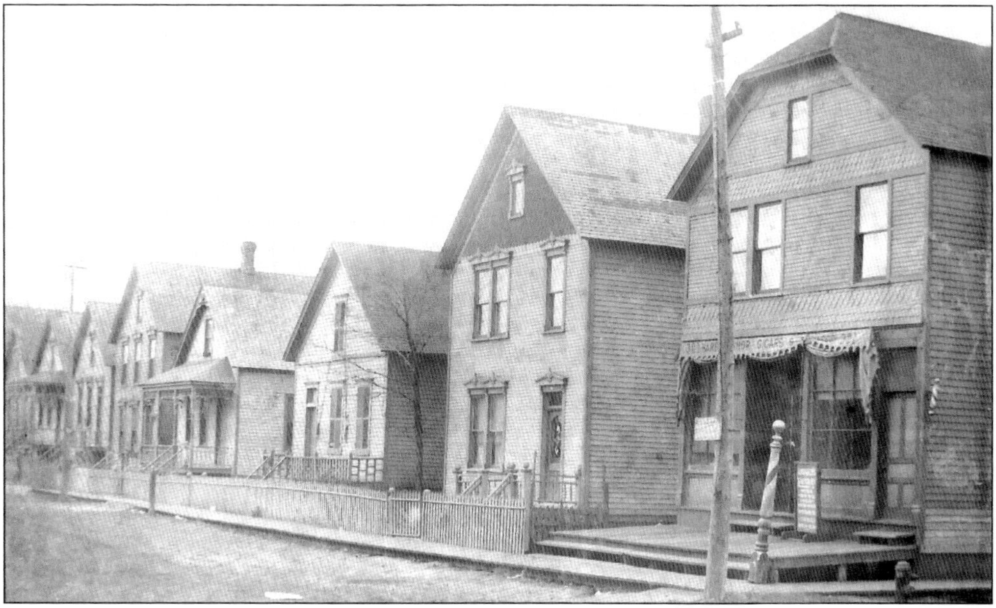

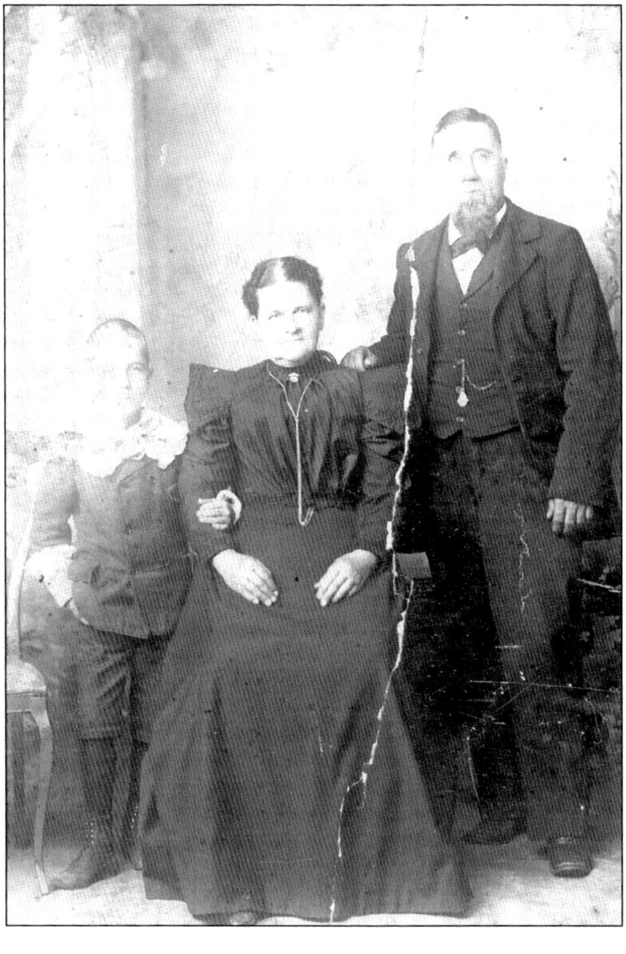

Lined with wooden sidewalks, Whiting resembled a frontier town in the 1890s, when these buildings were constructed. The store on the corner belonged to Fred and John Fischrupp. The sign above the store advertises cigar and tobacco products. Additional signs in front of the store indicate barbershop and laundry services, and the sign on the light pole advertises "Fischrupp Real Estate and Loans." (Whiting Historical Society.)

Attracted by job prospects at the Standard Oil refinery, the Schellenger family moved from New Jersey to Whiting in the late 1800s. (Sandrick family.)

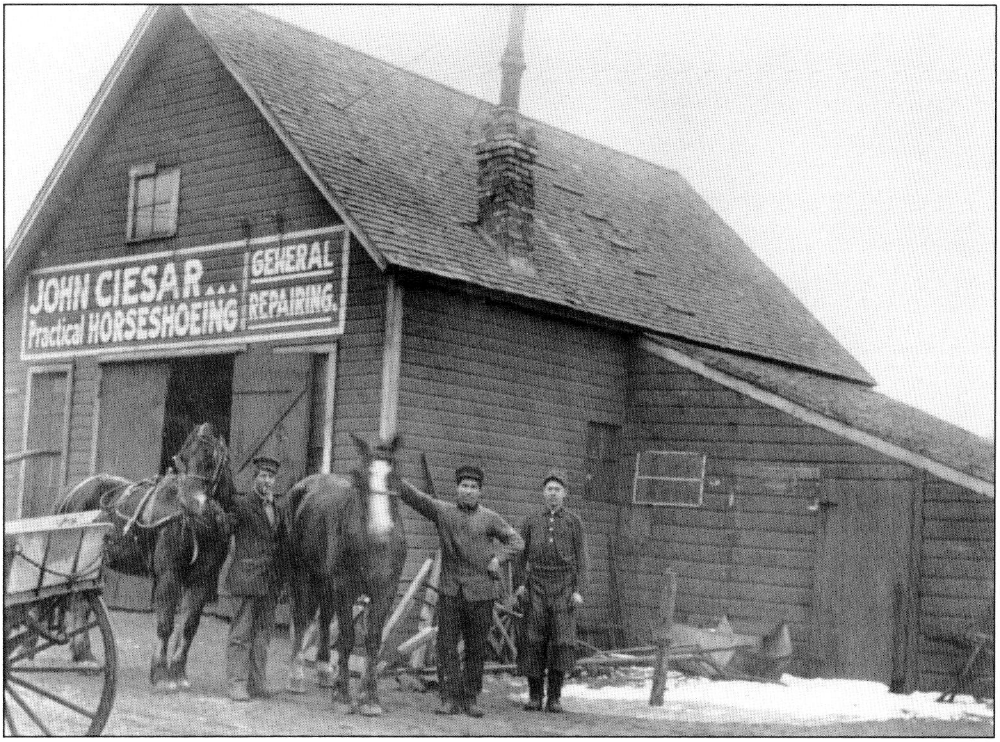

As the town of Whiting began to grow, immigrants found their niche by establishing shops that allowed them to apply talents and skills they had learned in their homeland. John Ciesar and Matt Ambroz, two such early citizens, set up a blacksmith shop on one of the area's main thoroughfares. The sign on their building advertised their services as "Practical Horseshoeing and General Repairing." (Whiting Historical Society.)

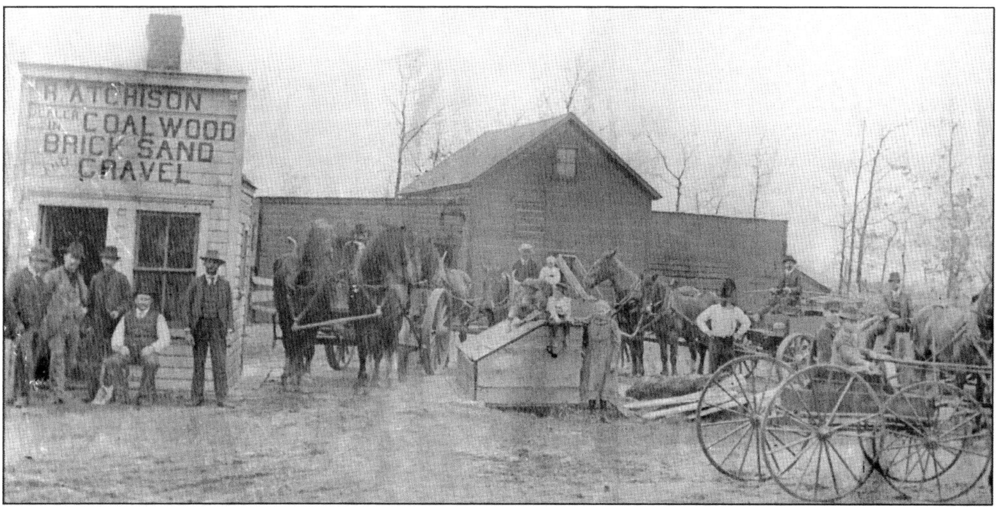

In this 1896 photograph, there was much activity in front of Robert Atchison's place of business. A dealer in coal, wood, brick, sand, and gravel, he settled in the area in the 1850s and provided many of the tools and resources needed to build the community. Atchison Street, the dividing line between Whiting and Robertsdale, was named after him. His youngest daughter, Pearl, married George Roberts, the biggest landowner in the area. (Whiting Historical Society.)

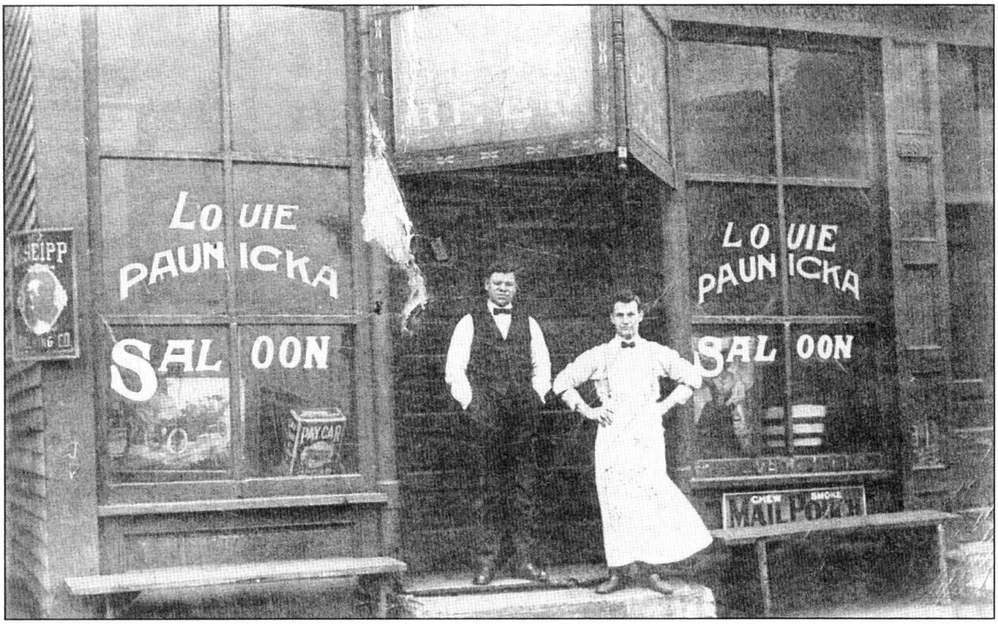

Louie Paunicka had been a page boy for Franz Joseph I of Austria before coming to the United States. His first business was a saloon on 119th Street near the Whiting refinery. He could speak seven languages, including Hungarian, Slovak, Polish, and Croatian, and could easily converse with the many different immigrant groups who patronized his establishment. (Dolores Paunicka Callahan.)

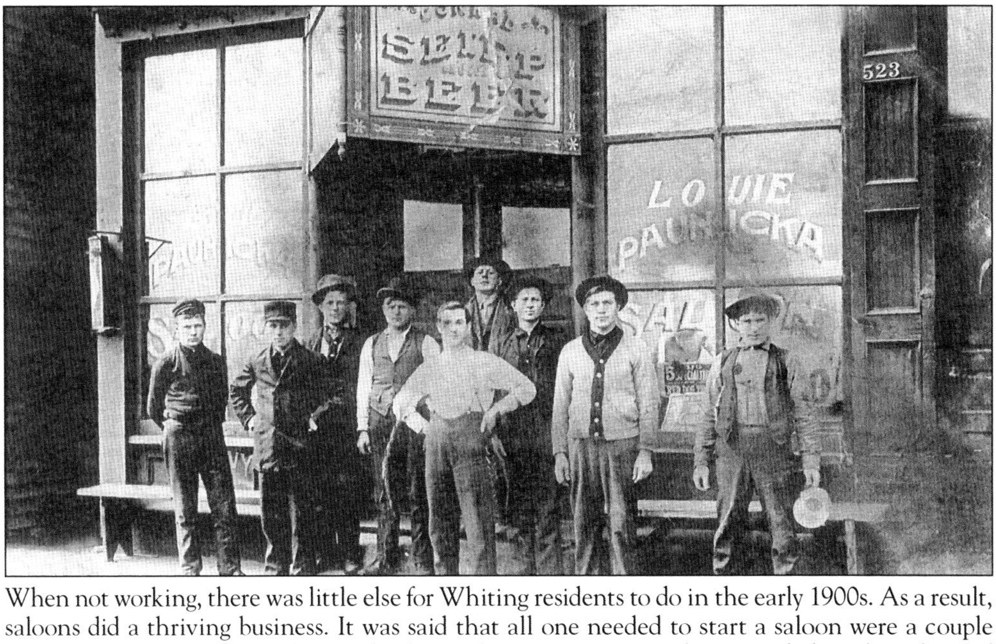

When not working, there was little else for Whiting residents to do in the early 1900s. As a result, saloons did a thriving business. It was said that all one needed to start a saloon were a couple kegs of beer, a bottle of whiskey, and a dozen glasses. Louie Paunicka expanded on that idea and created a place with an attractive storefront, good service, and plenty of Seipp Beer. (Dolores Paunicka Callahan.)

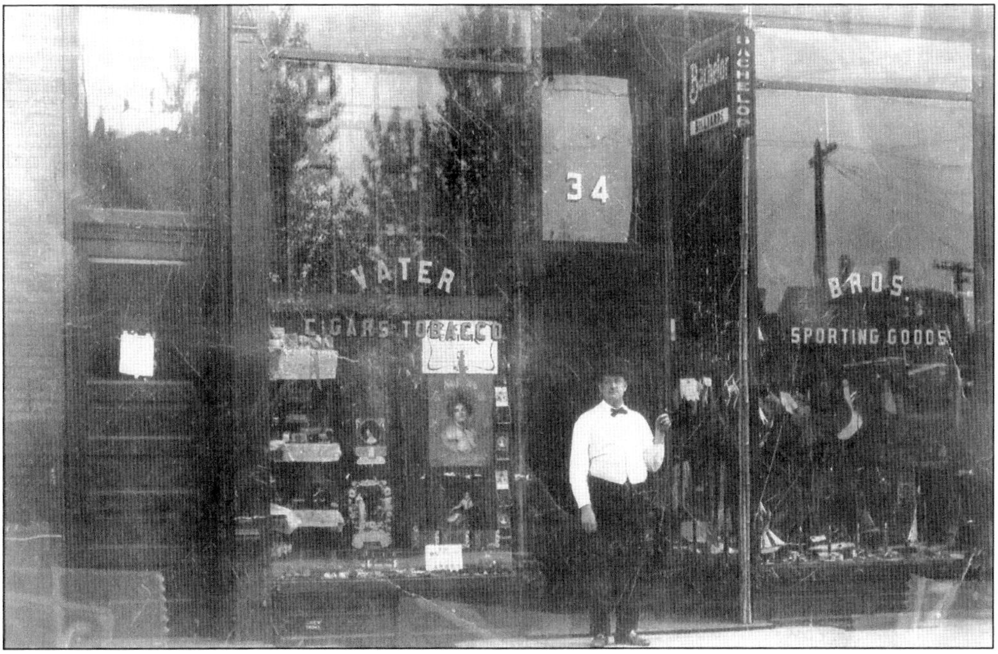

Herman F. Vater poses in front of the Vater Bros. shop on 119th Street. Cigars, tobacco, sporting goods, and billiards were among the goods found inside. According to a local advertisement, the store also sold "fire works in brilliant colored fires." (Judy Vater Sunderman.)

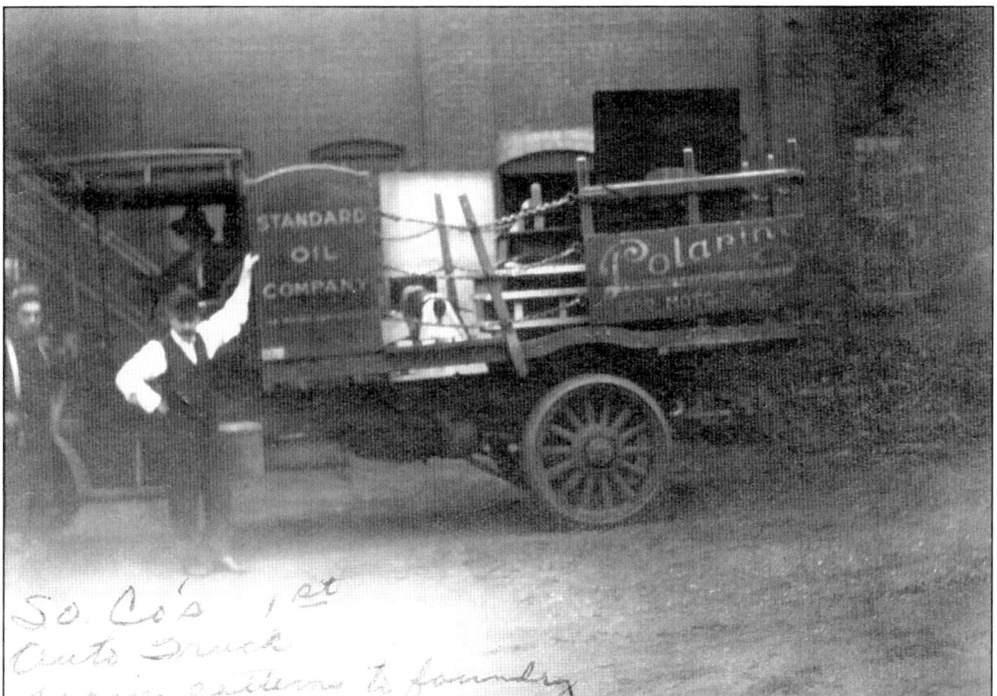

Standard Oil Company played a major role in the rapid growth of the community in its early days. Here is the company's first auto truck, which carried patterns to the foundry. (Whiting Historical Society.)

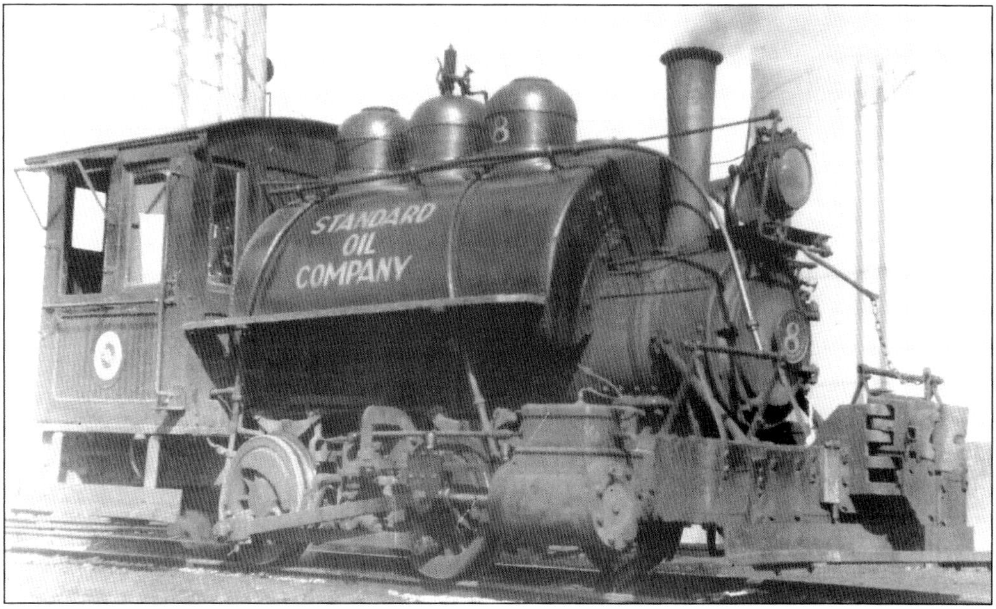

The region's proximity to the railways running to and from Chicago was one of the main reasons that Standard Oil Company chose Whiting as the site for one of its largest oil refineries. On Thanksgiving Day in 1890, the first shipment of 125 tank cars of kerosene left the refinery for the marketplace. The refinery has not ceased operations since that day. (Whiting Historical Society.)

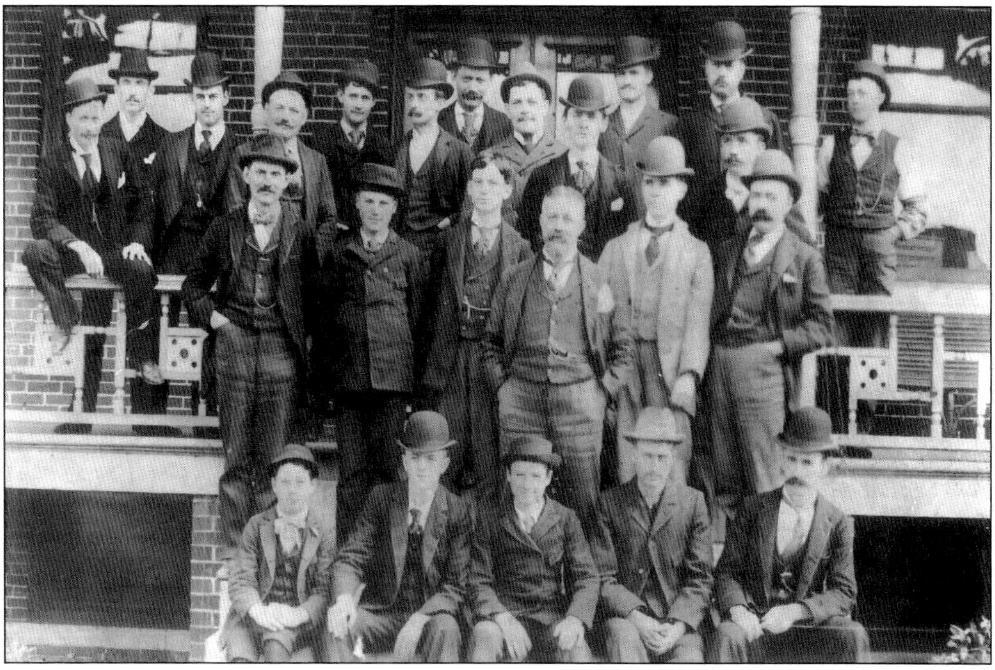

Office employees of the Whiting refinery are seen here in the 1890s. Because there was very little available housing in Whiting when Standard Oil began construction in 1889, the company built houses for its supervisory employees in an area that became known as "the Village." The company housing had modern conveniences like wooden sidewalks and running water. (Whiting Historical Society.)

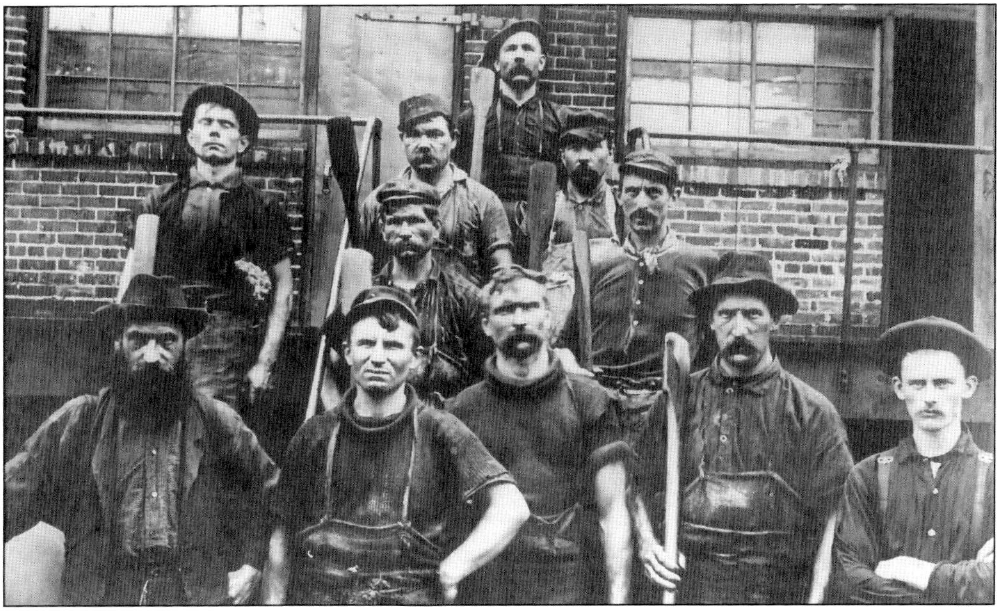

When the Whiting refinery began operations in 1890, many of the laborers who had been involved in the construction remained with the company to oversee various departments. As operations expanded, more laborers were added. In 1895, the highest daily wage was $4.50 for skilled labor and $2.50 for unskilled labor. The pay rate was among the best in the industry, and by 1896, nearly 3,000 people were employed at the refinery. (Whiting Historical Society.)

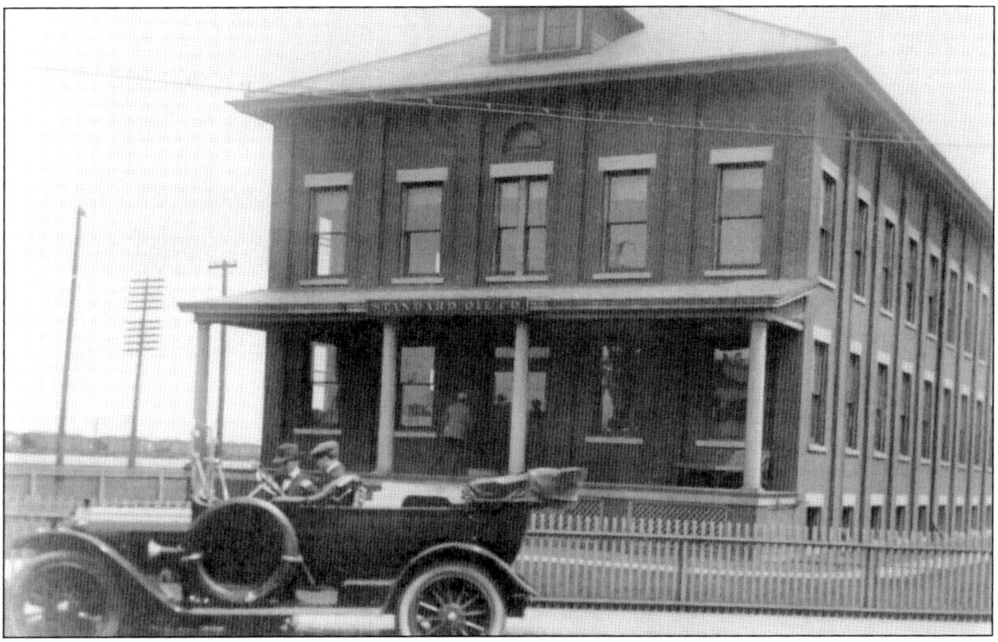

Whiting became the main hub for the Standard Oil Company of Indiana, with all of the company's offices located there except for the purchasing department, which was in nearby Chicago. In addition to constructing new office buildings such as this one, the company also transformed old farmhouses into laboratories and experimental sites as it began to hire chemists to perfect the refining process. (Whiting Historical Society.)

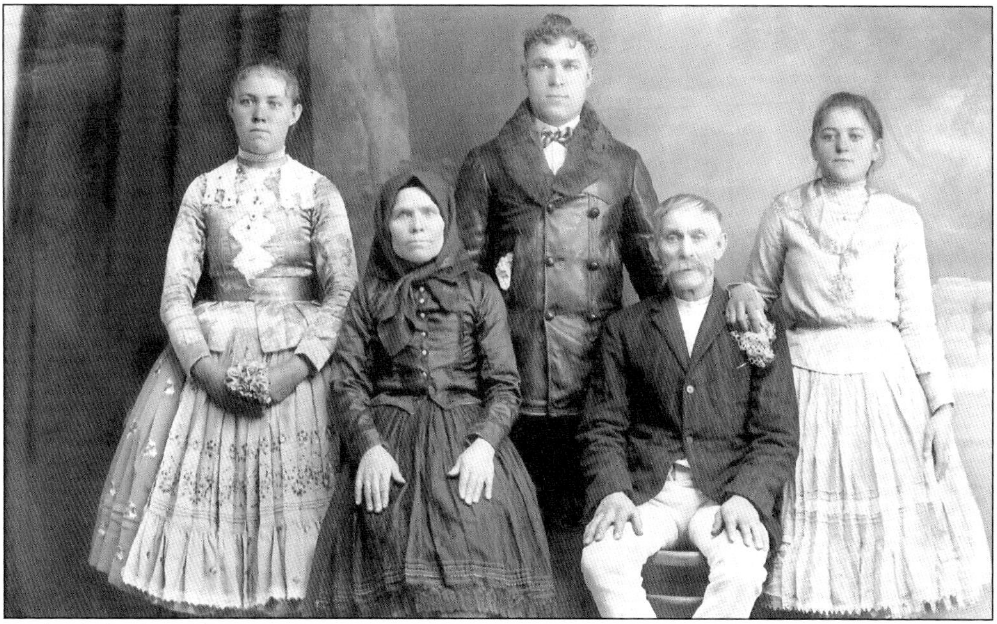

Michael Tkach and his wife, Mary, are seen here with three of their five children in Slovakia. Tkach came to the United States in 1888, seeking work in Pennsylvania. He soon moved to Whiting, where he worked as a laborer on the construction of the Whiting refinery. After several years in Whiting, Tkach returned to Slovakia with his family. His sons Michael and John later returned to the United States and raised their families in Whiting-Robertsdale. (Tkach family.)

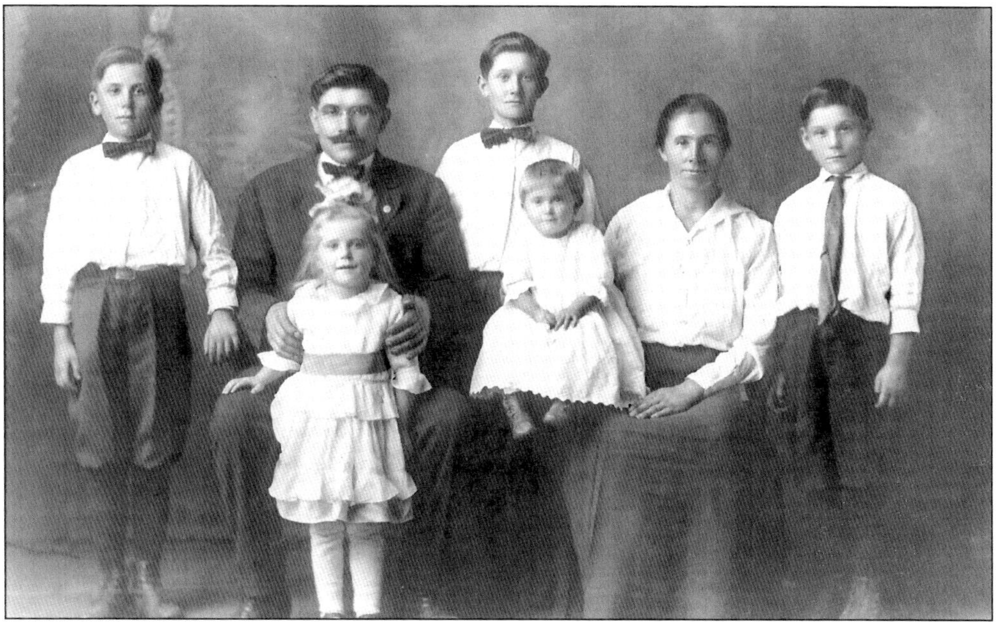

Andrew and Mary Vrabel came from Slovakia to Pennsylvania, where Andrew worked as a coal miner in the 1920s. Like many other Eastern European immigrants, they moved to the Whiting area in search of job opportunities in the growing industrial area of northwestern Indiana. They had six sons and two daughters and remained lifelong residents of the Whiting-Robertsdale community. (Vrabel family.)

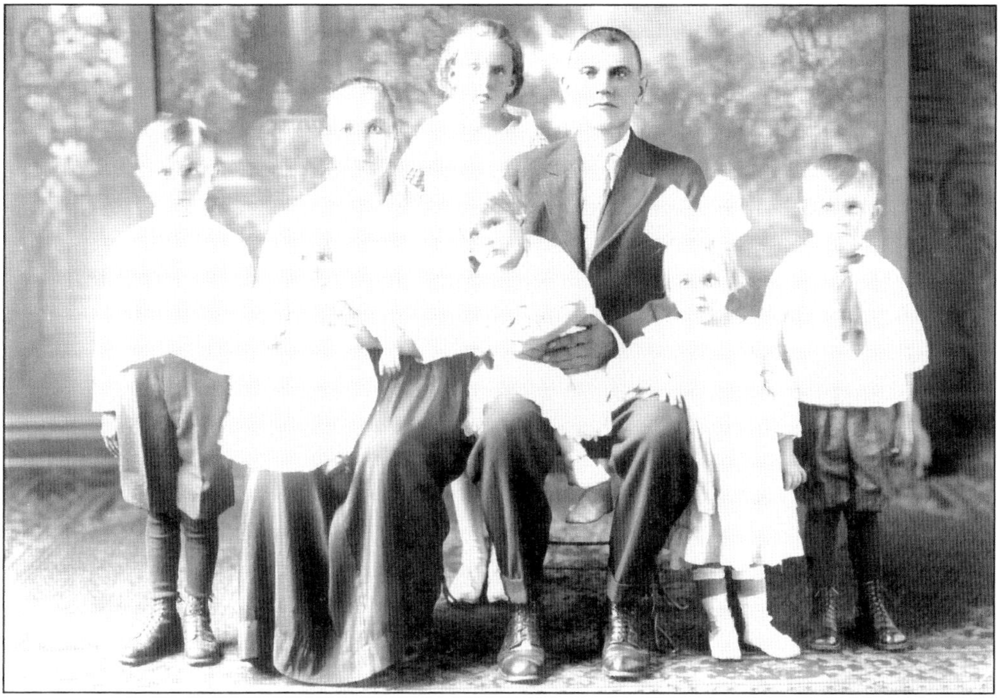

Joseph and Mary Svitko posed for this family portrait in 1920 in Slovakia. Their children are, from left to right, Joseph, Johanna, Margaret, Helen, and Andrew. Standing in the background is a young neighbor girl. The Svitkos immigrated to the United States and settled in the Whiting area, as did many other families of Slavic origin in the early 1900s. In 1910, forty-three percent of the community's population was foreign-born. (Svitko family.)

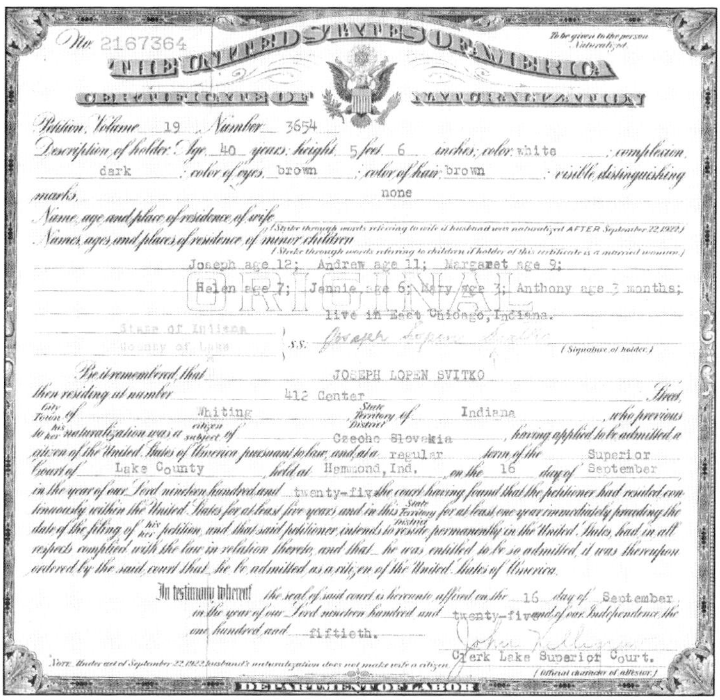

No. 2167364

To be given to the person Naturalized.

THE UNITED STATES OF AMERICA

CERTIFICATE OF NATURALIZATION

Petition, Volume 19 Number 3654

Description of holder: Age 40 years; height 5 feet 6 inches; color white; complexion dark; color of eyes brown; color of hair brown; visible distinguishing marks none

Name, age and place of residence of wife

(Strike through words referring to wife if husband was naturalized AFTER September 22, 1922.)

Names, ages, and places of residence of minor children

(Strike through words referring to children if holder of this certificate is a married woman.)

Joseph age 12; Andrew age 11; Margaret age 9;

Helen age 7; Jennie age 6; Mary age 3; Anthony age 3 months;

live in East Chicago, Indiana.

ORIGINAL

State of Indiana }
County of Lake } S.S.

(Signature of holder.)

Be it remembered, that JOSEPH LOPEN SVITKO then residing at number 412 Center Street, City Town of Whiting State Territory District of Indiana, who previous to his her naturalization was a citizen subject of Czecho Slovakia, having applied to be admitted a citizen of the United States of America pursuant to law, and at a regular term of the Superior Court of Lake County held at Hammond, Ind., on the 16 day of September in the year of our Lord nineteen hundred and twenty-five the court having found that the petitioner had resided continuously within the United States for at least five years and in this State Territory District for at least one year immediately preceding the date of the filing of his her petition, and that said petitioner intends to reside permanently in the United States, had in all respects complied with the law in relation thereto, and that he was entitled to be so admitted, it was thereupon ordered by the said court that he be admitted as a citizen of the United States of America.

In testimony whereof the seal of said court is hereunto affixed on the 16 day of September in the year of our Lord nineteen hundred and twenty-five and of our Independence the one hundred and fiftieth.

Clerk Lake Superior Court.

(Official character of attestor.)

Note: Under act of September 22, 1922, husband's naturalization does not make wife a citizen.

DEPARTMENT OF LABOR

Some immigrants came to Whiting seeking employment for a short time, with intentions of returning to their homeland. Many others came with the intention of making a new home in America. This is an example of a naturalization certificate, which many immigrants sought after they arrived. (Svitko family.)

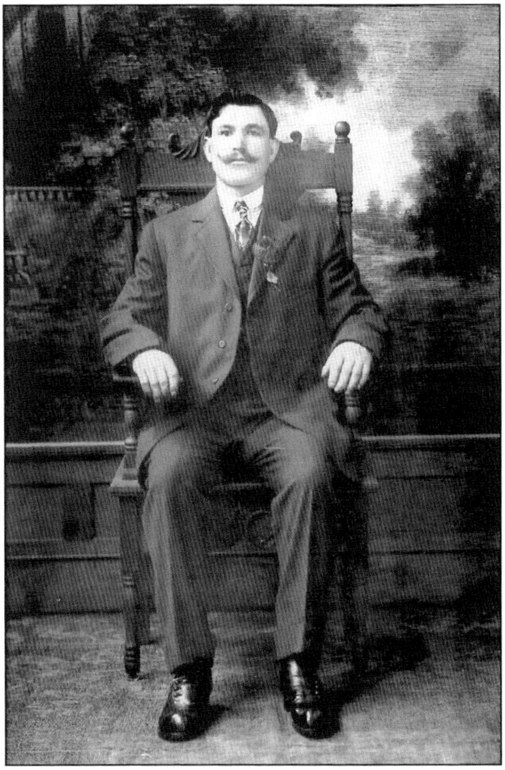

Personal portraits were a growing trend in the early 1900s and a luxury that immigrants did not have in the old country. Andras Lentvorszki poses here in 1917, shortly after arriving in the United States from Hungary. (Lentvorsky family.)

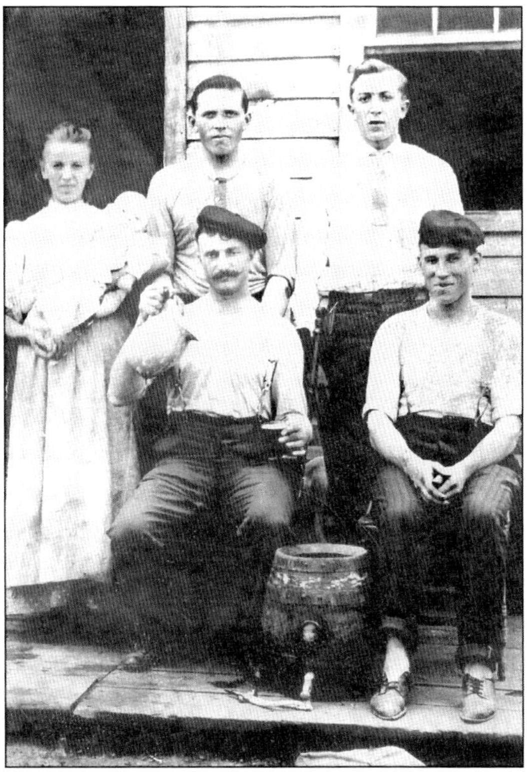

Ann Poracky Vrabel (left) poses with family and friends in front of her home in Whiting. (Vrabel family.)

This passport picture shows Anna Tkach at age 18, when she immigrated to the United States in 1929. She was one of many Slovak women who left behind family and friends in the old country to start a new life in America. Inherent in them was an intense devotion to family and faith. Many of the customs and traditions they brought with them are still honored and practiced in Whiting to this day. (Tkach family.)

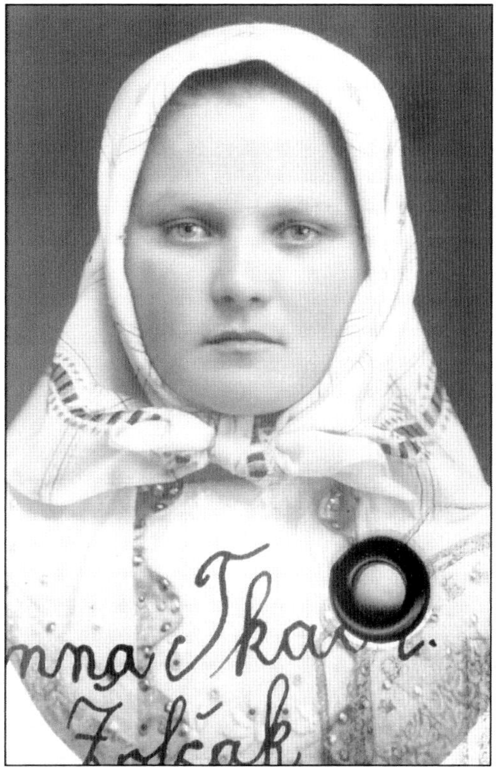

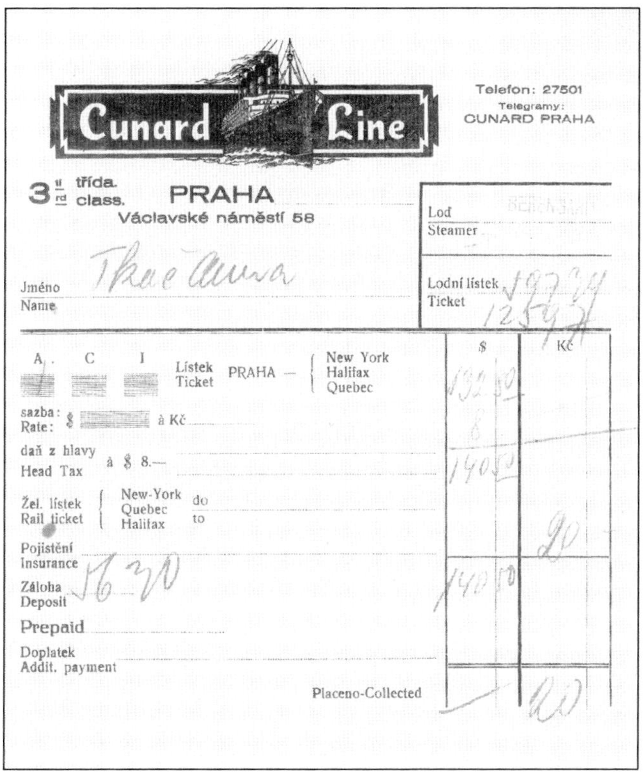

Cunard Line

Telefon: 27501
Telegramy:
CUNARD PRAHA

3 třída
class. PRAHA
Václavské náměstí 56

Jméno
Name Tkač Anna

Loď
Steamer

Lodní lístek
Ticket

A C I Lístek Ticket PRAHA — New York Halifax Quebec

sazba: Rate: $ à Kč

daň z hlavy
Head Tax à $ 8.—

Žel. lístek
Rail ticket New-York Quebec Halifax do to

Pojištění
Insurance

Záloha
Deposit

Prepaid

Doplatek
Addit. payment

Placeno-Collected

This is the receipt for Anna Tkach's passage on the ship *Berengaria* to join her husband, John Tkach, who had journeyed to Whiting ahead of her to make a home for them. By 1920, Slovaks were the largest of the ethnic groups in Whiting, followed by Poles and Hungarians. The proportion of Whiting's population claiming Slovak ancestry is still among the highest in the United States. (Tkach family.)

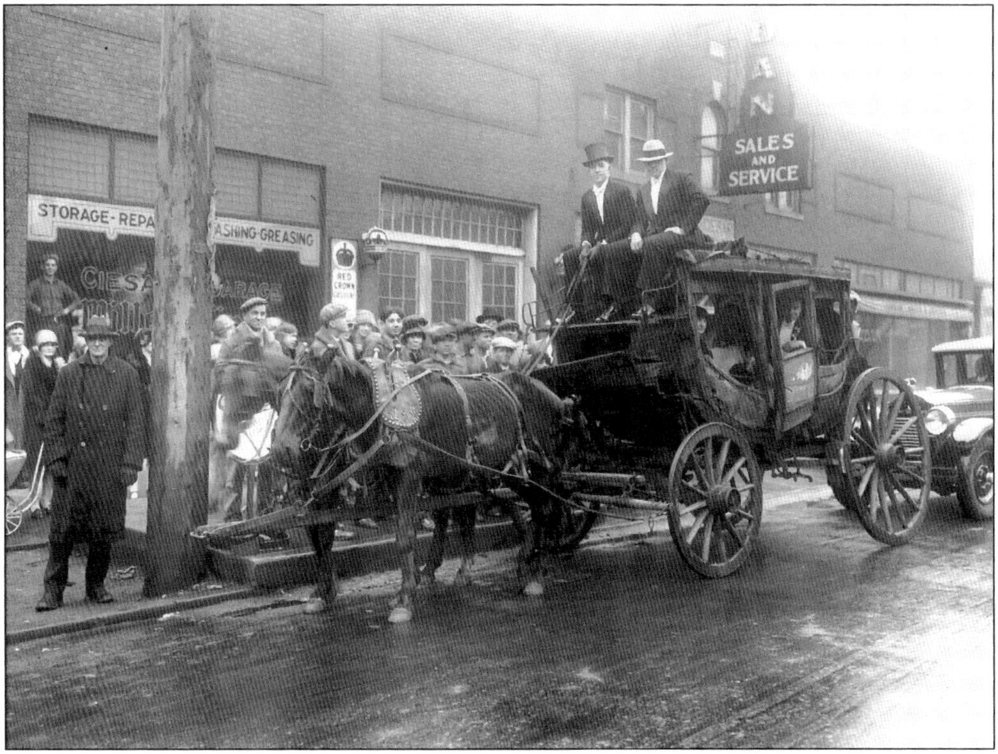

Even though automobiles had become more common by the 1920s, they still shared the road with horses and carriages. In the background of this image is Ciesar's Garage. John Ciesar, a blacksmith, made the move to the automobile business when he saw that trends were changing and the demand for his work as a blacksmith would diminish. (Whiting Historical Society.)

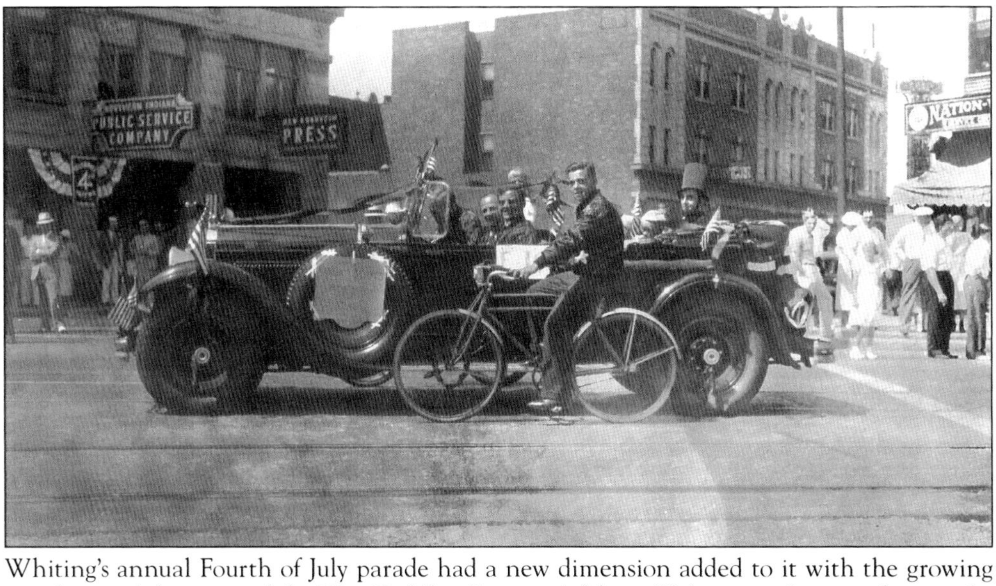

Whiting's annual Fourth of July parade had a new dimension added to it with the growing popularity of the automobile. The Cadillac Squires Athletic Club is seen here in the parade. Popular businesses in the background include Ben Franklin Press and the Northern Indiana Public Service Company. (Vrabel family.)

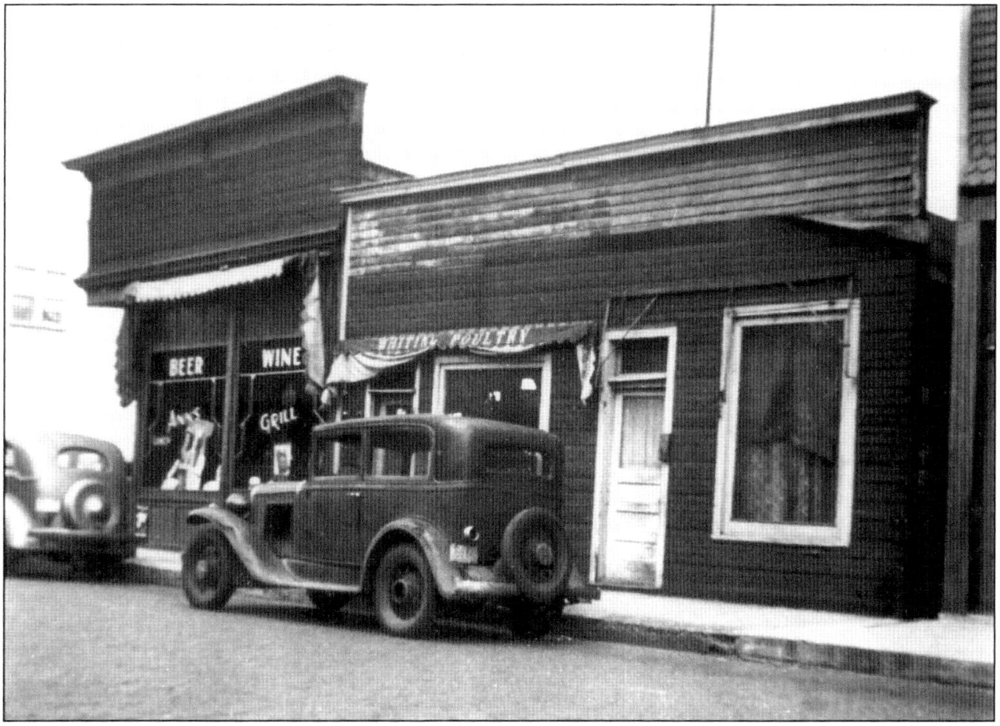

Small stores and businesses like Ann's Grill and Whiting Poultry, both seen here at New York and Fischrupp Avenues, could be found all over the community by the 1930s. (Whiting Historical Society.)

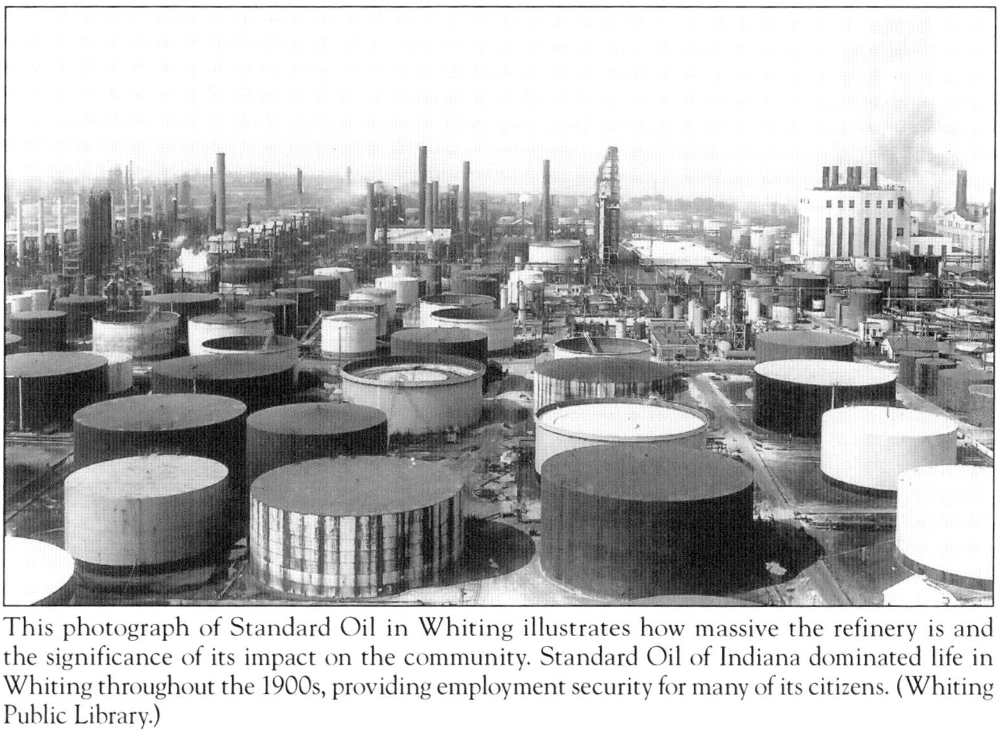

This photograph of Standard Oil in Whiting illustrates how massive the refinery is and the significance of its impact on the community. Standard Oil of Indiana dominated life in Whiting throughout the 1900s, providing employment security for many of its citizens. (Whiting Public Library.)

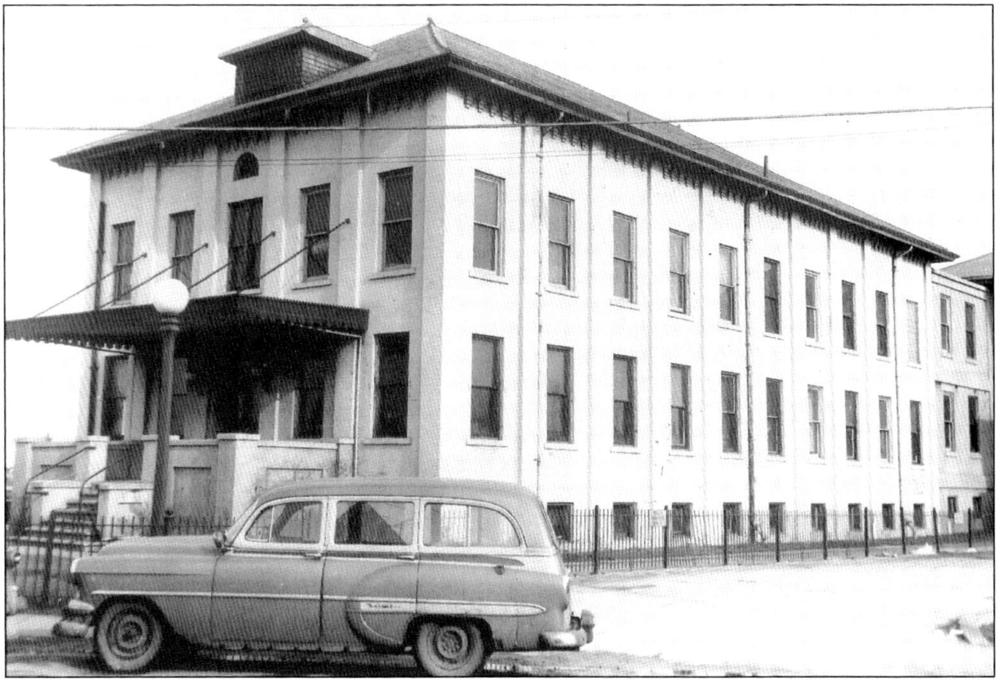

In 1919, Standard Oil began offering employee benefits such as health insurance and a stock-purchase plan. It was also one of the first American companies to provide pensions for its employees. Another one of its new office buildings, necessitated by the company's continued growth and expansion, is seen here. (Whiting Historical Society.)

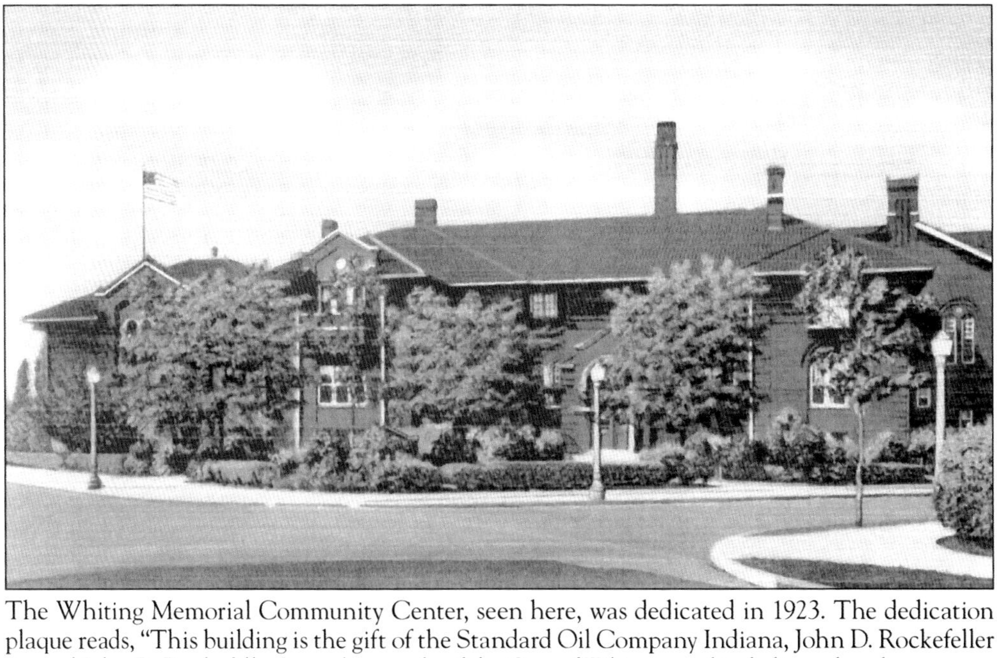

The Whiting Memorial Community Center, seen here, was dedicated in 1923. The dedication plaque reads, "This building is the gift of the Standard Oil Company Indiana, John D. Rockefeller Sr. and John D. Rockefeller Jr. to the people of the City of Whiting and is dedicated to the memory of those who served their country in the World War and to the perpetuation in this community of the principles for which they fought." (Whiting Historical Society.)

Two

BUILDING AND GROWING

By 1891, many of the cottages and cabins Standard Oil had built to house its employees were filled to capacity. Early settlers who already owned plots of land began to construct small houses and apartment buildings to rent to the growing number of new residents.

With the incorporation of Whiting came new services and the amenities of city life, including a public library, law enforcement, recreational facilities, and a lakefront park. Cement sidewalks started to replace wooden ones, street surfaces were smoothed out and cindered, and a sewer and sanitation system was built. Improvements such as shade trees, shrubbery, and flowers were incorporated into the sandy landscape. The community gradually lost the appearance of a frontier town and became a bustling modern city. The retail district that had started out on Front Street near the railroad tracks and the entrance to the refinery began to expand west along 119th Street, creating what would eventually become the community's main business district.

Churches of several denominations were formed to support the community's spiritual needs, and they also served as social centers where families with similar backgrounds could find comfort and a sense of belonging. Many of the churches and parishes also formed their own schools to provide religious instruction and to teach children about their heritage, traditions, and customs.

By 1907, Whiting had six banks and a few real estate agencies. Families who had been unable to purchase land in their old country were able to save money, obtain loans, and purchase land to build their own homes. By 1927, Whiting had five schools within its public school system, and the community would eventually have five parochial schools.

In 1896, the Standard Oil refinery in Whiting employed 2,500–3,000 laborers, and by 1900, the town had a population of almost 4,000. By the early 1920s, the refinery employed more than 4,000 workers, and the city population was approximately 10,000. Everyone still spoke their own language—Germans, Slovaks, Poles, Czechs, Hungarians, Turks, and Croatians among them—but an Americanization process had begun.

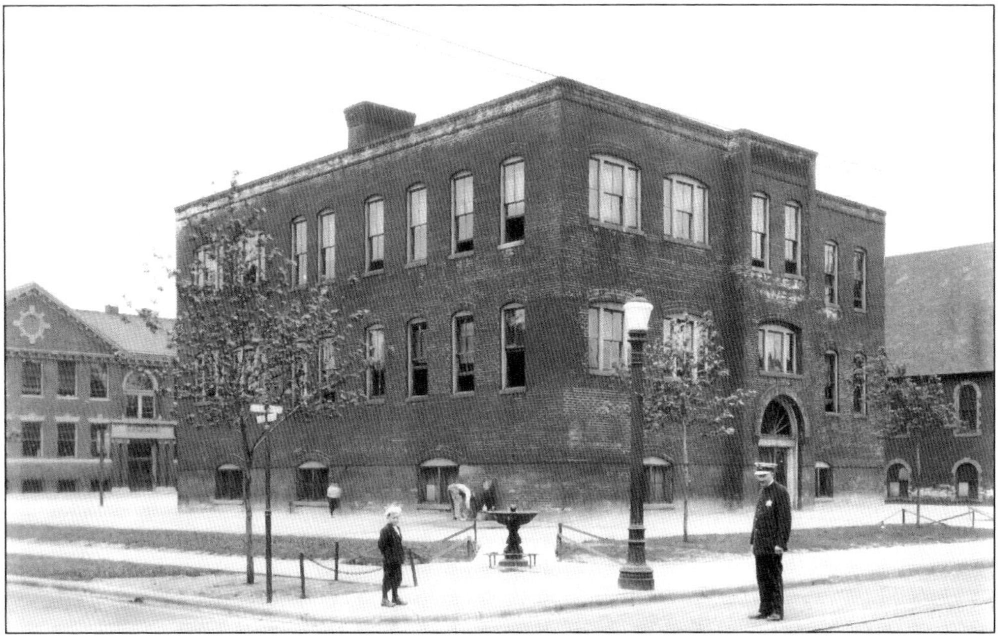

Whiting High School was established in 1898. The first building was located at the corner of 119th and Oliver Streets, along with a popular mineral spring fountain. (Whiting Public Library.)

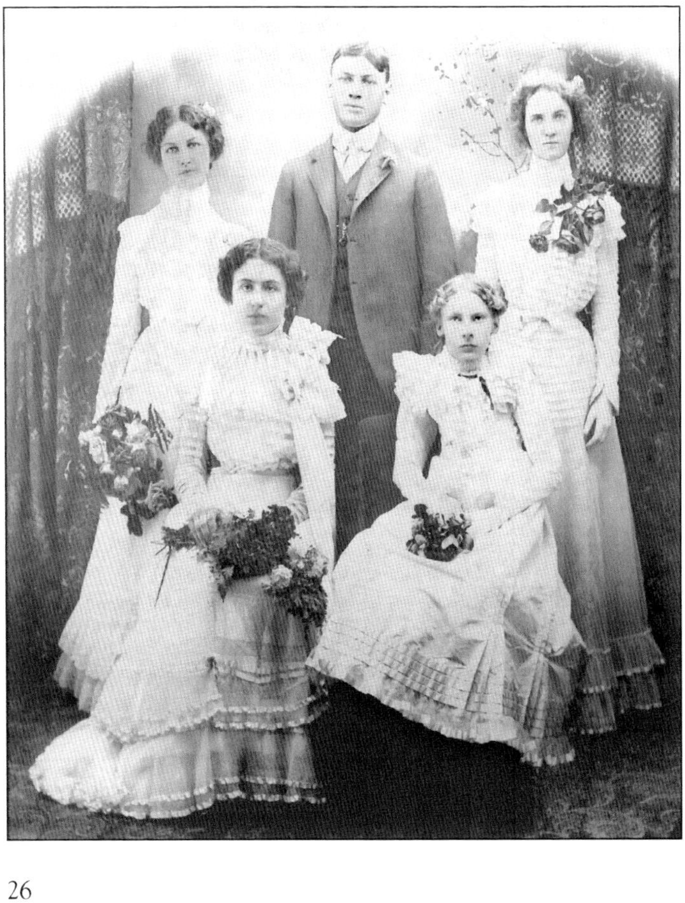

The Whiting High School Class of 1900 consisted of five students. They are, from left to right, (sitting) Constance Walsh and Florence Stewart; (standing) Leona Nanzer Reineman, Charles Klose, and Anna Bustine Gainer. (Whiting Public Library.)

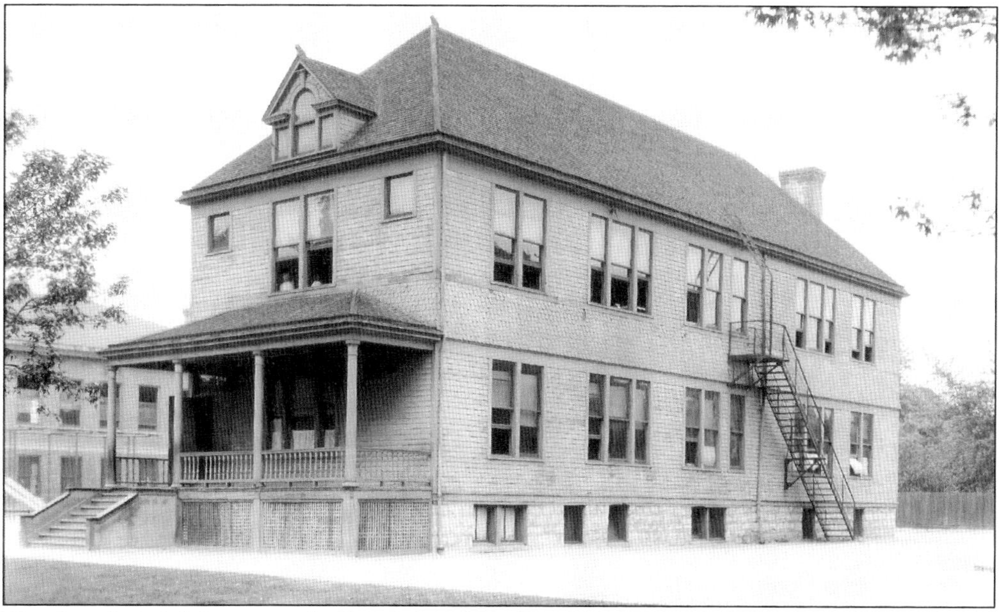

The Standard Oil Company deeded a plot of land to Whiting's public school system in 1900 for $1, as well as an adjoining lot for $1,260. Seen here is the old primary building, originally built for elementary school students. (Whiting Public Library.)

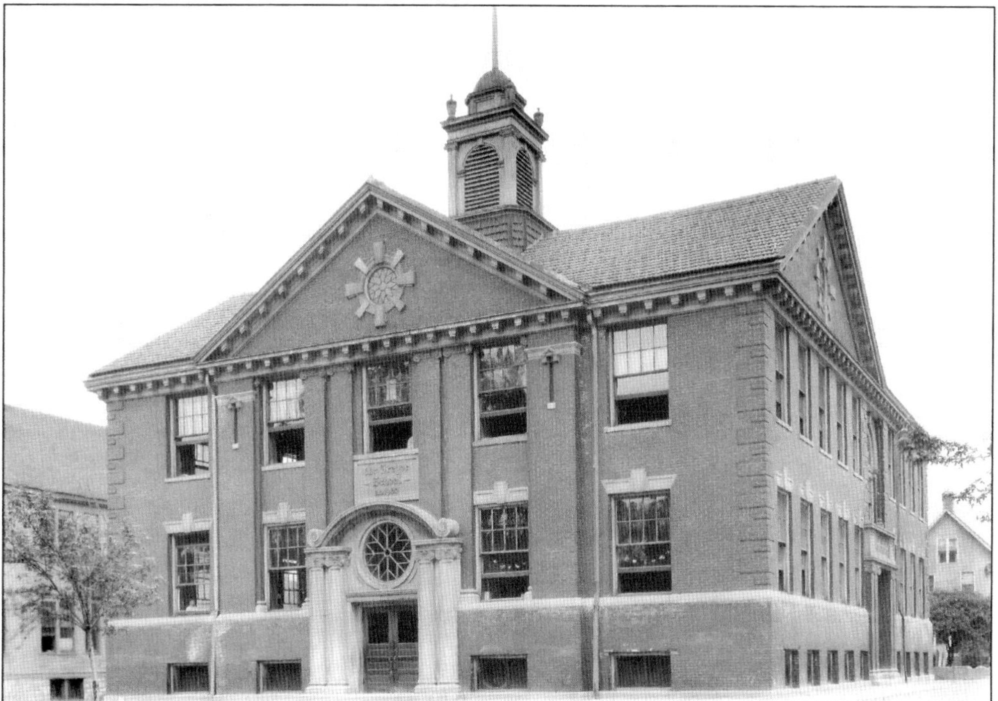

McGregor School, established in 1900 for the primary grades, opened this new building in 1909. It was named for Ambrose McGregor, the chairman of the manufacturing committee at Standard Oil of Indiana and the person responsible for overseeing general operations at the Whiting refinery. (Whiting Public Library.)

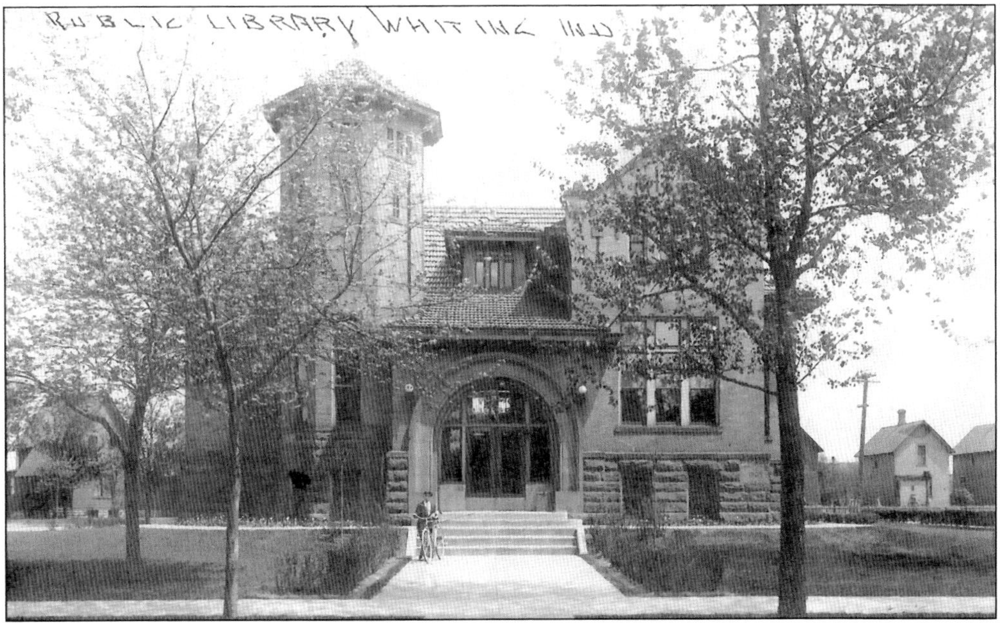

A library board was formed in 1904 to establish a public library for Whiting. The board approached Andrew Carnegie, who agreed to donate $15,000 for the construction. Standard Oil donated a piece of land at the corner of Ohio Avenue and Oliver Street, and in December 1905, the first stone was laid. It included an inscription that reads: "The Gift of Andrew Carnegie-A.D. 1905." (Whiting Public Library.)

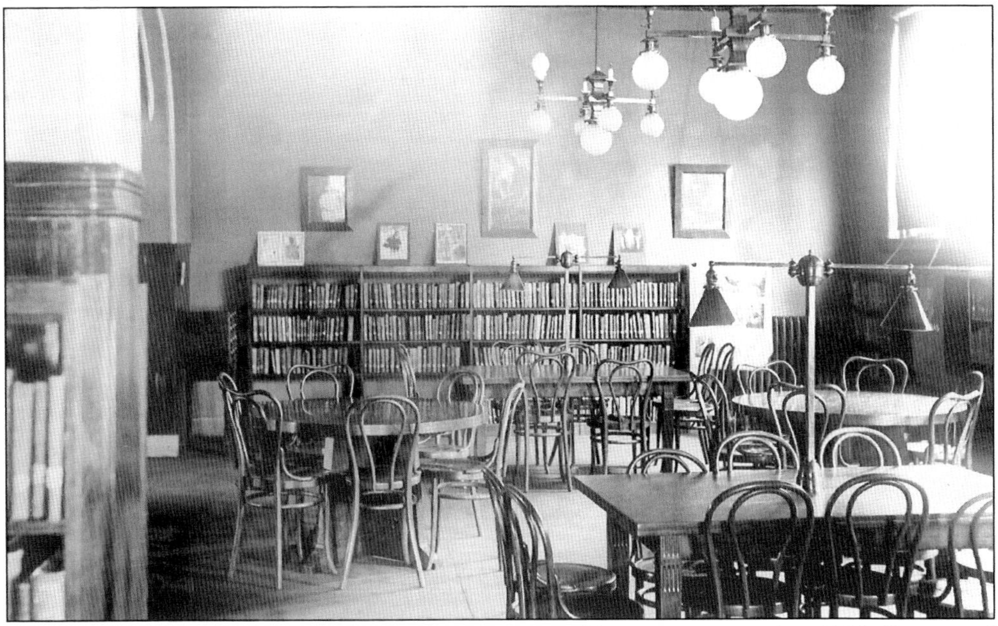

While the library was being constructed, a temporary library was opened at 119th Street and Sheridan Avenue to begin acquiring books. When the new library opened in July 1906, the shelves contained 2,588 volumes. The collection grew rapidly, and other branches eventually opened throughout the community. By the 1960s, the collection had grown to 52,000 volumes. A library expansion project was completed in 1982. (Whiting Public Library.)

St. John the Baptist Parish was established in 1897 by Fr. Benedict Rajcany. The meeting hall of the Slovak Catholic Union served as the parish's first church. By 1914, the church had to be expanded to accommodate the growing number of parishioners. Ground was broken for a new church on May 20, 1930, the cornerstone was laid in July, and it took nearly a year to construct the much larger, more magnificent structure. (St. John the Baptist Parish.)

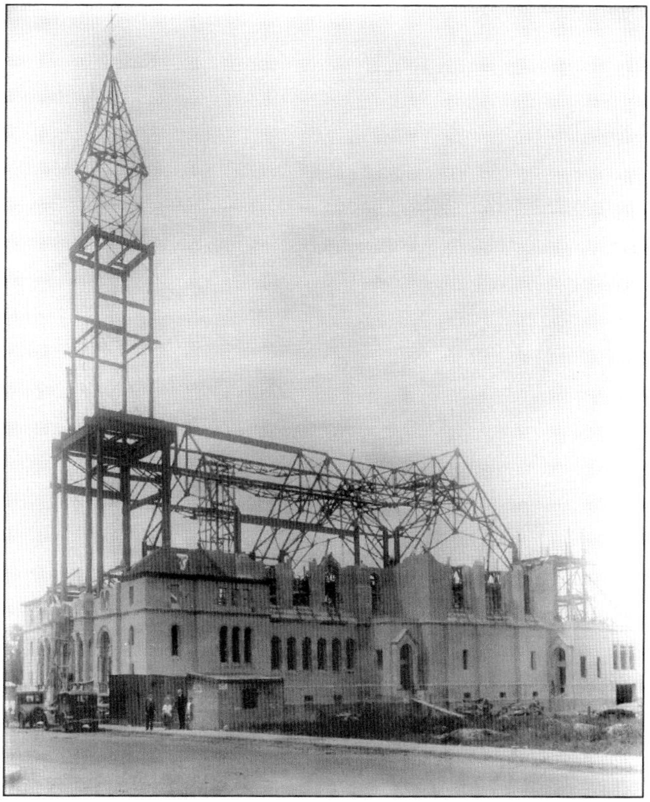

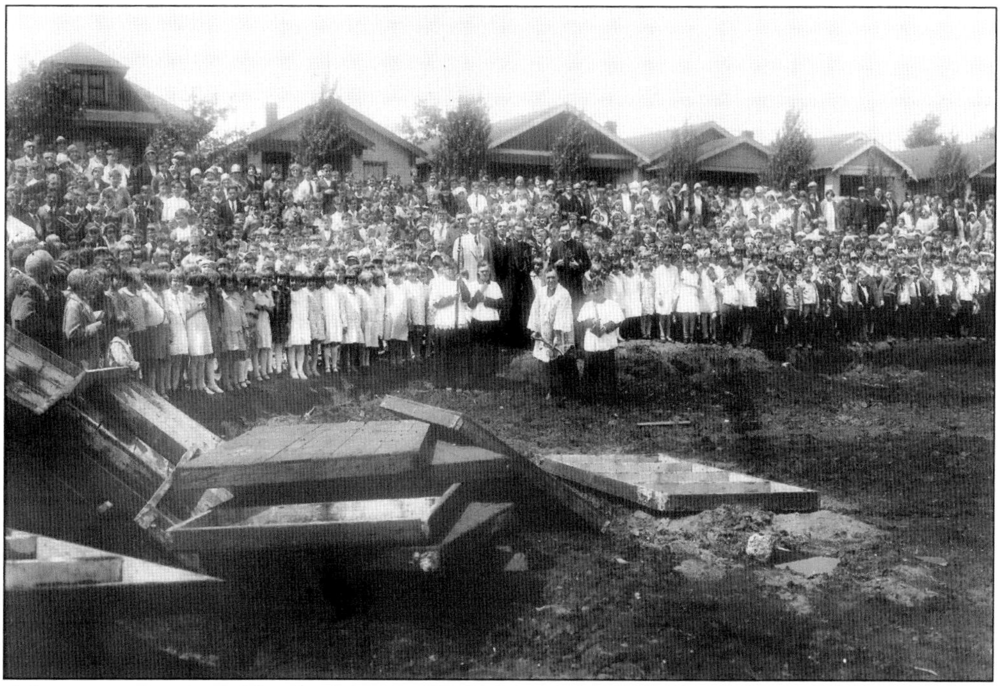

A large crowd gathered for the laying and blessing of the cornerstone for the new St. John the Baptist School in 1948. (Vrabel family.)

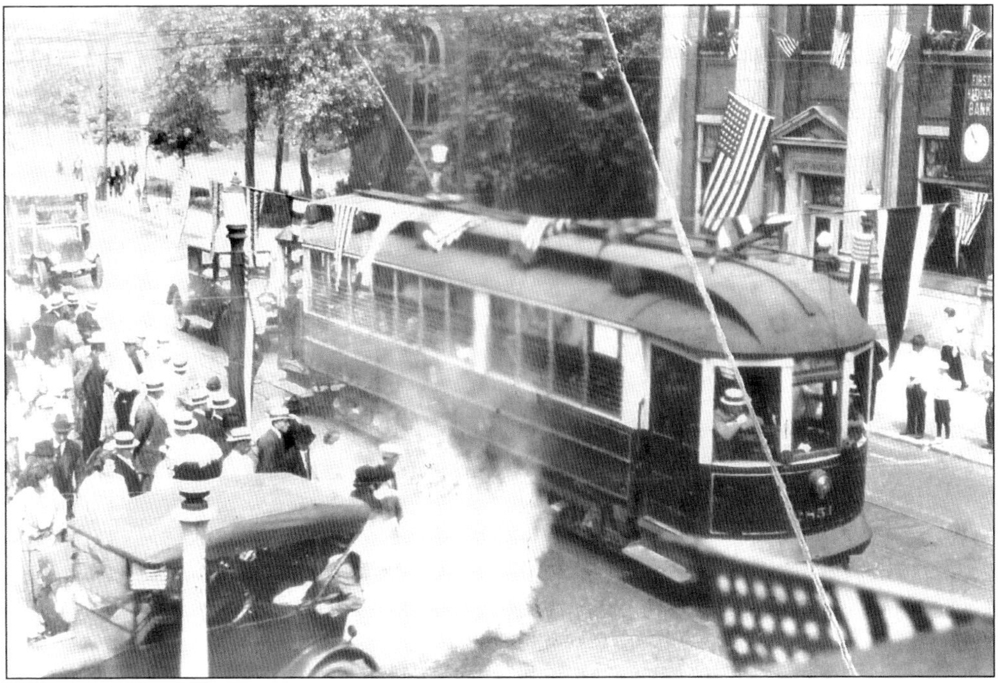

A streetcar makes its way down 119th Street on a busy day in Whiting. For several years, streetcar parties were held during the summer months. A streetcar was chartered, round-trip tickets were sold, and passengers dressed in costumes enjoyed a band on board. The streetcar made periodic stops for riders to disembark and purchase special treats along the way. (Whiting Historical Society.)

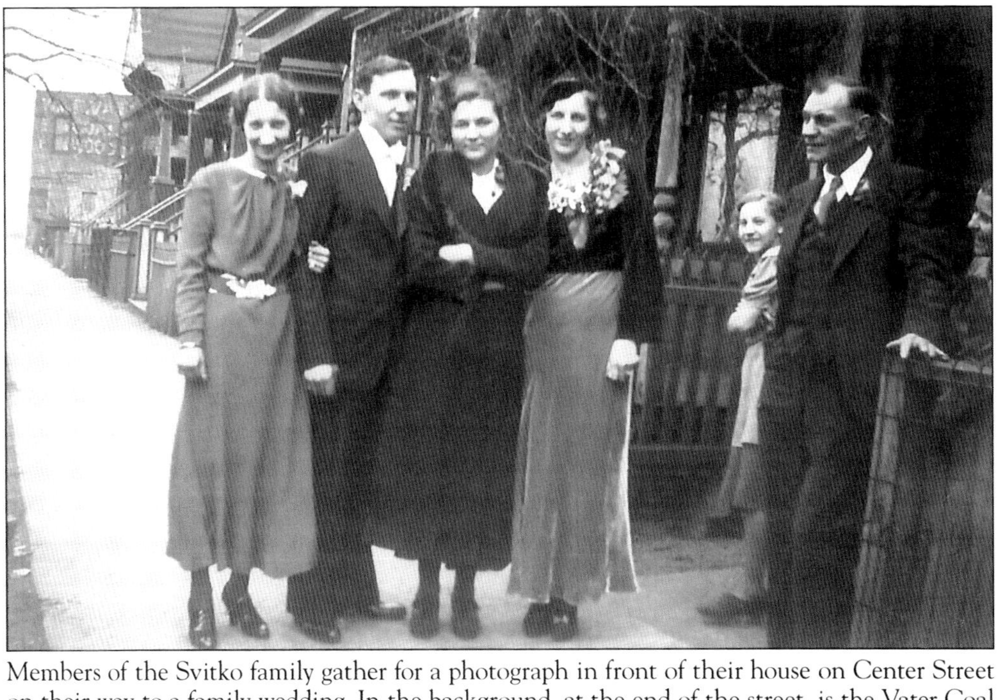

Members of the Svitko family gather for a photograph in front of their house on Center Street on their way to a family wedding. In the background, at the end of the street, is the Vater Coal Company. (Svitko family.)

Established in 1920, American Trust & Savings Bank was a long-standing institution in Whiting. It provided traditional banking services as well as foreign exchange and steamship departments, which were both important services for the growing immigrant population. Note the hours on this bankbook cover: 9:00 a.m. to 3:00 p.m. on weekdays, 9:00 a.m. to noon on Saturdays, and extended hours of 8:30 a.m. to 8:00 p.m. on Standard Oil paydays. (Tkach family.)

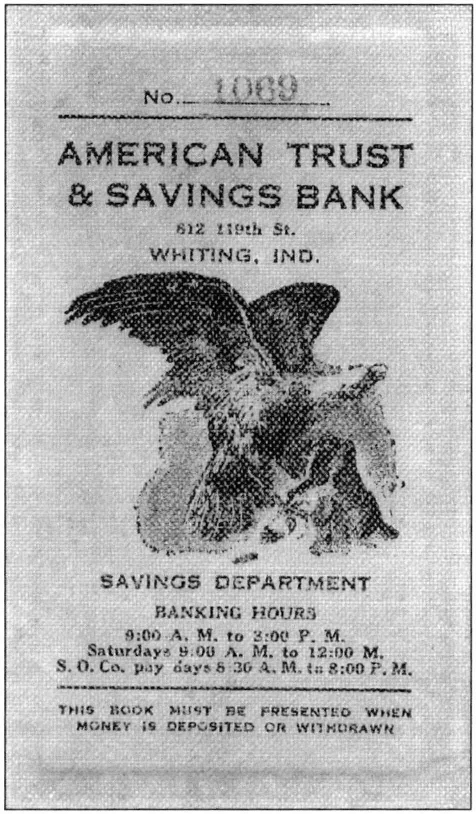

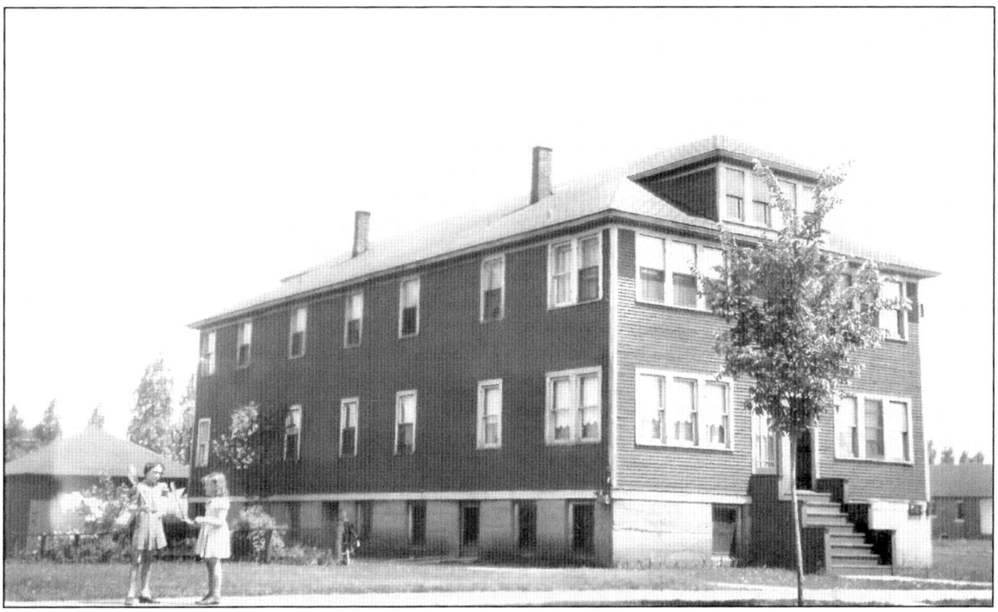

Due to the rapid growth in Whiting-Robertsdale in the early 1900s, there was not adequate housing for many of the families moving into the area. Some managed to pool their resources and purchase land on which they constructed apartment buildings such as this one, where family members could live close together and rent to others in need of a place to call home. (Tkach family.)

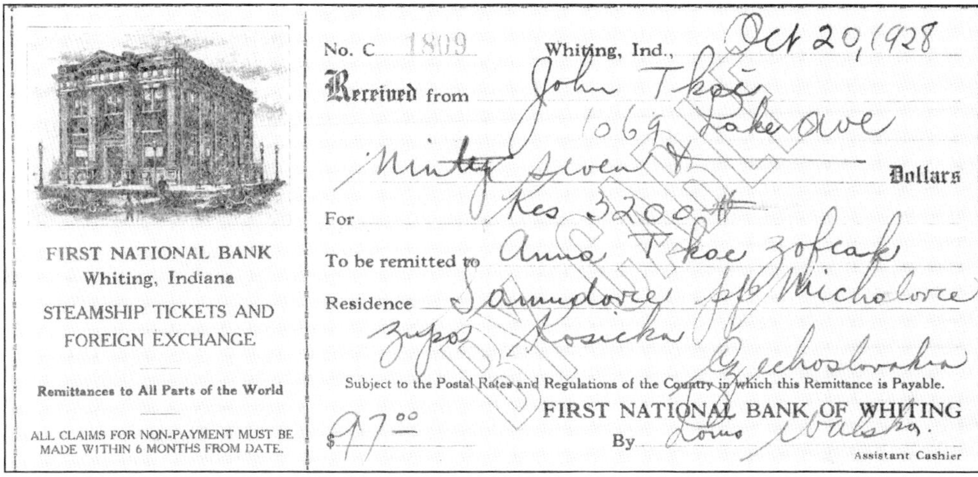

FIRST NATIONAL BANK
Whiting, Indiana
STEAMSHIP TICKETS AND
FOREIGN EXCHANGE
Remittances to All Parts of the World
ALL CLAIMS FOR NON-PAYMENT MUST BE MADE WITHIN 6 MONTHS FROM DATE.

No. C 1809 Whiting, Ind., Oct 20, 1928
Received from John Tkoč
1069 Lake ave
Ninety seven Dollars
For Kcs 3200
To be remitted to Anna Tkoc Zofcak
Residence
Czechoslovakia
Subject to the Postal Rates and Regulations of the Country in which this Remittance is Payable.
FIRST NATIONAL BANK OF WHITING
$97.00 By
Assistant Cashier

Banks in Whiting offered special services for clients who wished to send money to relatives in their homeland. Here is a receipt from the First National Bank in Whiting, where John Tkach made arrangements to send money to his wife, Anna, in Slovakia until she was able to join him in America. (Tkach family.)

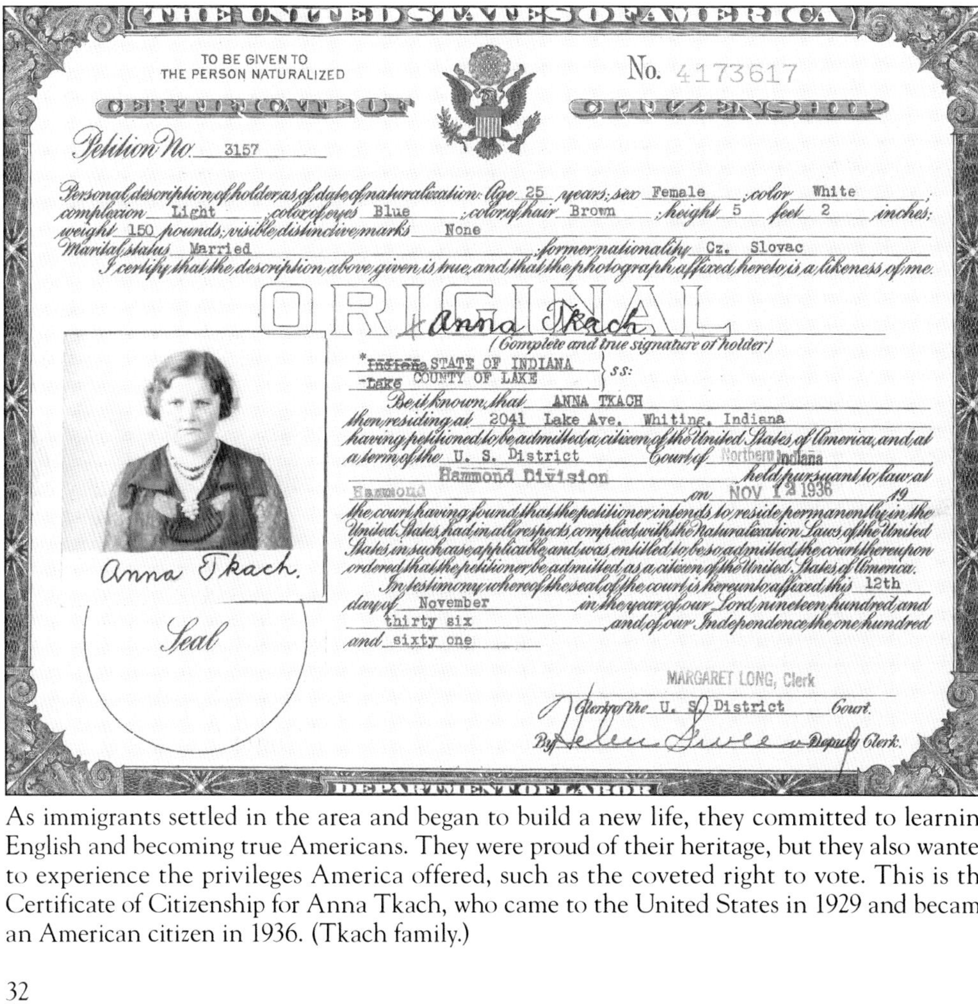

THE UNITED STATES OF AMERICA
TO BE GIVEN TO THE PERSON NATURALIZED
No. 4173617
CERTIFICATE OF CITIZENSHIP
Petition No. 3157
Personal description of holder as of date of naturalization: Age 25 years; sex Female ; color White ; complexion Light ; color of eyes Blue ; color of hair Brown ; height 5 feet 2 inches; weight 150 pounds; visible distinctive marks None
Marital status Married ; former nationality Cz. Slovac
I certify that the description above given is true, and that the photograph affixed hereto is a likeness of me.
ORIGINAL
Anna Tkach
(Complete and true signature of holder)
STATE OF INDIANA
COUNTY OF LAKE } ss:
Be it known, that ANNA TKACH
then residing at 2041 Lake Ave. Whiting, Indiana
having petitioned to be admitted a citizen of the United States of America, and at a term of the U. S. District Court of Northern Indiana
Hammond Division held pursuant to law at
Hammond on NOV 12 1936 19
the court having found that the petitioner intends to reside permanently in the United States, had in all respects complied with the Naturalization Laws of the United States in such case applicable, and was entitled to be so admitted, the court thereupon ordered that the petitioner be admitted as a citizen of the United States of America.
In testimony whereof the seal of the court is hereunto affixed this 12th day of November in the year of our Lord nineteen hundred and thirty six and of our Independence the one hundred and sixty one
Anna Tkach.
Seal
MARGARET LONG, Clerk
Clerk of the U. S. District Court.
By Helen Siwec Deputy Clerk.
DEPARTMENT OF LABOR

As immigrants settled in the area and began to build a new life, they committed to learning English and becoming true Americans. They were proud of their heritage, but they also wanted to experience the privileges America offered, such as the coveted right to vote. This is the Certificate of Citizenship for Anna Tkach, who came to the United States in 1929 and became an American citizen in 1936. (Tkach family.)

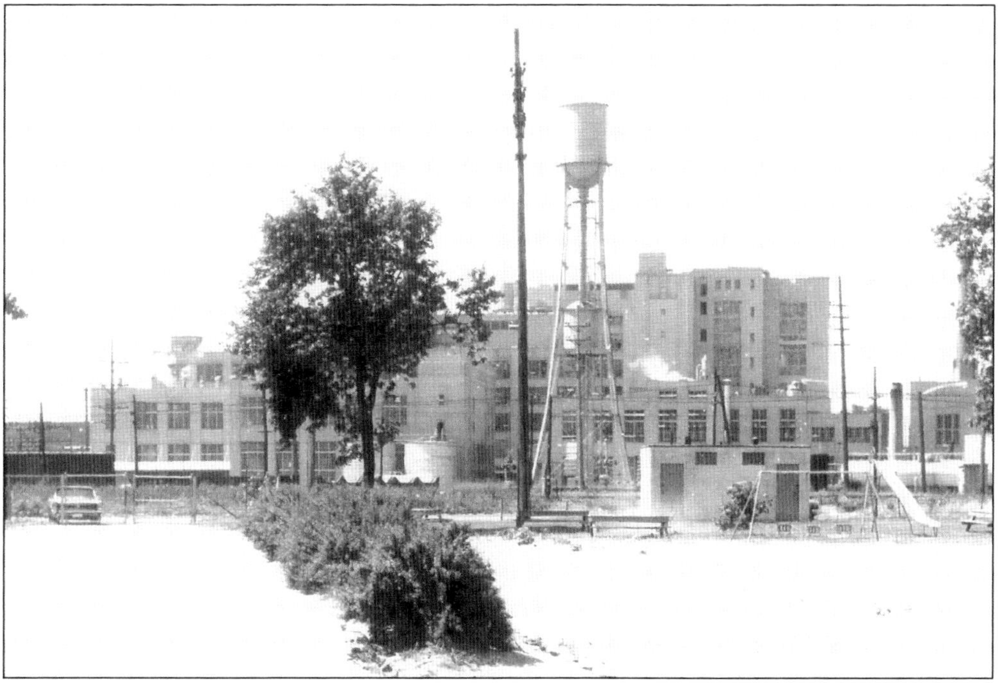

With the explosive growth of the railroads and the Standard Oil Company in the 1890s and early 1900s, Whiting-Robertsdale quickly became home to a variety of other industries. Seen here is Lever Brothers, a manufacturer of soaps and other cleaning products, which began operations in 1930. Views of industrial settings such as this became commonplace from several vantage points in the community. (Domasica family.)

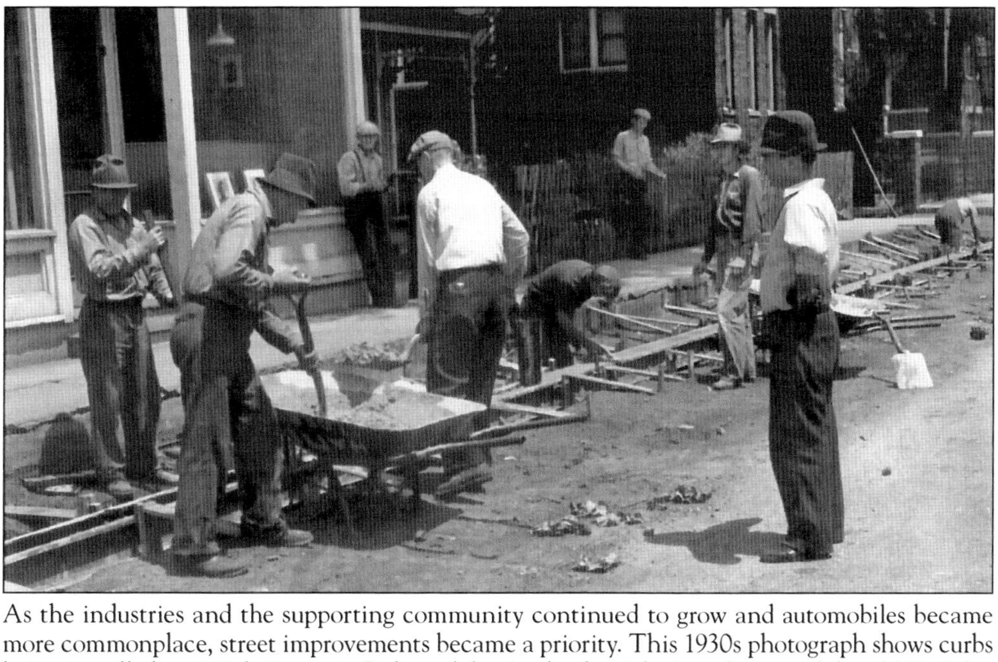

As the industries and the supporting community continued to grow and automobiles became more commonplace, street improvements became a priority. This 1930s photograph shows curbs being installed on 119th Street in Robertsdale. At the far right is a glimpse of the old St. John the Baptist School. (Vrabel family.)

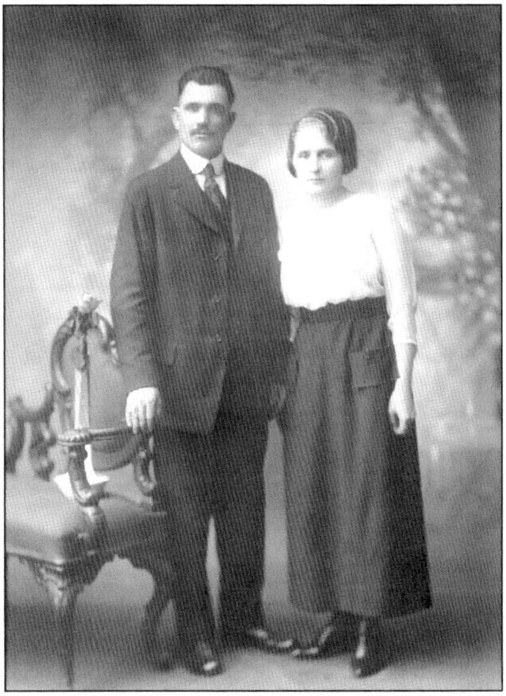

Andras Lentvorszki and Maria Miskrych both immigrated to the United States from Hungary. They met and were married in Whiting. (Lentvorsky family.)

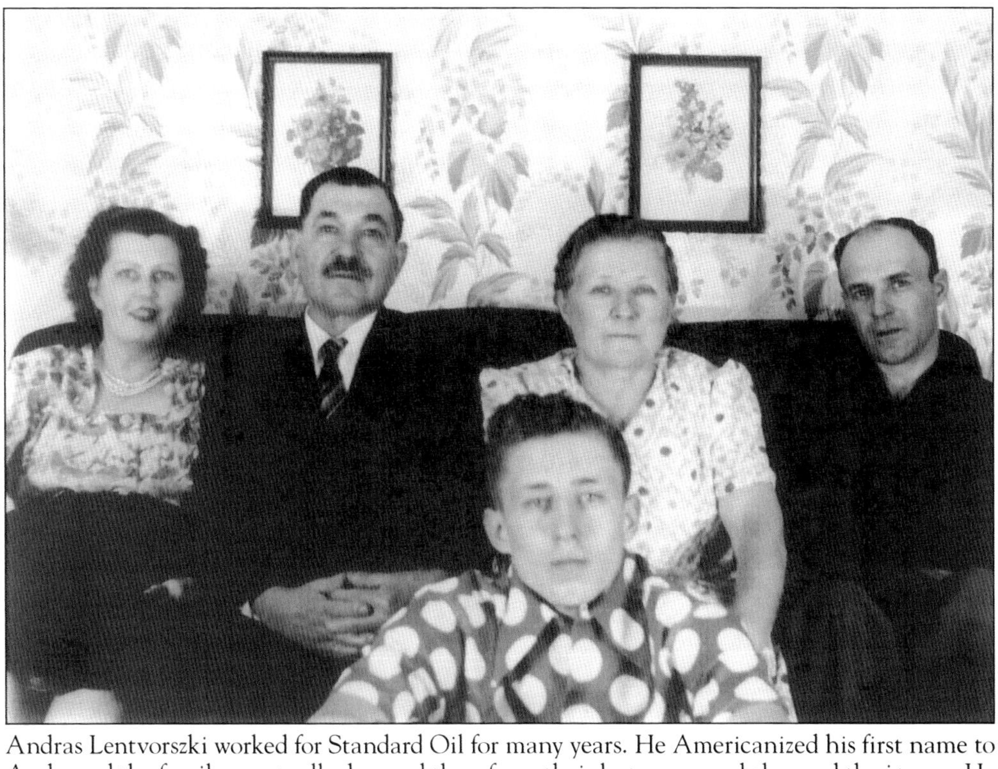

Andras Lentvorszki worked for Standard Oil for many years. He Americanized his first name to Andy, and the family eventually dropped the *z* from their last name and changed the *i* to a *y*. He is seen here in the 1950s with his wife, Maria "Mary," his daughter-in-law Irene (far left), his son Stephen (far right), and his grandson Francis (front). (Lentvorsky family.)

John and Anna Tkach pose for their first photograph together in America. John was born in Whiting in 1901 while his father was working at Standard Oil but returned to Slovakia as a young child. He came back to Whiting in 1923 to work at Standard Oil as his father had and married Anna Zofcak in Slovakia in 1926. This photograph was taken shortly after Anna arrived in the United States in 1929. (Tkach family.)

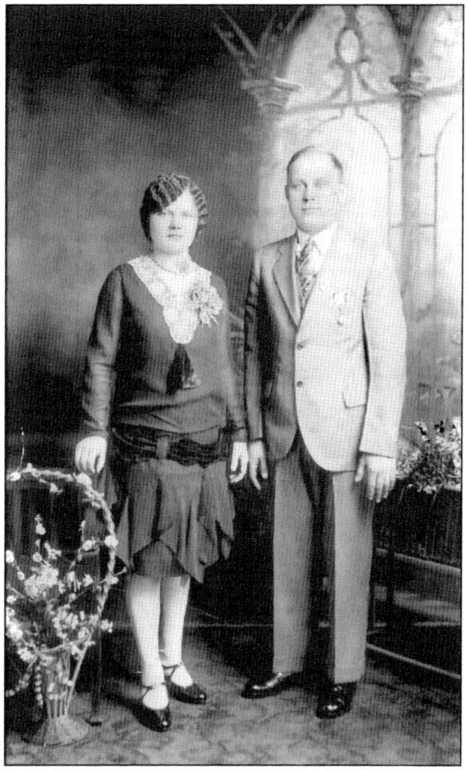

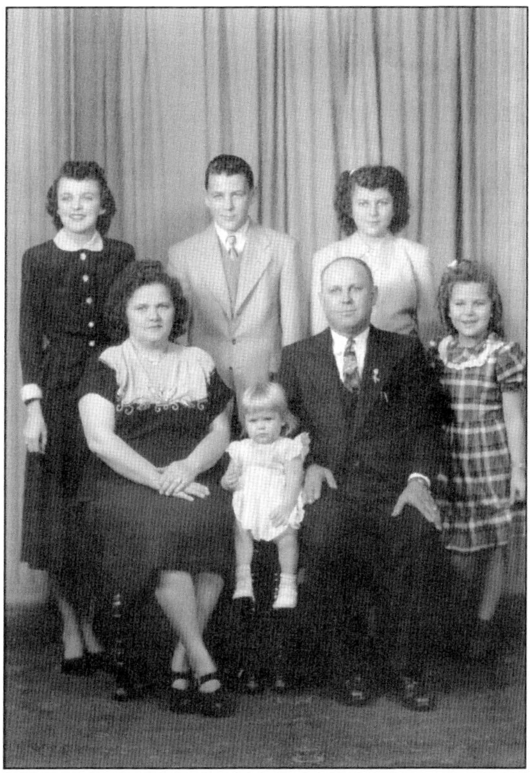

John and Anna Tkach pose for a family photograph with their children in the 1940s. Standing from left to right are Anna, John, Rosemary, and Nancy. Sitting in front is Ruth. Photographs such as these were sent to relatives in their homeland so they could be introduced to their growing families. Unfortunately, many first-generation Americans never had the opportunity to meet their grandparents; they only knew them through letters and photographs. (Tkach family.)

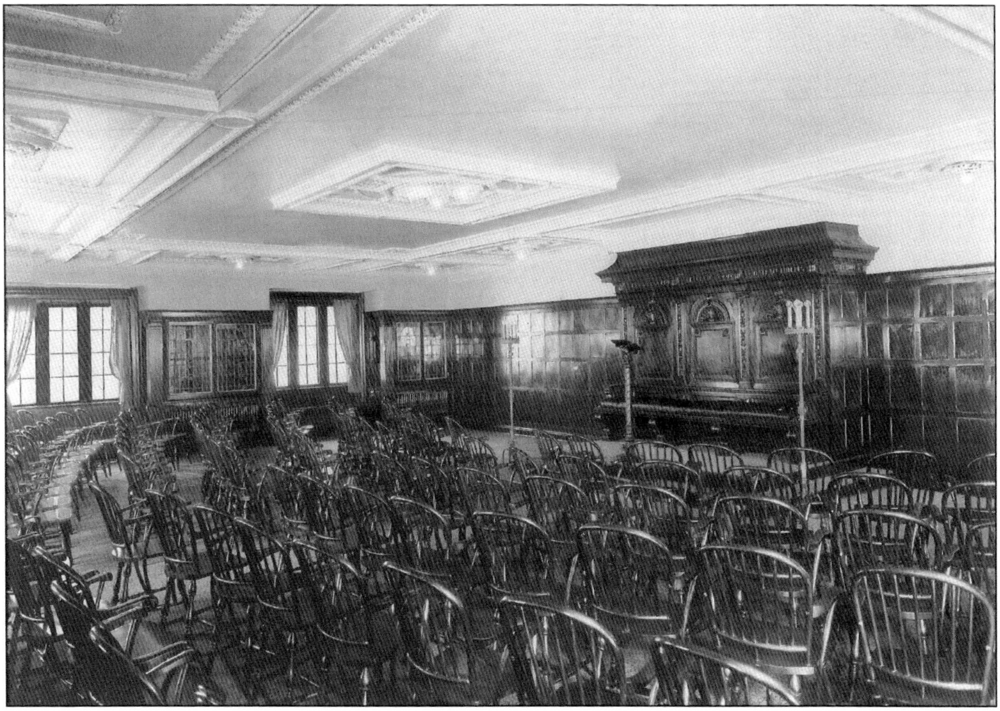

The Whiting Memorial Community Center became the social hub of Whiting and Robertsdale. This meeting room featured the beautiful architecture, woodworking, and furnishings that graced the building's interior. (Whiting Historical Society.)

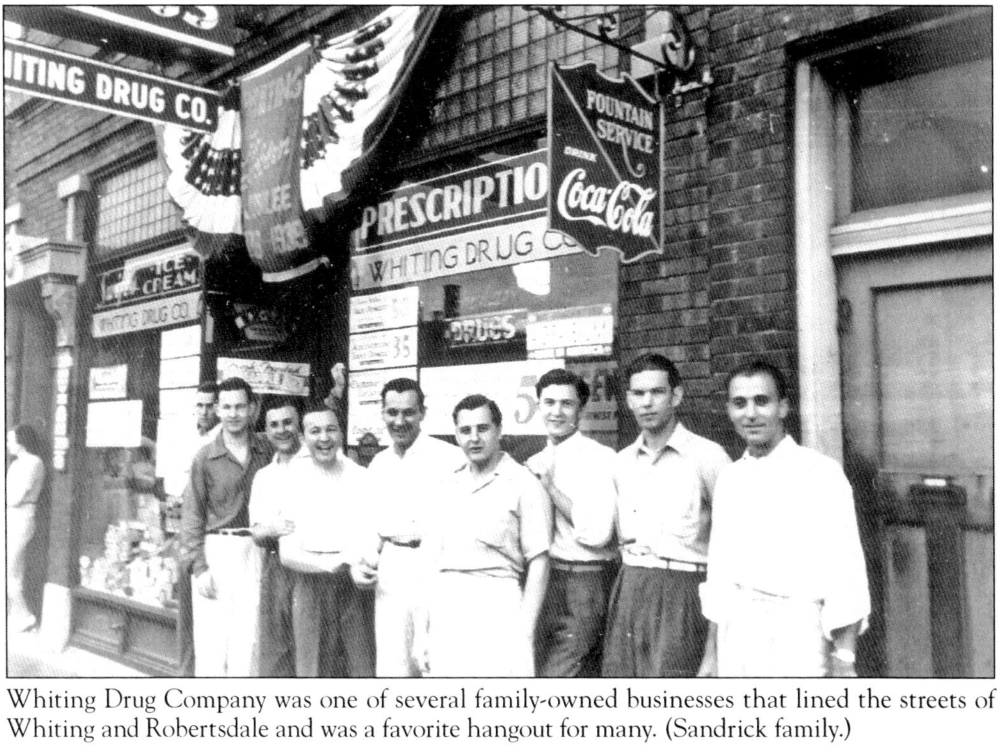

Whiting Drug Company was one of several family-owned businesses that lined the streets of Whiting and Robertsdale and was a favorite hangout for many. (Sandrick family.)

One of the largest complete refineries in the world, Standard Oil's Whiting location has seen much growth and evolution since it began operations in 1890. In this 1959 photograph, a crane puts a new piece of equipment into place. (Bill Harbour.)

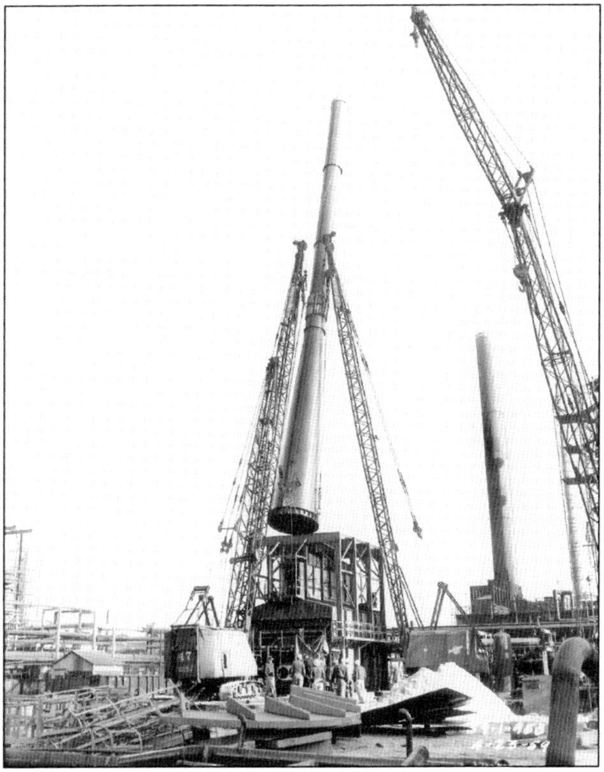

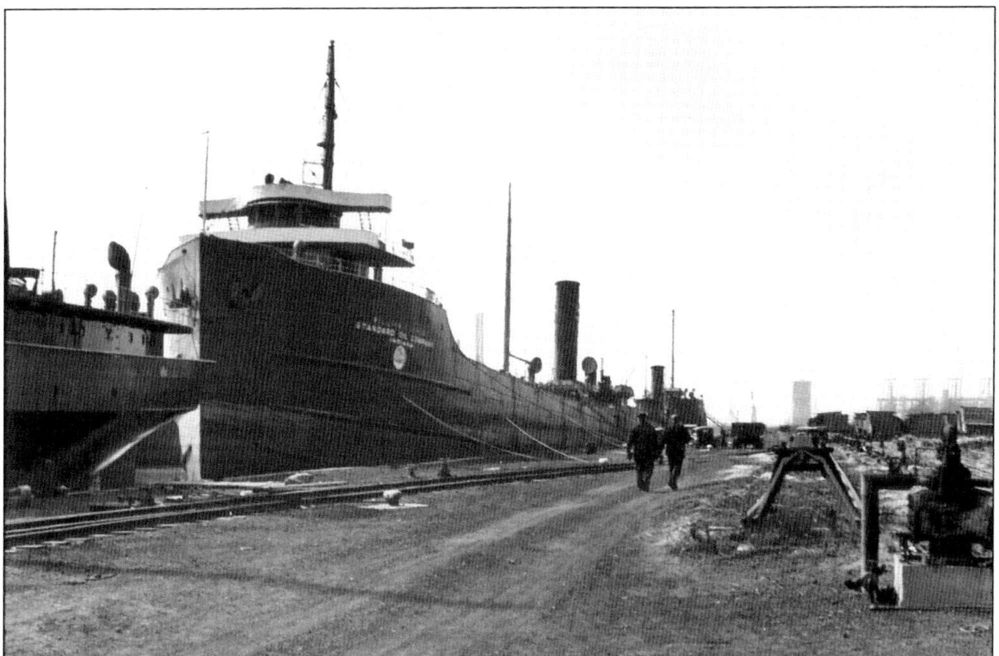

Situated along the southern shore of Lake Michigan, the Whiting refinery is able to distribute products easily by boat and by the many railways that crisscross the area. Here, the SS *William P. Cowan* sits at the docks ready for its next shipment. (Whiting Public Library.)

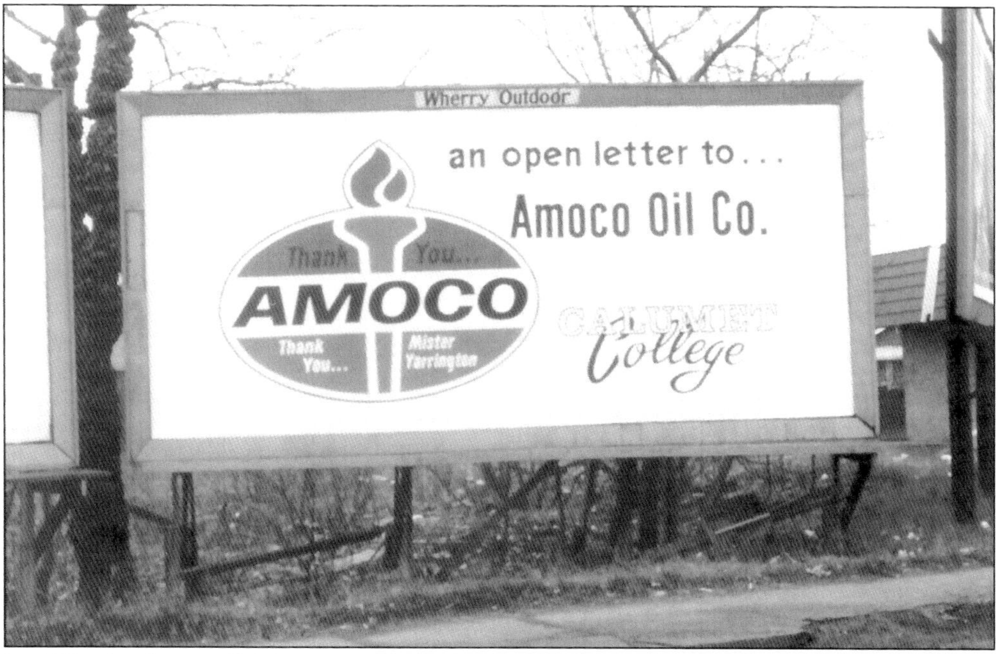

In 1973, the Amoco Oil Company, formerly the Standard Oil Company, deeded 256 acres of land in Robertsdale to Calumet College. The land included research-and-development buildings that had previously been used by the refinery. In 1976, the college moved to its newly renovated location at 2400 New York Avenue. (Specker Library, Calumet College of St. Joseph.)

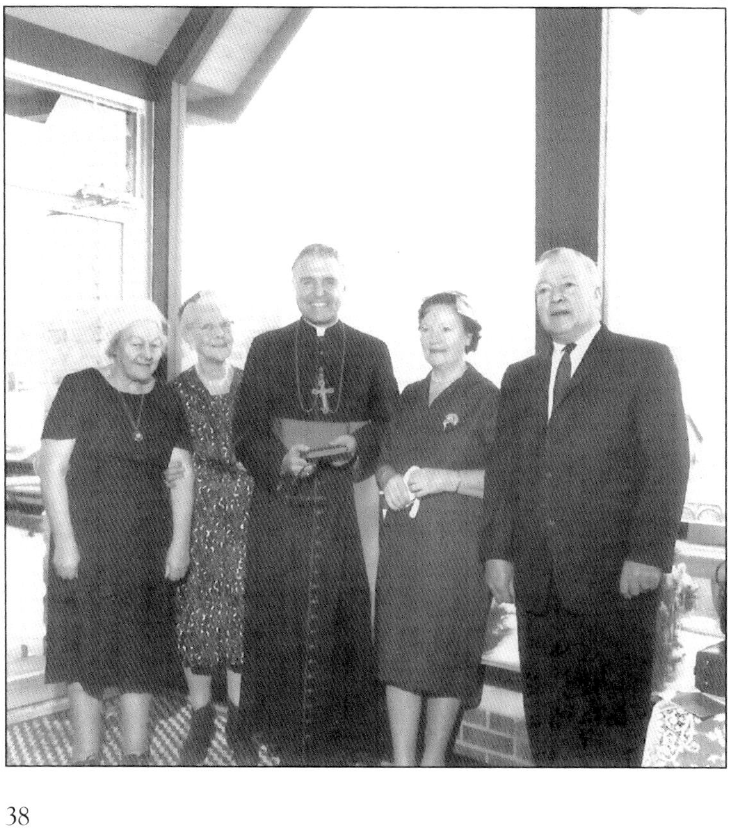

In 1963, Calumet College dedicated its library to the Specker family in honor of their support of the institution. Renamed Calumet College of St. Joseph in 1987 to reconnect with its Catholic roots, the college is sponsored by the Cincinnati Province of the Missionaries of the Precious Blood. It offers several degree programs and plays an integral role in the growth of the community. (Specker Library, Calumet College of St. Joseph.)

Three

Living and Learning

In 1920, thirty-six percent of Whiting residents were foreign-born and only 24 percent were American citizens. Many of the immigrants still spoke their own language, and as a result, the process of Americanization became more prevalent. Churches and community groups began to conduct classes to teach the new residents English and prepare them to become citizens.

Grocery stores began to pop up on nearly every corner, serving not just as sources of groceries but also as social centers where neighbors could gather and catch up on news about friends and relatives. The stores tended to cater to their own ethnic groups, and grocers came to know the needs and habits of their customers.

The family backyard was a haven for vegetable gardens, fruit trees, grape arbors, and small plots of flowers, and some families even raised chickens. The backyard was also the place where clothes were hung out to dry and neighbors visited with one another across the fence. And, of course, it served as a safe haven for children to play with their friends.

The war eras of the 1940s and 1950s had a significant impact on the community, heightening patriotism and bonding families in support of a common cause. Teachers saw it as a duty to their country to teach students and their parents how to be good Americans. To be prepared in case of an emergency, children's blood types were tattooed on their sides, and families received literature on how to build an air raid shelter.

Victory gardens became popular as part of Americans' commitment to assist the war effort by growing their own food, thereby freeing up food in the marketplace to be used for the troops. Rationing and recycling efforts also became commonplace, and the sale of war bonds became popular.

Families gathered on Sundays and imparted the values of their heritage and traditions. Children were content to play hide-and-go-seek, hopscotch, marbles, and jacks.

Community newspapers kept residents informed, starting with the *Congregationalist* in 1890. It was eventually followed by a series of other daily and weekly publications, including the *Whiting Standard*, *Whiting News*, *Ben Franklin News*, and *Whiting Times*. The community is now served by the monthly *WRite Stuff* newsletter.

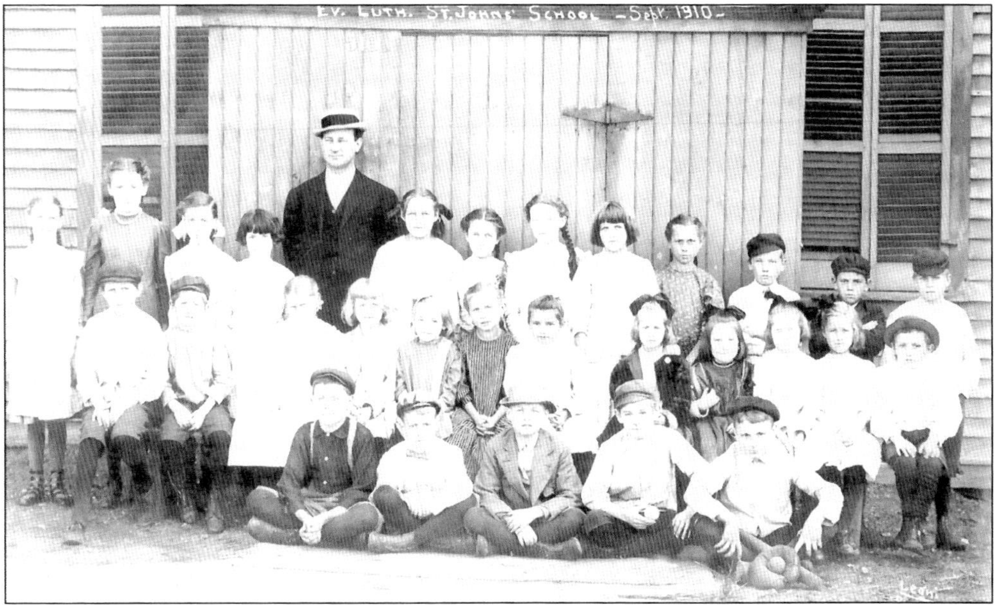

As early as 1866, German families gathered in a little schoolhouse near the present site of the Whiting refinery in what were the beginnings of Whiting's St. John's Evangelical Lutheran Church. Social and educational organizations began to form as well. A Lutheran day school was built and remained in use until 1911. This class gathered for a photograph in September 1910. (Whiting Historical Society.)

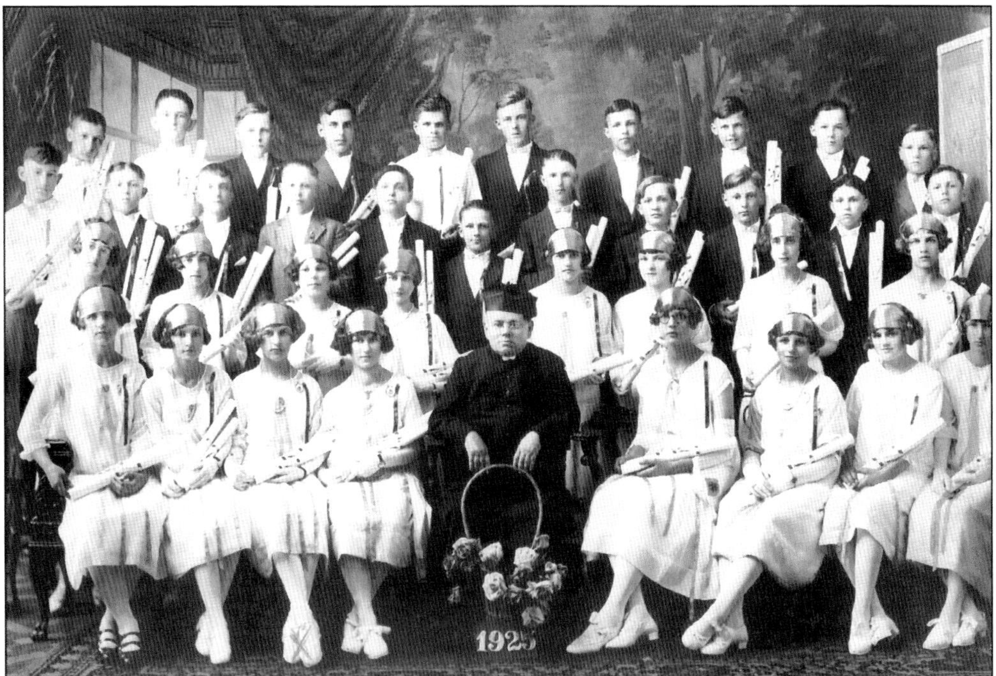

The 1925 class at St. John the Baptist School poses with the parish's founding pastor, Fr. Benedict Rajcany. The school opened in 1901 with 75 pupils. Students were taught by the Sisters of Providence from St. Mary's of the Woods. (Whiting Historical Society.)

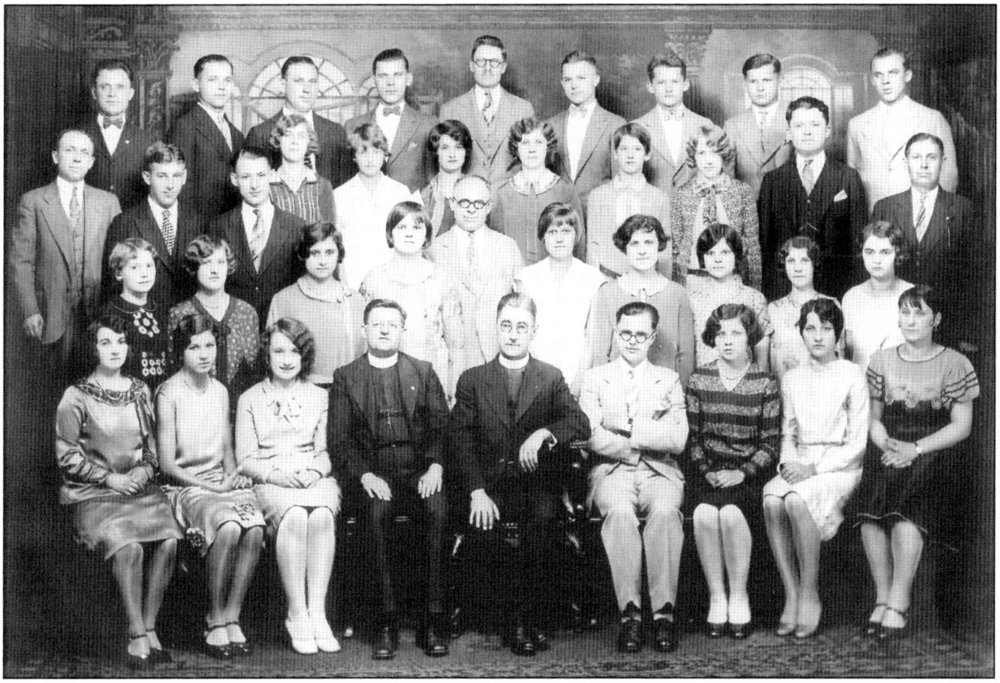

Church choirs provided a social and artistic outlet for parishioners. The choir group from St. Mary's Assumption Church in Whiting is seen here. (Whiting Historical Society.)

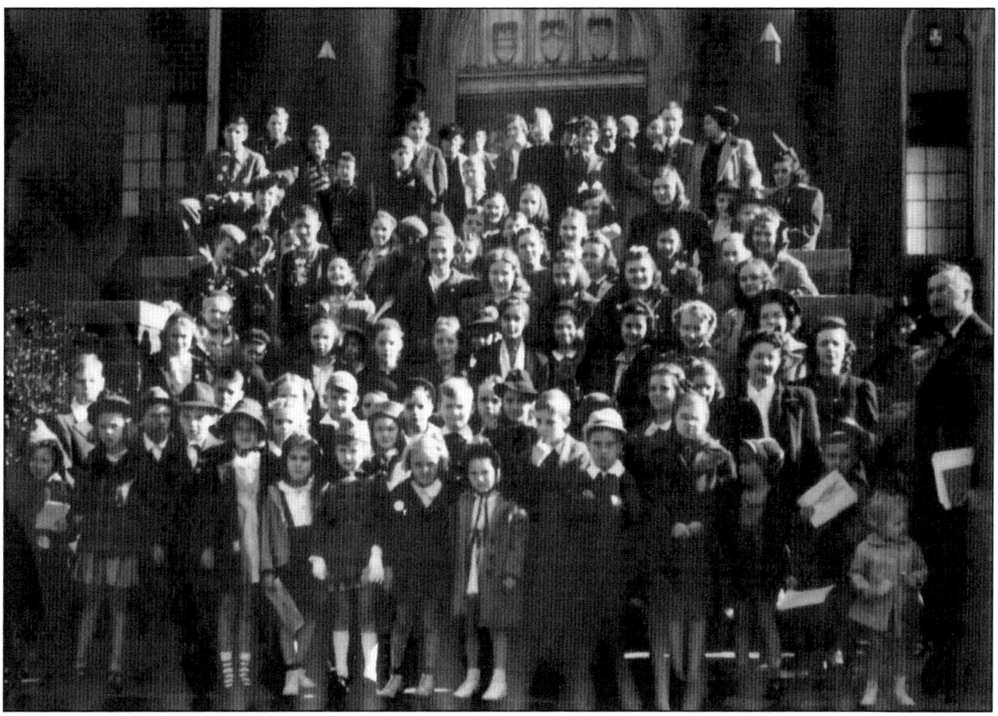

The Plymouth Congregational Church, at the corner of Stanton Avenue and 119th Street, provided religious instruction for the children of its congregation under the leadership of Richard McClaughry Sr. and Elizabeth Elster. (Whiting Historical Society.)

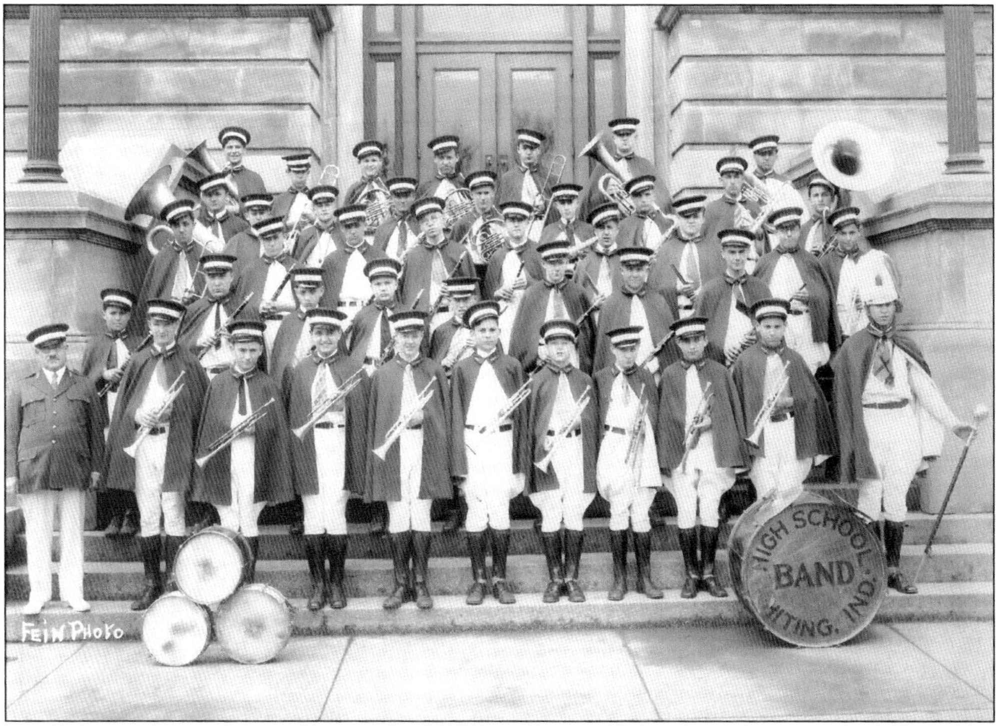

The Whiting High School boys' and girls' bands pose on the steps of Whiting High School in 1930. (Both, Whiting Public Library.)

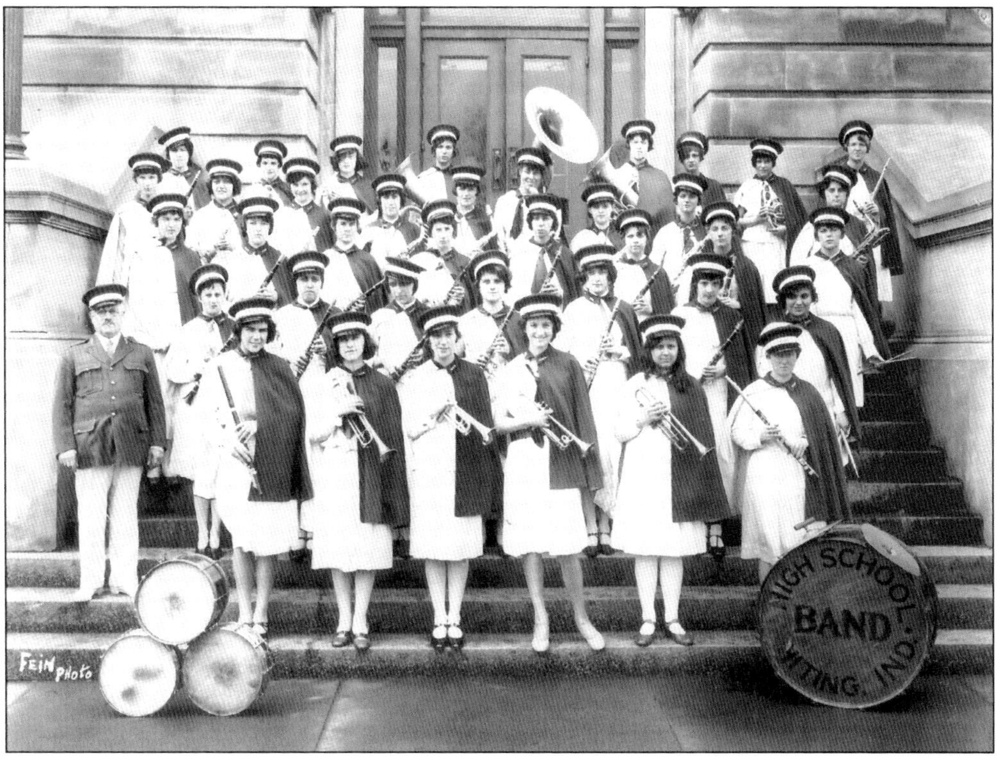

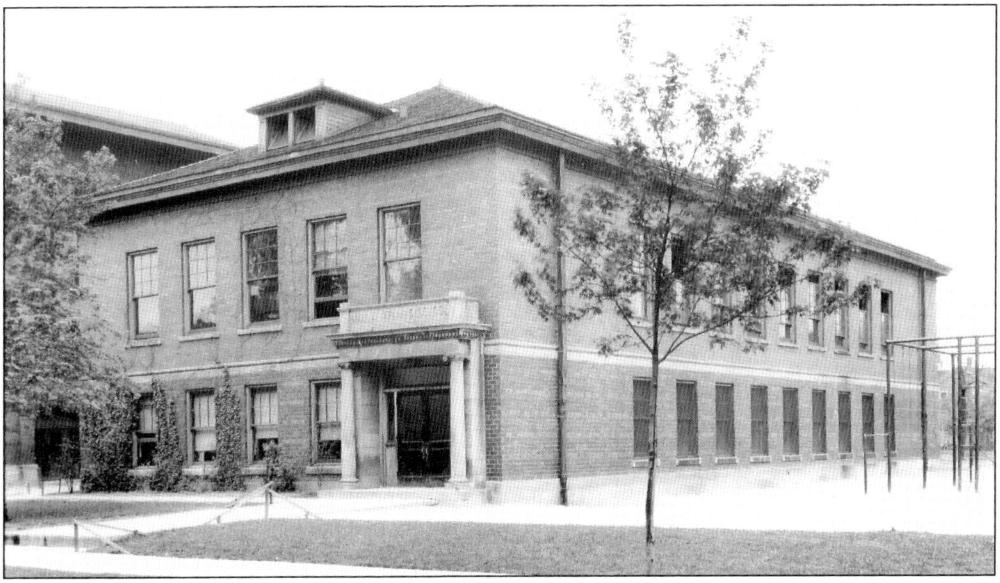

The Manual Training School was on Oliver Street next to the primary school. Whiting was among the first school districts in the Calumet Region to make manual training and domestic arts part of the school curriculum. Boys in grades five through eight were required to work one hour each week at manual training, and girls were required to spend the same amount of time on activities such as sewing. (Whiting Public Library.)

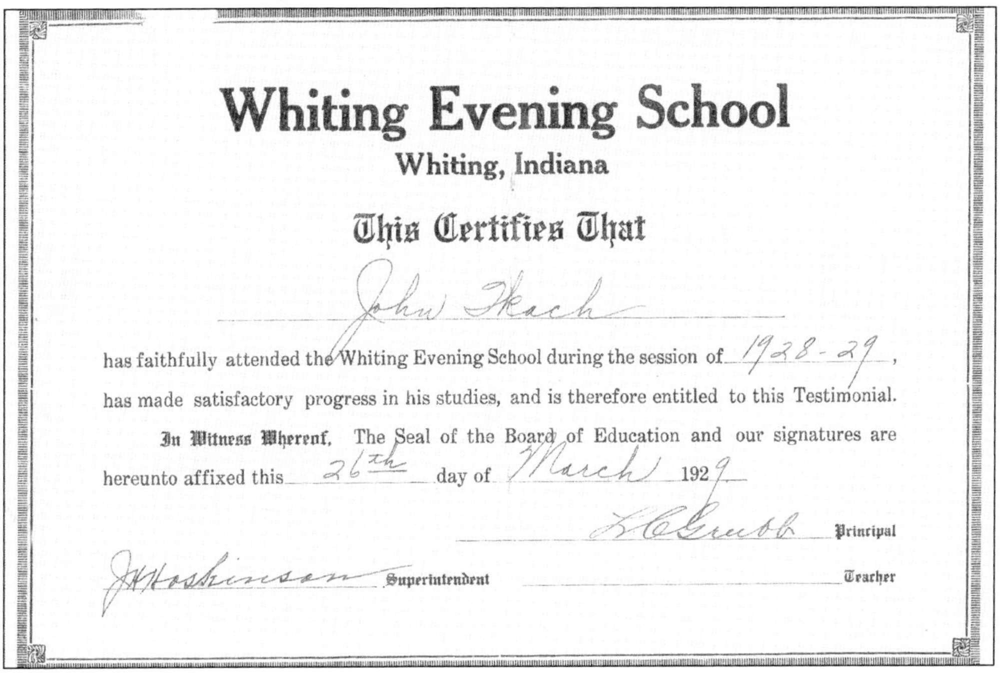

Whiting Evening School

Whiting, Indiana

This Certifies That

John Tkach

has faithfully attended the Whiting Evening School during the session of 1928-29,

has made satisfactory progress in his studies, and is therefore entitled to this Testimonial.

In Witness Whereof, The Seal of the Board of Education and our signatures are hereunto affixed this 26th day of March 1929.

L C Grubb **Principal**

JH Hoskinson **Superintendent** **Teacher**

In the 1920s, when many laborers were foreign-born, schools began to offer adult education, teaching English, American history, and government. Standard Oil also sponsored an Americanization program as a benefit to its employees. In order to better communicate in the workplace and in the community, John Tkach took advantage of the Whiting Evening School and earned this certificate in March 1929. (Tkach family.)

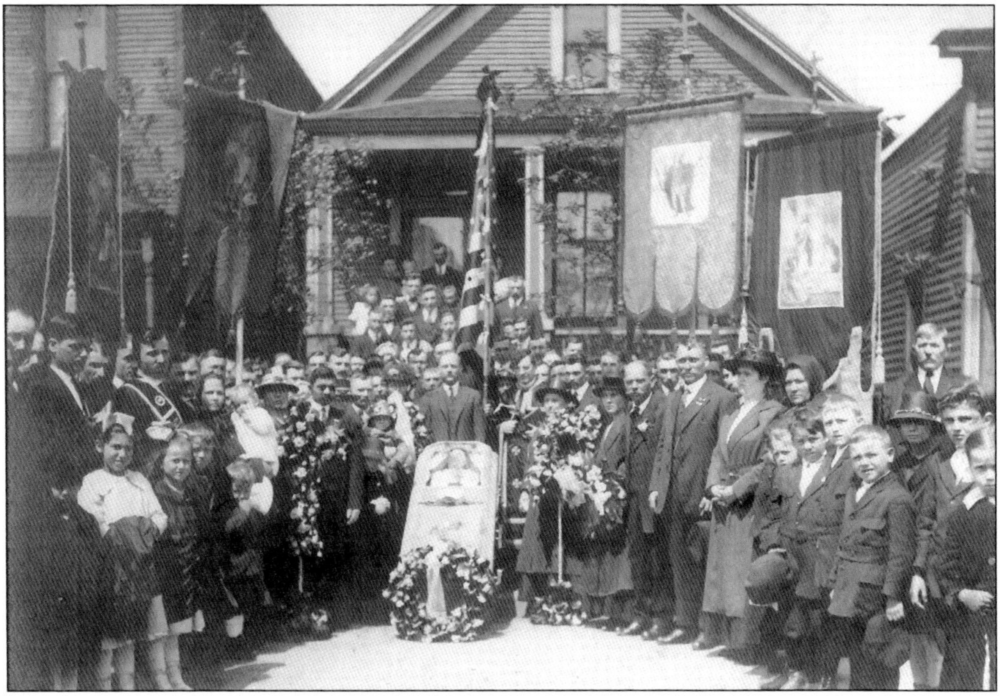

In the early 1900s, deceased family members were waked in the living rooms of their houses and surrounded by bouquets, vases of flowers, memorial wreaths, and casket sprays. This photograph was taken in 1918. (Lentvorsky family.)

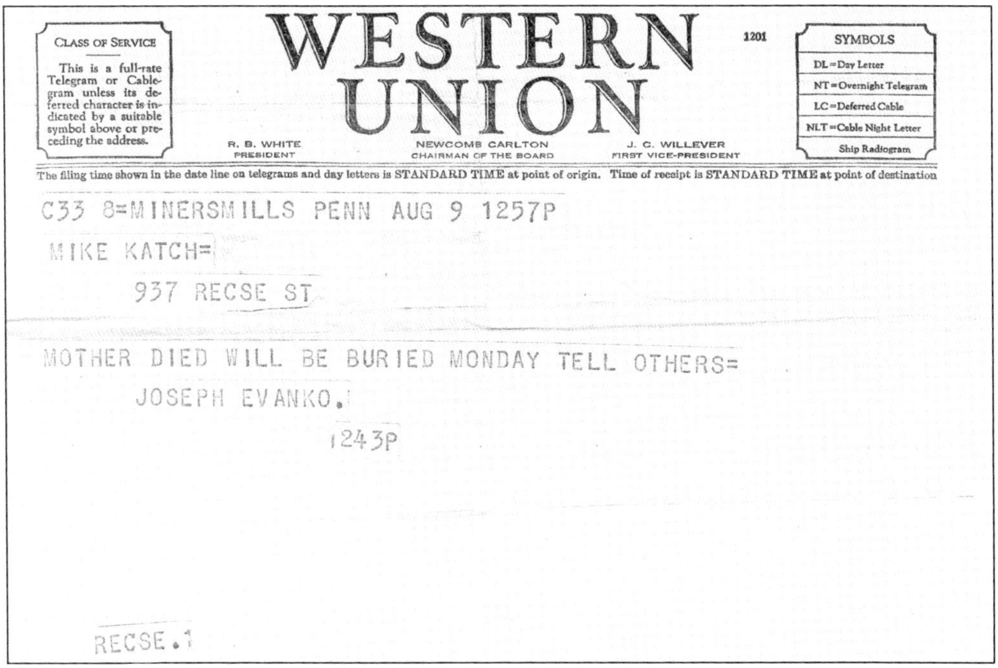

CLASS OF SERVICE
This is a full-rate Telegram or Cablegram unless its deferred character is indicated by a suitable symbol above or preceding the address.

WESTERN UNION

1201

SYMBOLS
DL = Day Letter
NT = Overnight Telegram
LC = Deferred Cable
NLT = Cable Night Letter
Ship Radiogram

R. B. WHITE, PRESIDENT — NEWCOMB CARLTON, CHAIRMAN OF THE BOARD — J. C. WILLEVER, FIRST VICE-PRESIDENT

The filing time shown in the date line on telegrams and day letters is STANDARD TIME at point of origin. Time of receipt is STANDARD TIME at point of destination

C33 8=MINERSMILLS PENN AUG 9 1257P
MIKE KATCH=
937 RECSE ST

MOTHER DIED WILL BE BURIED MONDAY TELL OTHERS=
JOSEPH EVANKO.

1243P

RECSE.1

Many immigrants to the United States left behind family members whom they never had the opportunity to see again. They often learned of their passing through notices from other family members, such as this one sent via Western Union. (Tkach family.)

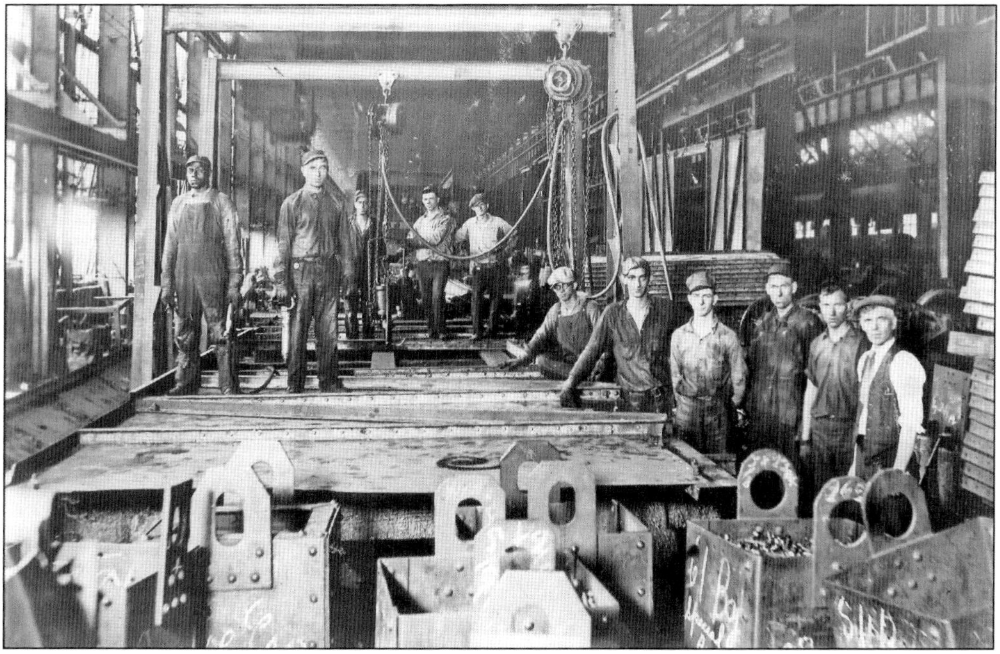

Men from several ethnic backgrounds learned to work together as a team within the confines of the Standard Oil refinery. While their languages, cultures, and traditions varied, they shared common bonds of a strong work ethic and pride in workmanship. (Domasica family.)

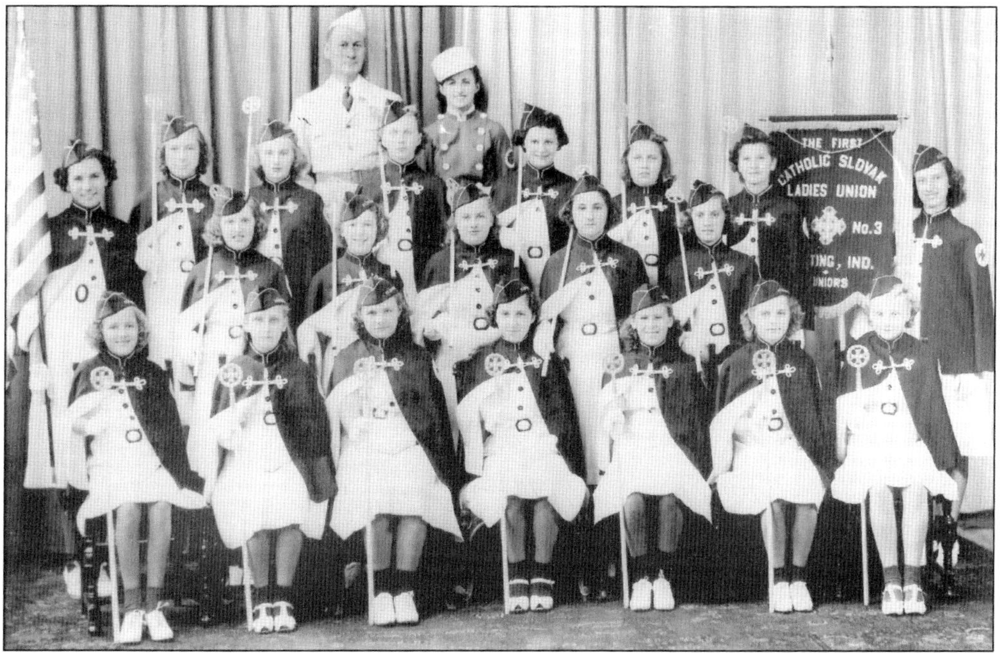

The purpose of the First Catholic Slovak Ladies Union of America was to provide friendly aid, mutual sympathy, and financial assistance while preserving and perpetuating the doctrines of their Catholic faith. The commonality of their Slovak background gave them a sense of belonging, allowed them to take pride in their heritage, and gave them an outlet for their social and organizational skills. (Whiting Historical Society.)

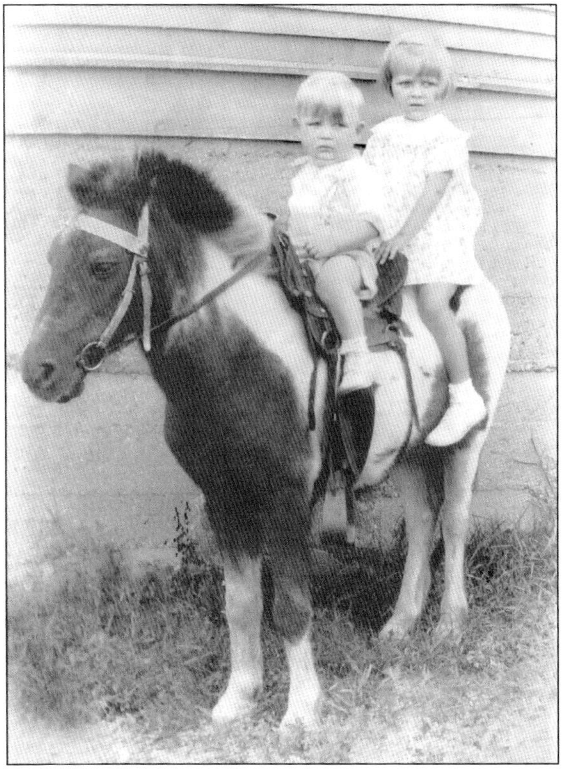

John and Anna Tkach pose on a Shetland pony outside their home on Lake Avenue in 1934. As cameras became more portable in the 1930s, photographers began traveling through neighborhoods with props such as this pony. The opportunity to sit on a pony was enticing to children, and for immigrant parents who had grown up in pastoral settings, it was reminiscent of home. To the families back in Europe to whom this photograph may have been sent, it conveyed a comforting message about what life was like in America. (Tkach family.)

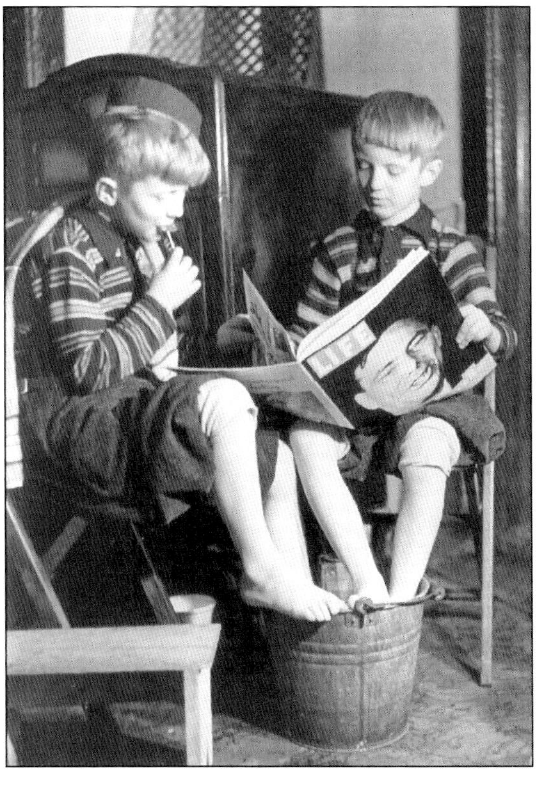

Twins James (left) and Donald Vrabel were common subjects of their father's photography. This photograph shows them reviewing the pages of the March 20, 1939, issue of *Life* magazine and soaking their tired feet from a hard day at play. (Vrabel family.)

This group of girls is all dressed up and ready to celebrate at a neighborhood birthday party. Cindy Hric stands in the front. Behind her are, from left to right, Peggy Jo Powell, Suzanne Vater, and Judy Hric. (Tkach family.)

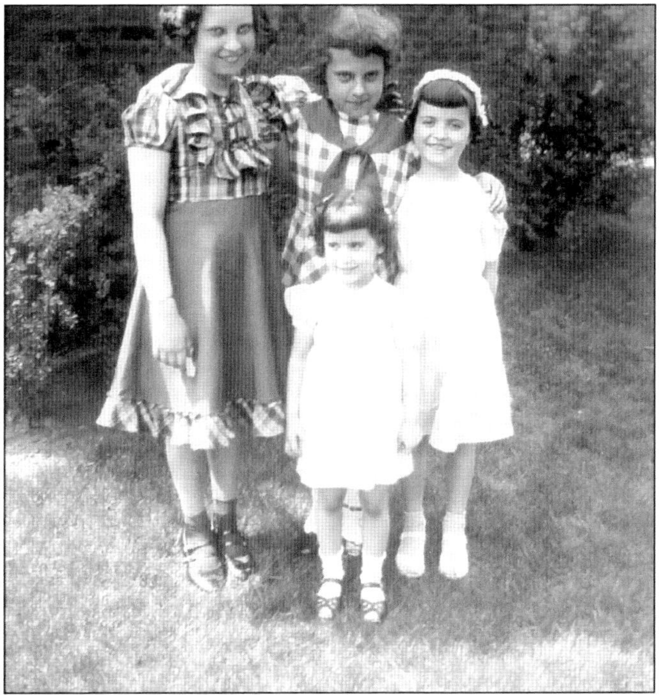

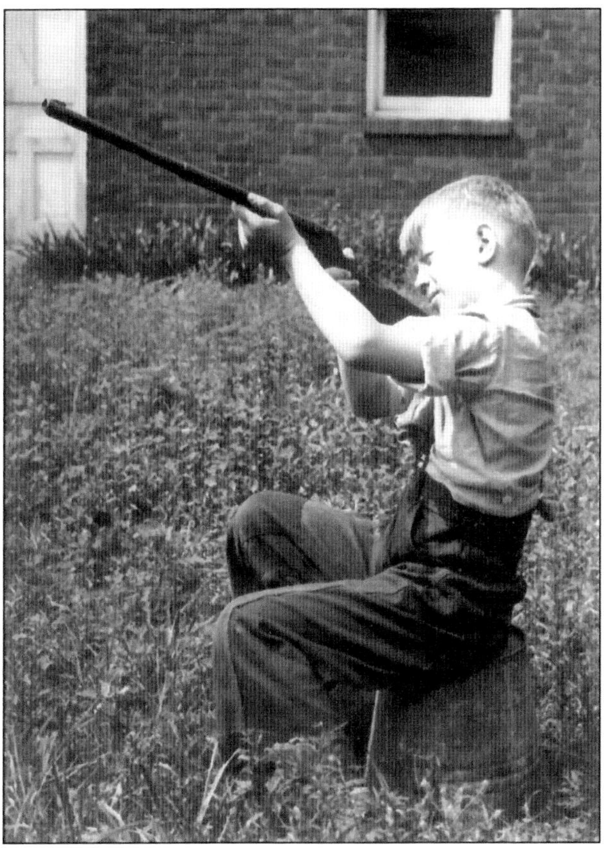

This photograph could have easily been the inspiration for the line, "Oh no, you'll shoot your eye out, kid," which was made famous by the movie *A Christmas Story*, based on the childhood memories of author Jean Shepherd, who grew up in nearby Hammond. The Red Ryder BB gun was first made available in 1938 and was coveted by young boys throughout the Calumet Region. (Vrabel family.)

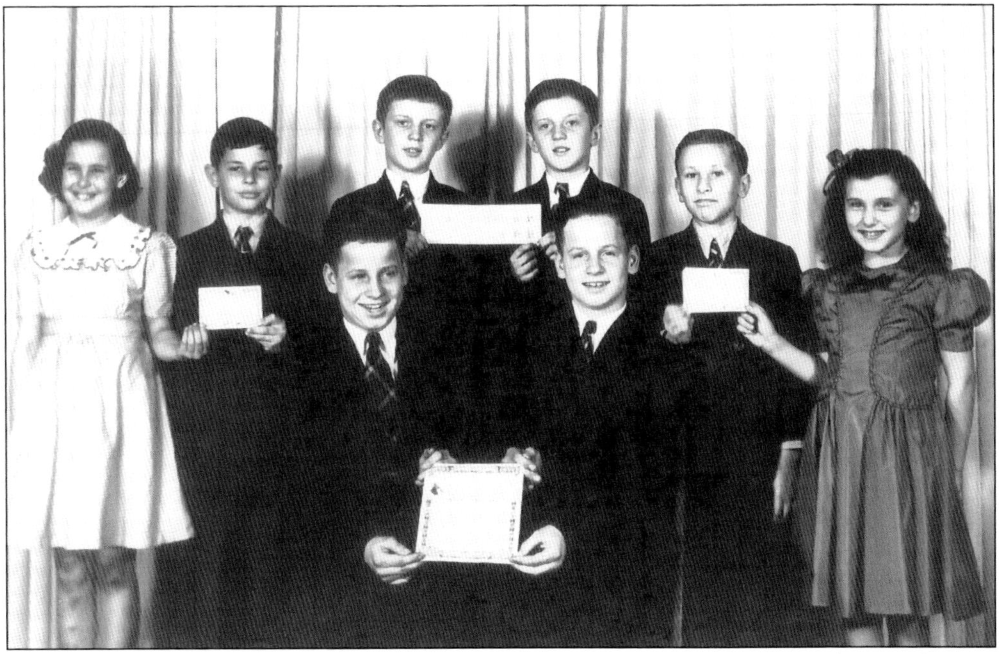

The industries of the Calumet Region provided much support during World War II by transforming their production lines to generate supplies and materials to support the troops overseas. Patriotism ran high in Whiting-Robertsdale, and even the children got involved in selling war bonds. By saving their nickels and dimes, citizens could buy stamps that could later be traded for a war bond. (Vrabel family.)

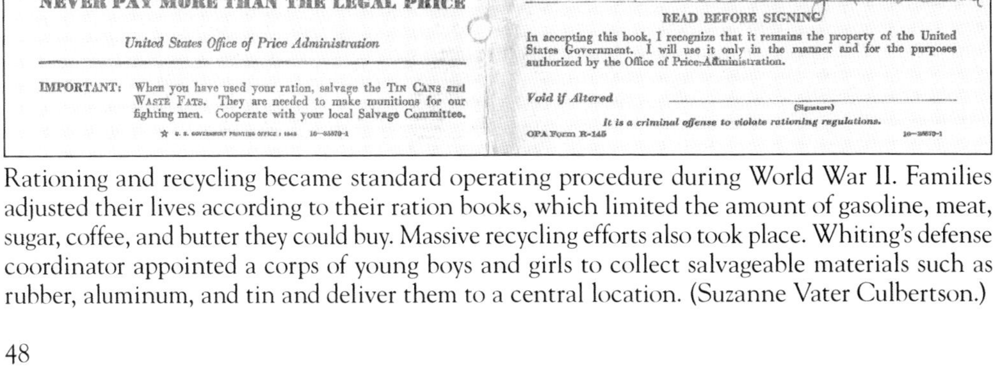

NEVER BUY RATIONED GOODS
WITHOUT RATION STAMPS

NEVER PAY MORE THAN THE LEGAL PRICE

United States Office of Price Administration

IMPORTANT: When you have used your ration, salvage the TIN CANS and WASTE FATS. They are needed to make munitions for our fighting men. Cooperate with your local Salvage Committee.

4

422262 BH

UNITED STATES OF AMERICA
OFFICE OF PRICE ADMINISTRATION

OPA

WAR RATION BOOK FOUR

Issued to ____
(Print first, middle, and last names)

Complete address ____

READ BEFORE SIGNING

In accepting this book, I recognize that it remains the property of the United States Government. I will use it only in the manner and for the purposes authorized by the Office of Price Administration.

Void if Altered ____
(Signature)

It is a criminal offense to violate rationing regulations.

OPA Form R-145

Rationing and recycling became standard operating procedure during World War II. Families adjusted their lives according to their ration books, which limited the amount of gasoline, meat, sugar, coffee, and butter they could buy. Massive recycling efforts also took place. Whiting's defense coordinator appointed a corps of young boys and girls to collect salvageable materials such as rubber, aluminum, and tin and deliver them to a central location. (Suzanne Vater Culbertson.)

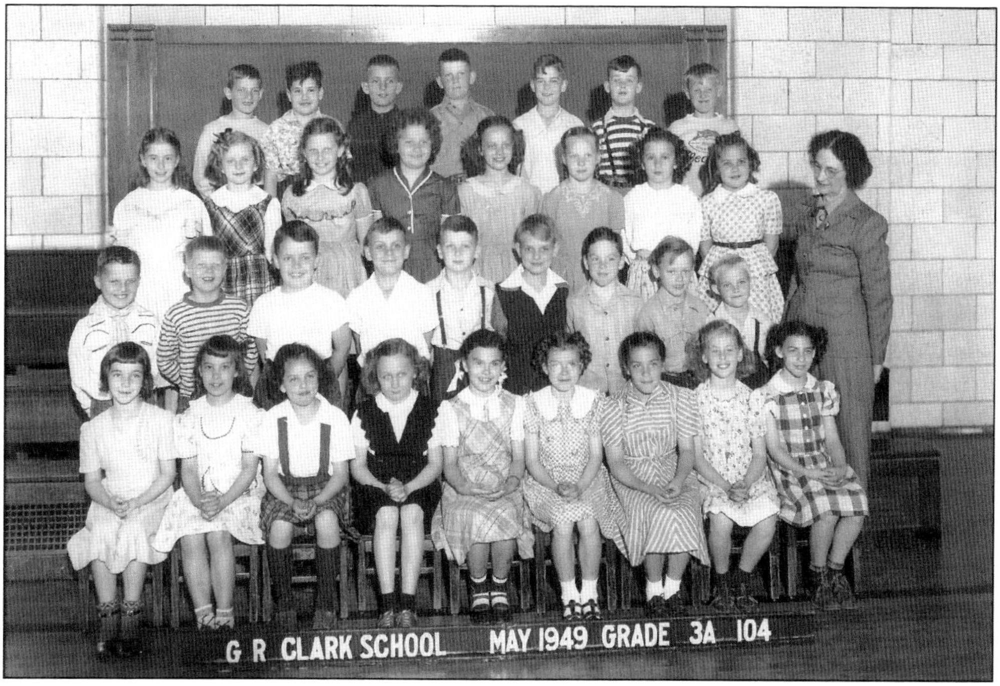

Elementary school children who lived in Robertsdale attended George Rogers Clark School, which was originally founded as West Park School in 1922 and was located at 120th Street and Davis Avenue. The school building, now located at 1921 Davis Avenue, was founded in 1932 and was enlarged in 1939. (Tkach family.)

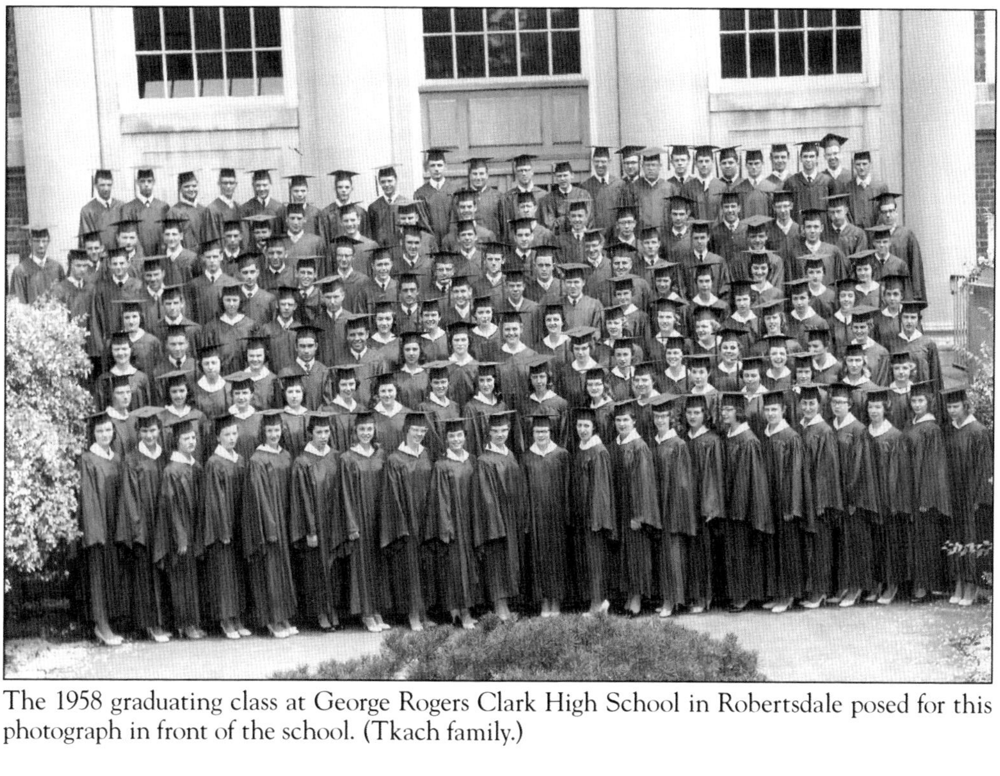

The 1958 graduating class at George Rogers Clark High School in Robertsdale posed for this photograph in front of the school. (Tkach family.)

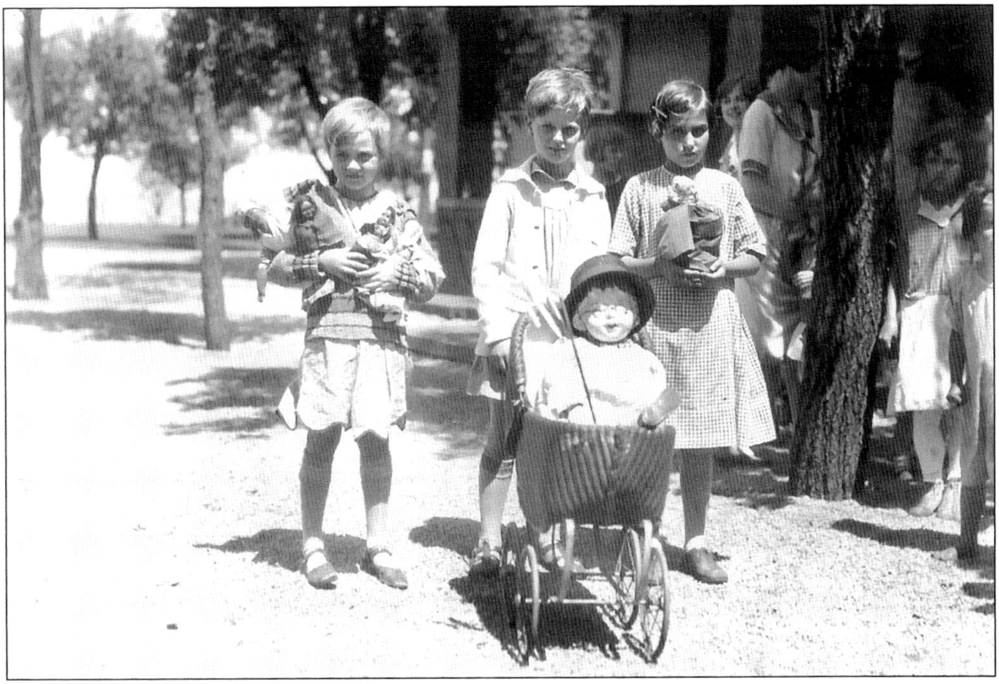

These young girls are at the annual doll show sponsored by the Whiting Community Center at Whiting Park. They were already well on their way to embracing the skills and traditions being taught to them by their mothers and grandmothers. (Whiting Historical Society.)

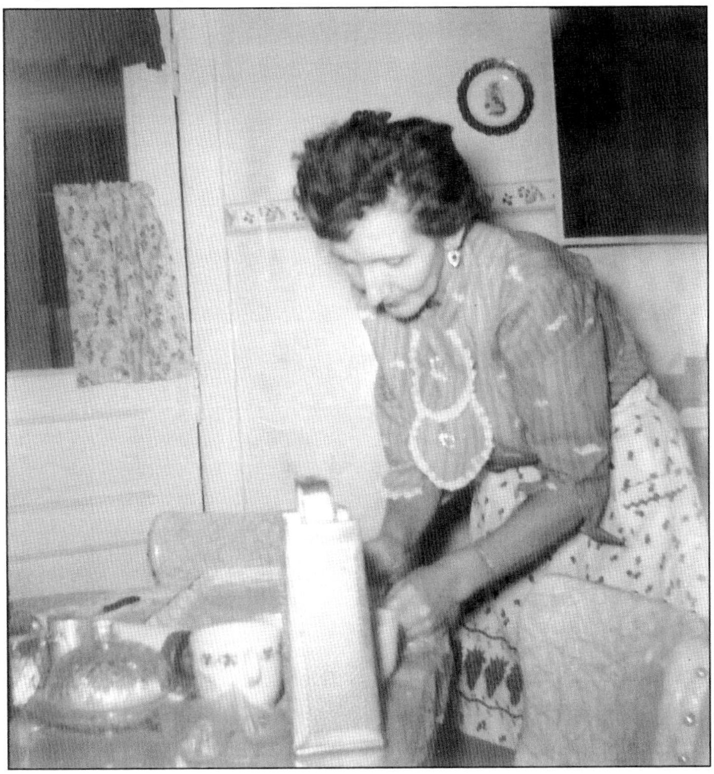

Women in the community were master chefs and highly skilled at creative cooking, stretching ingredients, and putting in just the right amount based on experience. Mondays were for washing, Tuesdays for ironing, Fridays for cleaning, and Saturdays for baking. The best day was Sunday, when everyone attended church and then gathered as a family to partake of delicious food and enjoy a day of rest. (Tkach family.)

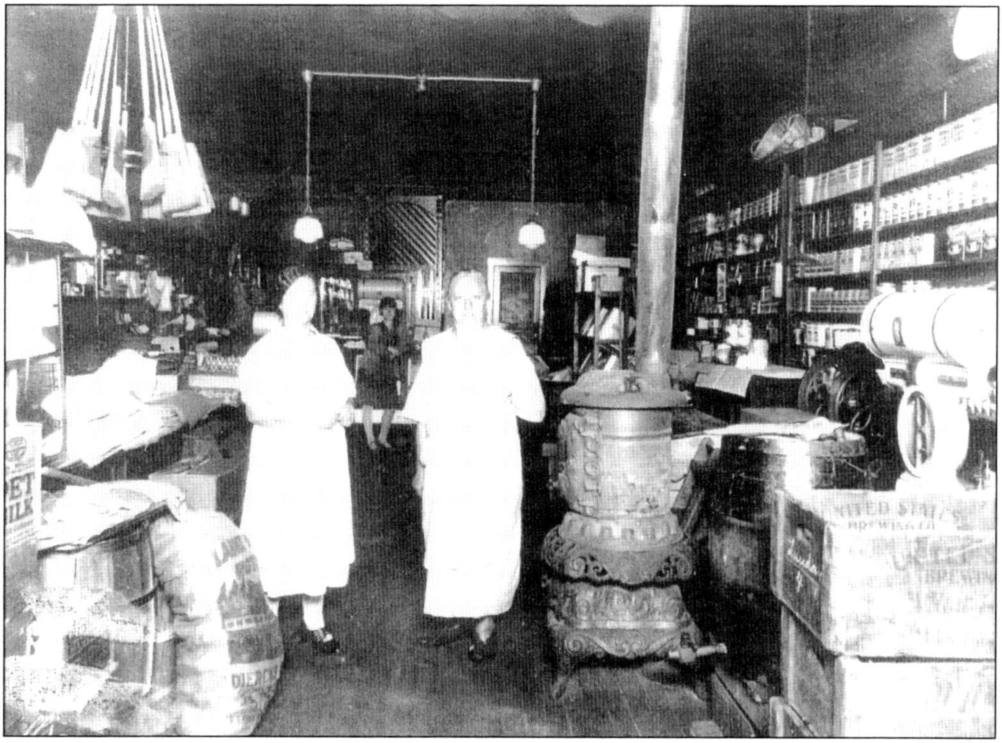

Mom-and-pop grocery stores were on nearly every corner in Whiting and Robertsdale. Paunicka's, at the corner of 121st Street and Superior Avenue, served many of the neighboring Slovaks, while Lucasek's, across the street, served the Polish population. (Dolores Paunicka Callahan.)

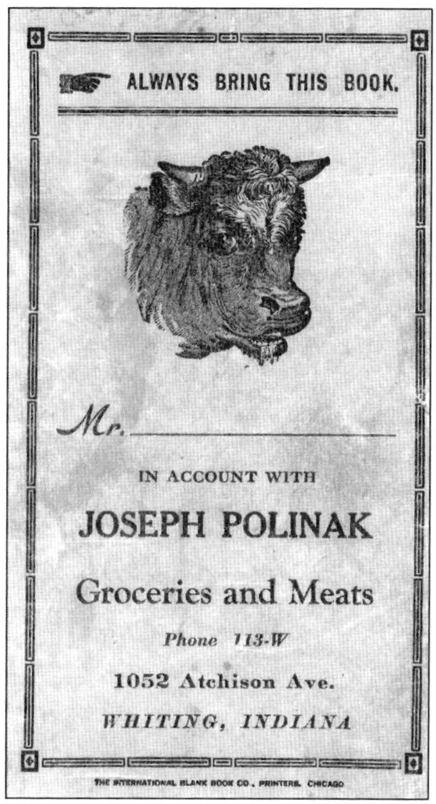

"Put it on the book" was a common phrase in the era of corner grocery stores. Mothers could send children to the store to pick up a few items without having to send money with them. The clever ones soon figured out they could add a few things to the order and not have to pay for it. When payday came and it was time to settle the account, the children learned a quick lesson about credit. (Tkach family.)

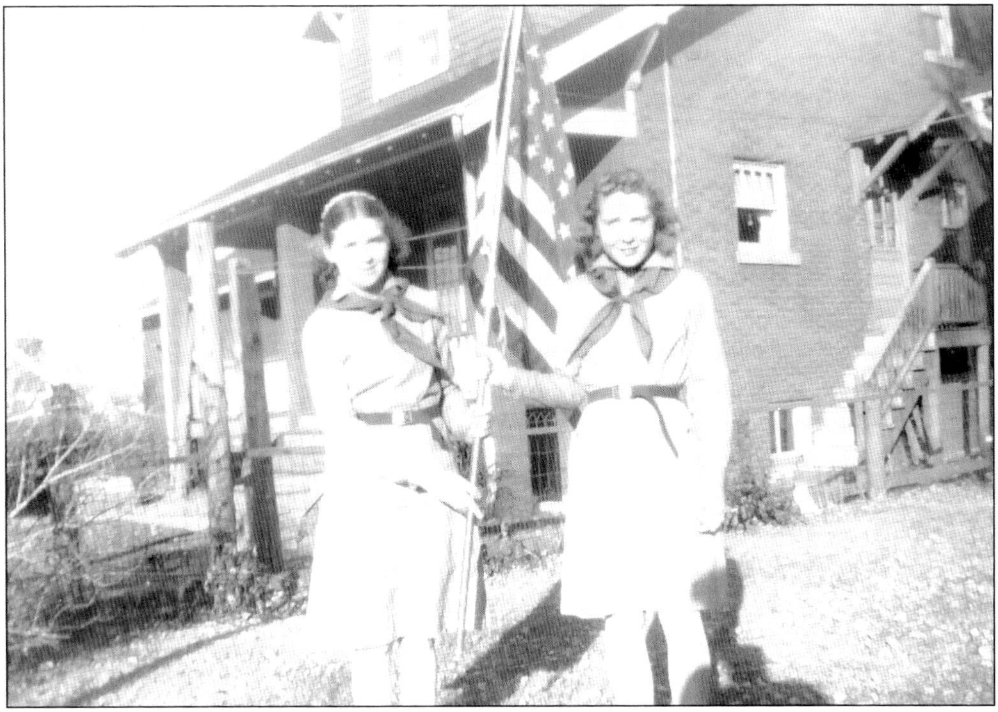

Girl Scouts was a popular activity for young girls. Elaine Gehring (left) and Phyllis Blohm are seen here in their Scout uniforms proudly clutching the American flag. (Elaine Gehring.)

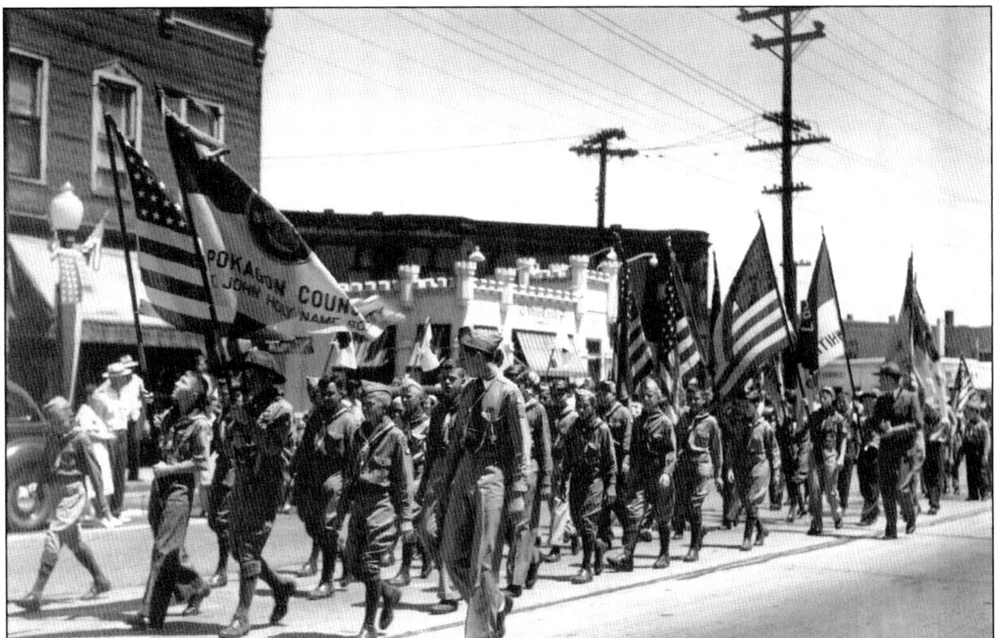

The Boy Scouts of the Pokagon Council, sponsored by St. John the Baptist's Holy Name Society, march down Indianapolis Boulevard in the annual Fourth of July parade. (St. John the Baptist Parish.)

Francis Lentvorsky, a student at Whiting High School, was one of many responsible young men who learned to serve their community at a young age as patrol boys. They were charged with assisting schoolchildren crossing the street and were formally identified by their white cloth belts. Those who served in leadership roles also received special badges and emblems to wear on their chest straps, as seen here. (Lentvorsky family.)

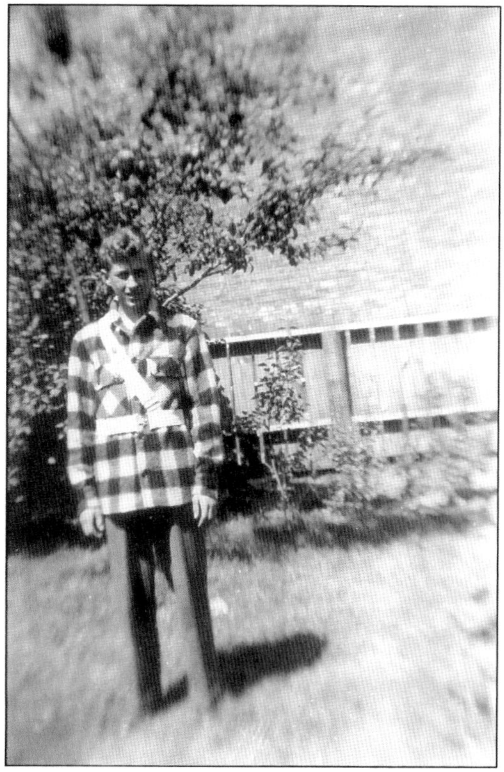

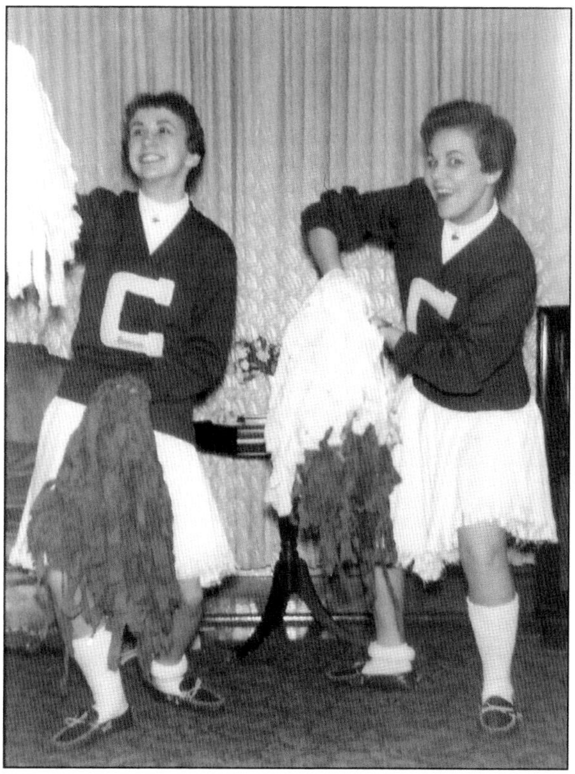

Gerri Kacer (left) and Nancy Tkach were cheerleaders for George Rogers Clark High School and were very successful at keeping their school spirit alive. (Tkach family.)

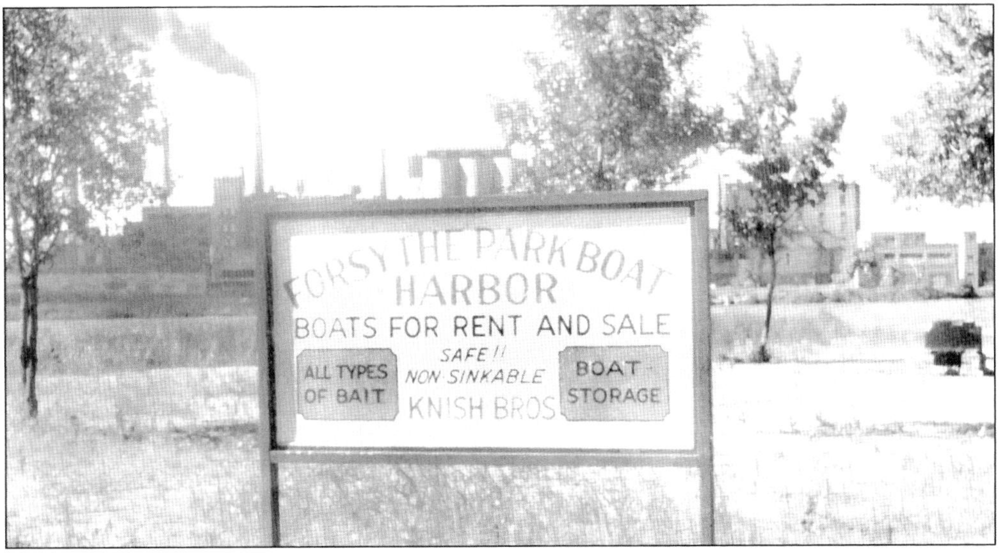

Located on the north side of Wolf Lake, Forsythe Park offers facilities for children and adults alike. In the background are the industries visible from the park and typical of the Calumet Region. (Whiting Historical Society.)

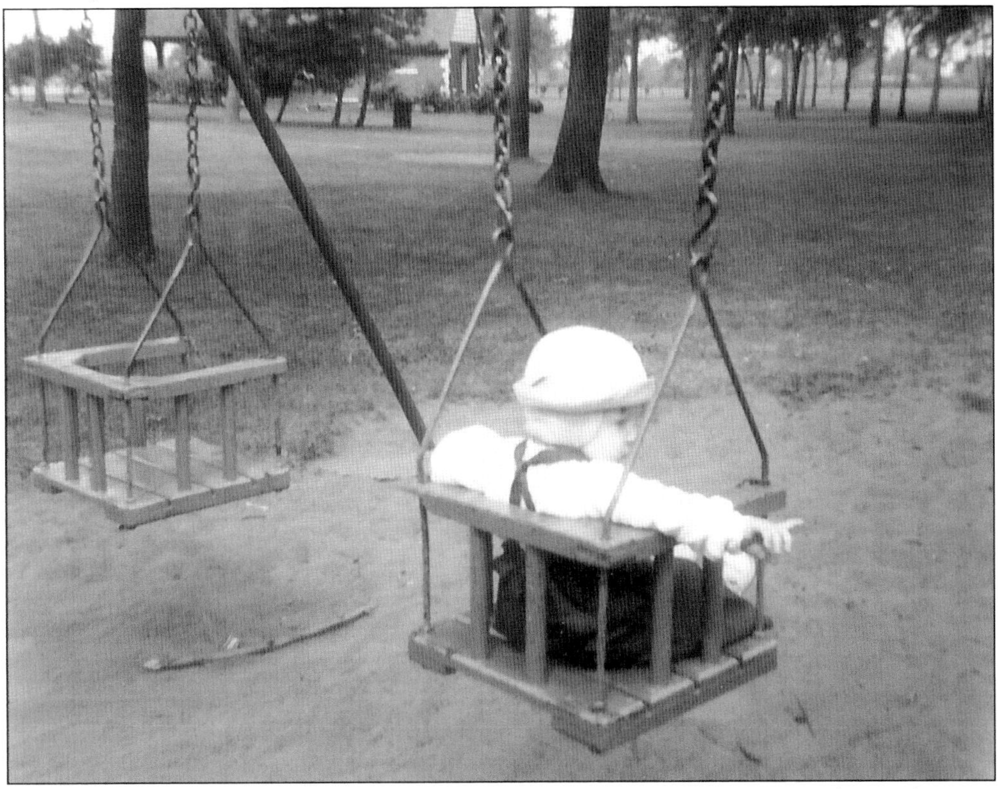

Forsythe Park has long been a favorite destination for family picnics, reunions, and special events. It provides a peaceful setting despite the neighboring industry and is a pleasant place to enjoy the area's natural habitat. Greg Domasica, seen here as a baby, and his family have visited the park for many years. (Domasica family.)

Four

Socializing

The small community of Whiting-Robertsdale, which started out as frontier-like town, soon began to offer social activities that rivaled those of the larger communities surrounding it. The Owl's Club and the Fortnightly Club were among Whiting's earliest organizations, formed in the 1890s to fight the boredom of the early settlers. They sponsored dances, outings, sporting events, and theatrical productions and set the stage for numerous other social and fraternal organizations founded since then.

To accommodate these activities, several halls and auditoriums were constructed, including Vater's Hall, St. Mary's Hall, Frankowski's Hall, and the Slovak Dom. The Whiting Greys baseball team was the first of many sports teams to be formed, and for the outdoorsmen, there were boating and hunting clubs.

Another source of social activity was at Five Points, the intersection of Indianapolis Boulevard, Calumet Avenue, and 114th Street near the Indiana-Illinois state line. Attractions there in the early 1900s included an amusement park, a roller rink, a beach, a dance hall, and a marina.

In 1909, Whiting purchased land along the Lake Michigan shore to develop a lakefront park. A beach house, a pavilion, a baseball field, and a man-made lagoon were constructed, and swings and slides were added along the beach's shoreline. Weekly concerts and dances were held at the pavilion, and Whiting Park became a popular site for social events.

Once the Whiting Community Center opened in 1923, it became the hub of social activities, offering contests and special events for children and adults all year long. Common activities included kite-flying tournaments, marble tournaments, bowling, Easter egg hunts, and Christmas parties.

Theaters and movie houses were also popular attractions. Over the years, Whiting operated four movie houses and an opera house: the Palace, the Star Theatre, the Princess Theatre, the Capitol Theatre, and the Hoosier Theatre. The Hoosier became Whiting's finest cinema and continues to operate to this day.

Groups such as the Knights of Columbus, the Elks Club, and the Lions Club provided fellowship opportunities for the community's residents while also contributing to many charitable causes. Churches formed numerous women's clubs, bands, theater groups, drama clubs, and other organizations.

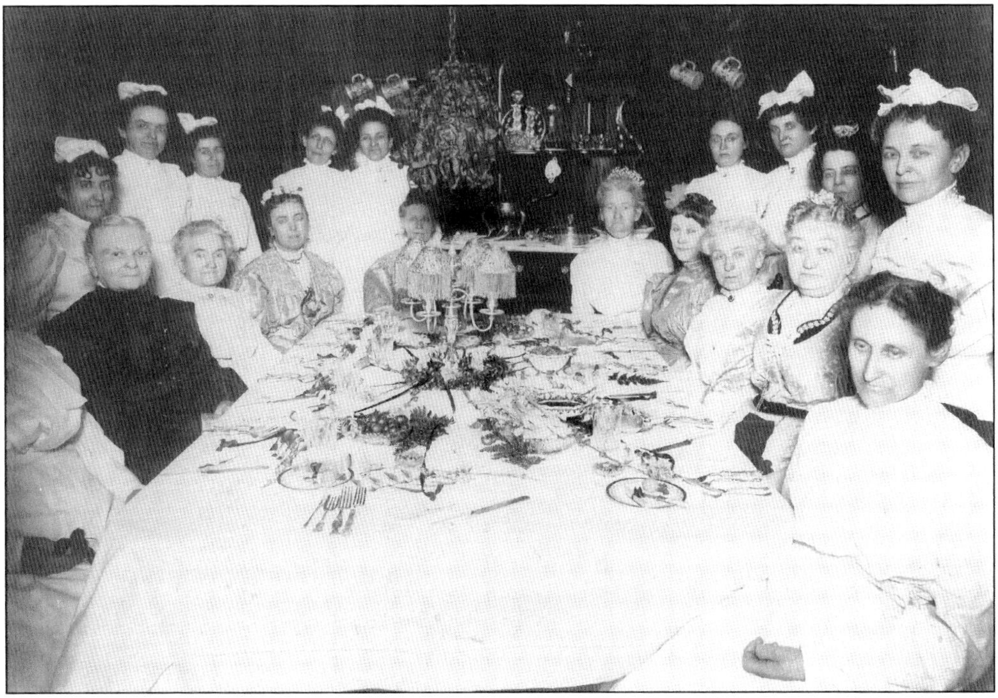

This group of women gathers for a Ladies Aid banquet at the Warwick home on Oliver Street in the early 1900s. (Whiting Public Library.)

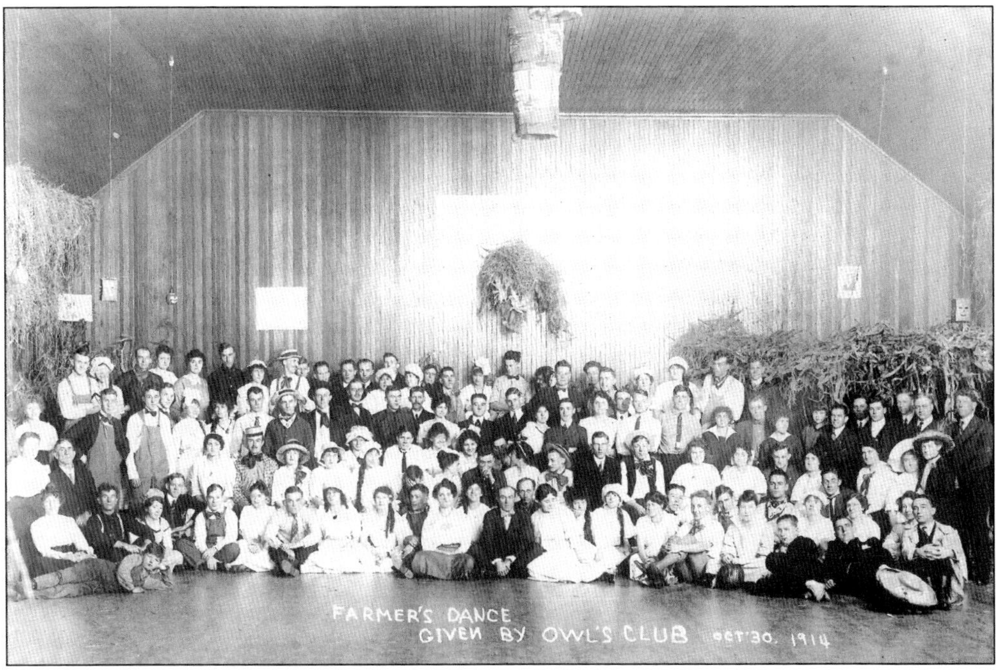

The Owl's Club was established in 1893 by a group of young men working at the Standard Oil refinery. Their purpose was to provide a social outlet for the early citizens of Whiting. They organized a variety of activities such as bicycle outings, dances, and sporting events. This group gathered for a Farmer's Dance given by the Owl's Club in 1914. (Whiting Public Library.)

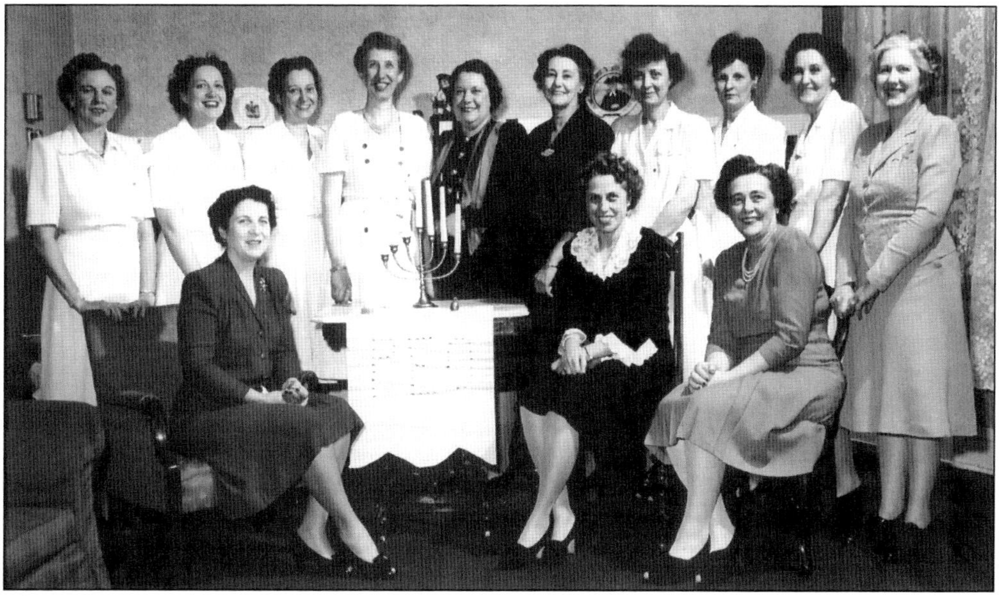

The PEO Sisterhood is a philanthropic education organization founded in 1869. These charter members of Chapter AH in Whiting gathered for a group photograph at one of their meetings. (Whiting Public Library.)

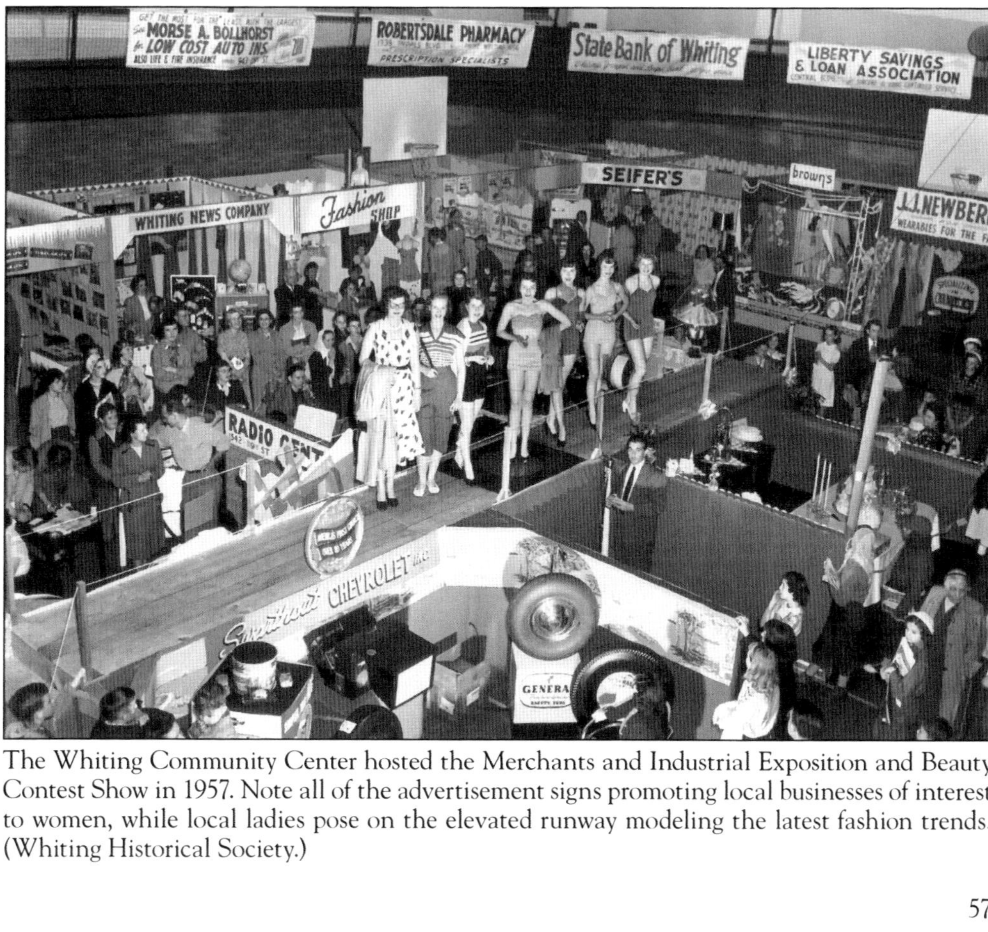

The Whiting Community Center hosted the Merchants and Industrial Exposition and Beauty Contest Show in 1957. Note all of the advertisement signs promoting local businesses of interest to women, while local ladies pose on the elevated runway modeling the latest fashion trends. (Whiting Historical Society.)

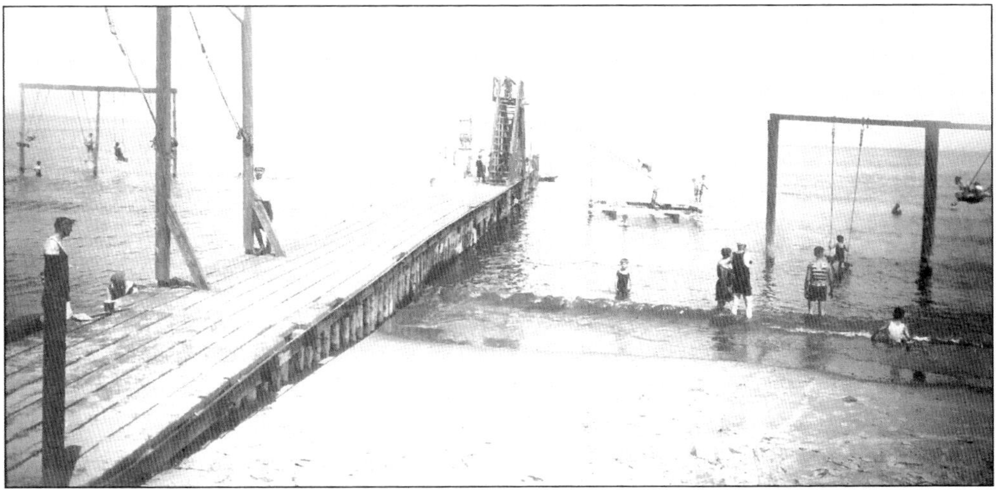

The bathing beach at Whiting's Lakefront Park in 1931 featured swings along the shoreline as well as a large slide and a pier to add to beachgoers' enjoyment. (Whiting Historical Society.)

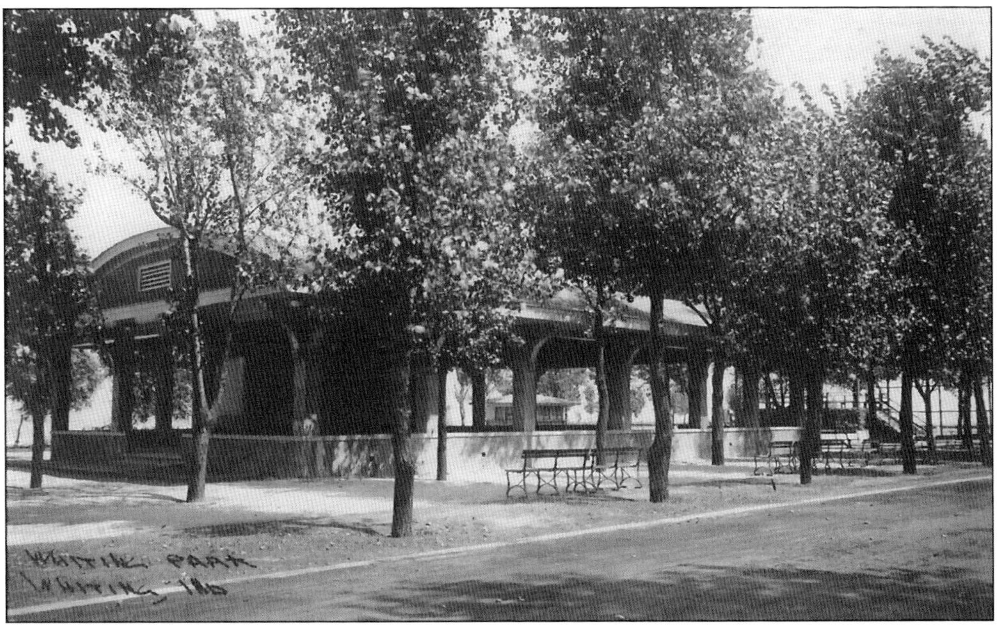

Whiting Park was established in 1909 after 22 acres were purchased from the Forsythe estate. Attractive walkways and roads were built to guide visitors through the area, and a bridge was built to span a man-made lagoon. By 1916, weekly concerts and dances were being held at the pavilion, and in 1920, a concrete pavilion was built to replace the wooden one. (Sandrick family.)

This advertisement promotes a boxing and wrestling show sponsored by St. John's Athletic Association and featuring members of the parish, including four-year-old twins James "Jimmie" and Donald Vrabel, who competed at the welterweight level. (Vrabel family.)

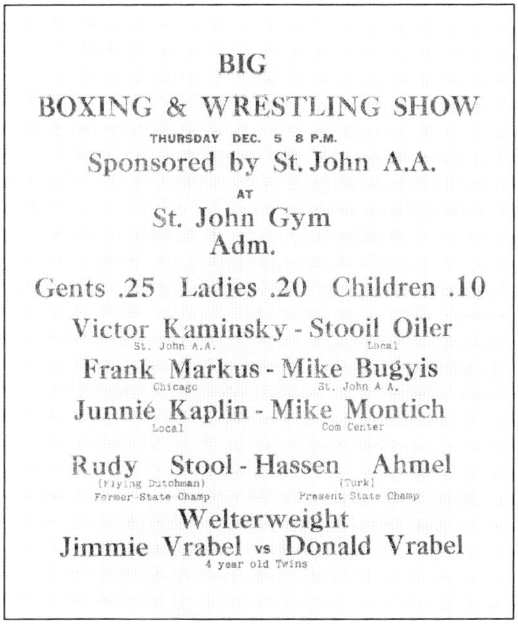

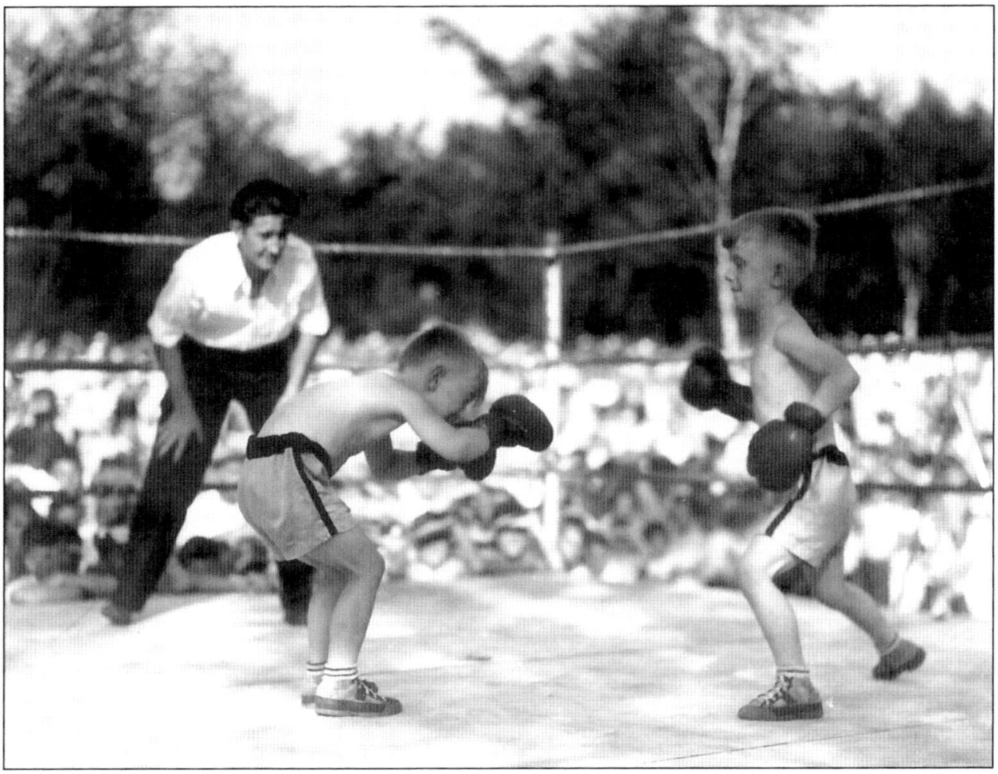

The Whiting Athletic Association sponsored an Annual Field Day each year on the Fourth of July at Whiting Park, providing a full day of recreation and activities for all of the Calumet Region to enjoy. Four-year-old twins Donald and James Vrabel fought it out in the ring in front of a large crowd at the annual picnic in 1935. Their father, George Vrabel, served as the official. (Vrabel family.)

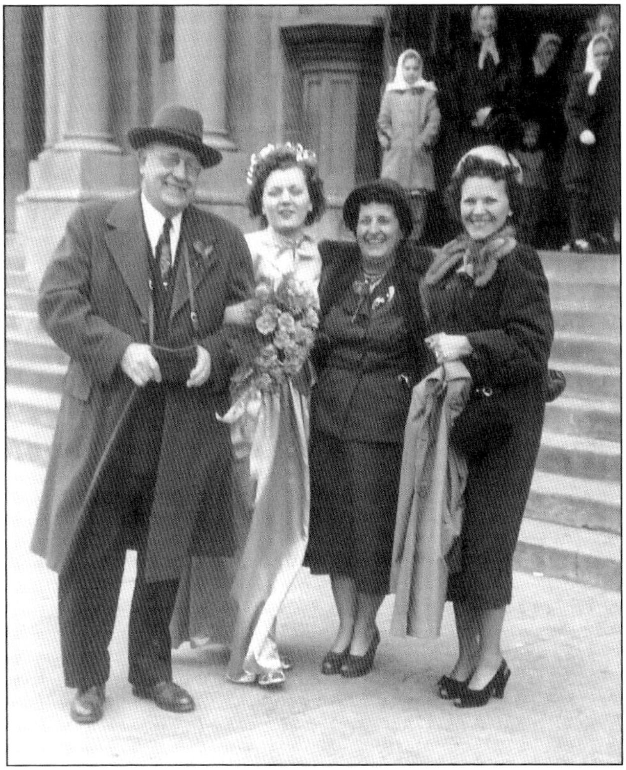

Harry Glair, an executive at Standard Oil, and his wife pose with friends at a Svitko family wedding. They are, from left to right, Harry Glair, Irene Svitko Morgan, Hortense Glair, and Margaret Svitko Kmetz, who worked for the Glair family. (Svitko family.)

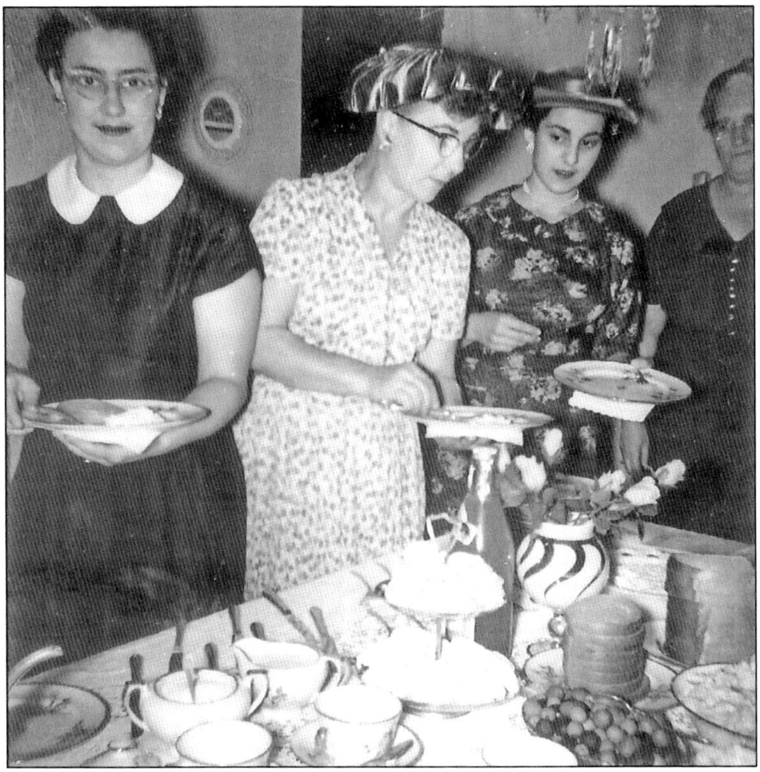

Friends gather for a special occasion, as evidenced by the spread on the dining room table, the use of the good china, and the hats worn by the women. Food is at the center of just about every special event held in Whiting-Robertsdale, no matter how large or small. (Tkach family.)

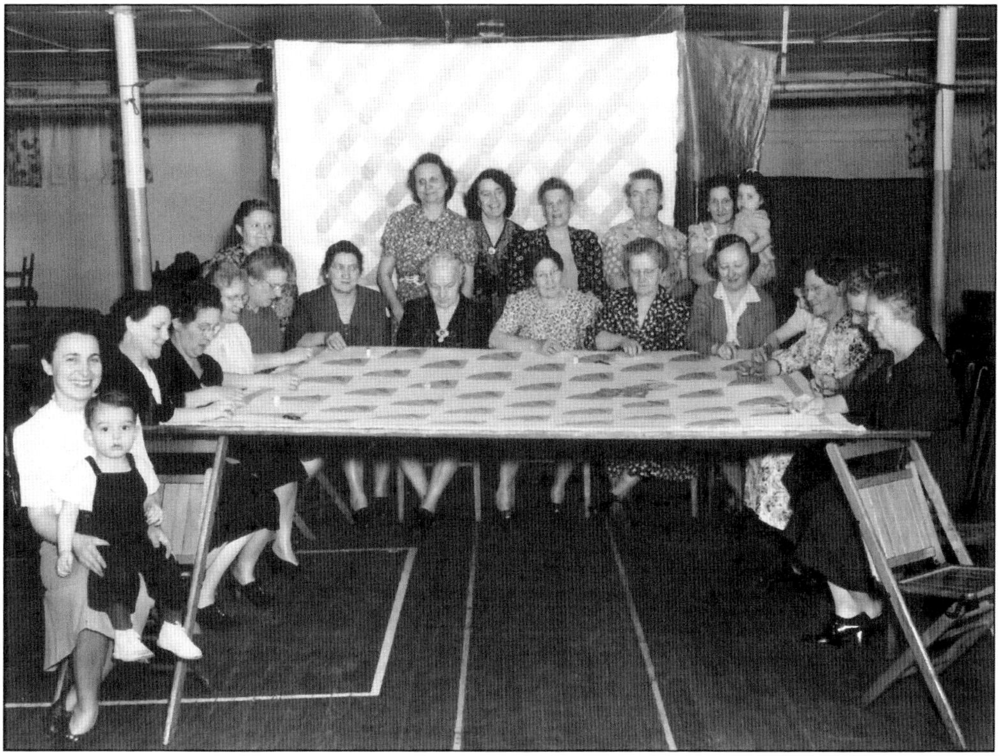

Women from St. John's Evangelical Lutheran Church pool their talents for beautiful quilting projects like this one. (Whiting Historical Society.)

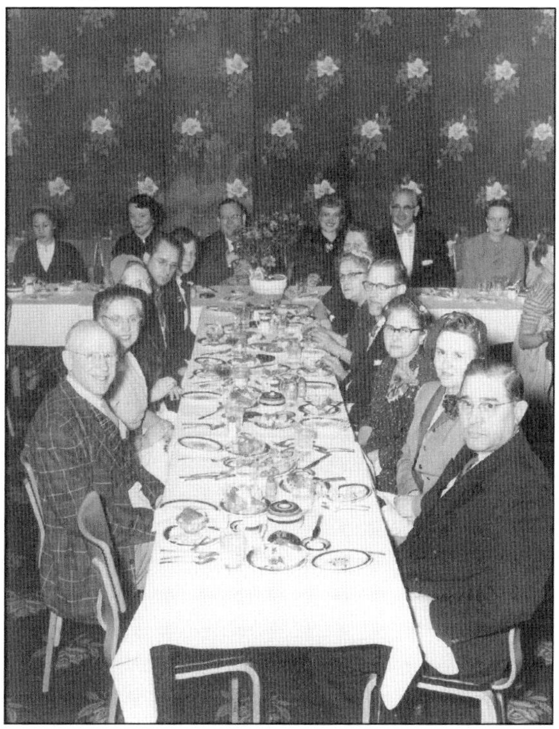

Phil Smidt's restaurant was a popular destination for dining and an ideal place to hold special events. Its signature family-style relish trays and side dishes of cottage cheese, beets, and potato salad line the center of the tables as this group awaits the main course. (Specker Library, Calumet College of St. Joseph.)

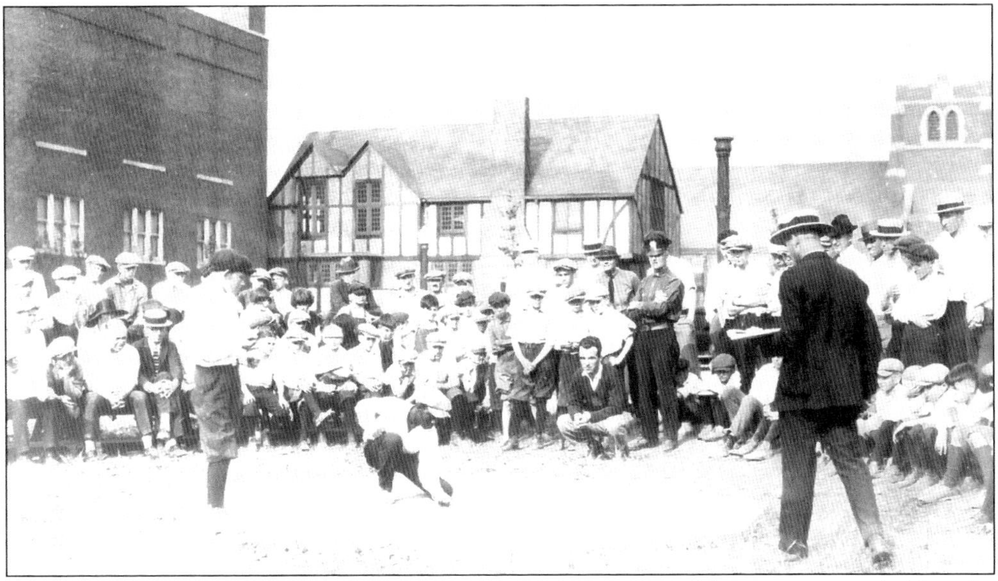

An official cleans the ring during the semifinals of the State Marble Tournament, held at the Whiting Community Center in June 1925. The idea of the game is to shoot from outside the large circle and knock a marble out of the small circle, thereby winning the marble. The game is played until someone wins all the marbles. In the background are the Masonic temple and the Methodist church. (Whiting Historical Society.)

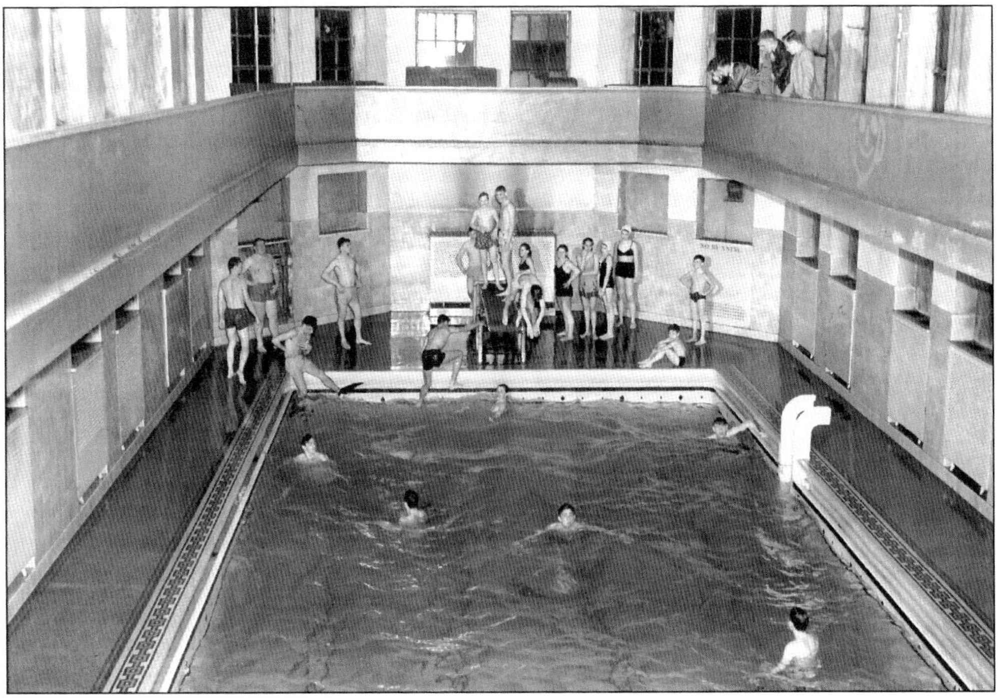

The Whiting Community Center features an indoor swimming pool that has always been a popular destination for residents, especially when the lakes are too cold for swimming. For many years, a cleanliness check was performed by the lifeguard before anyone was allowed to swim. (Whiting Historical Society.)

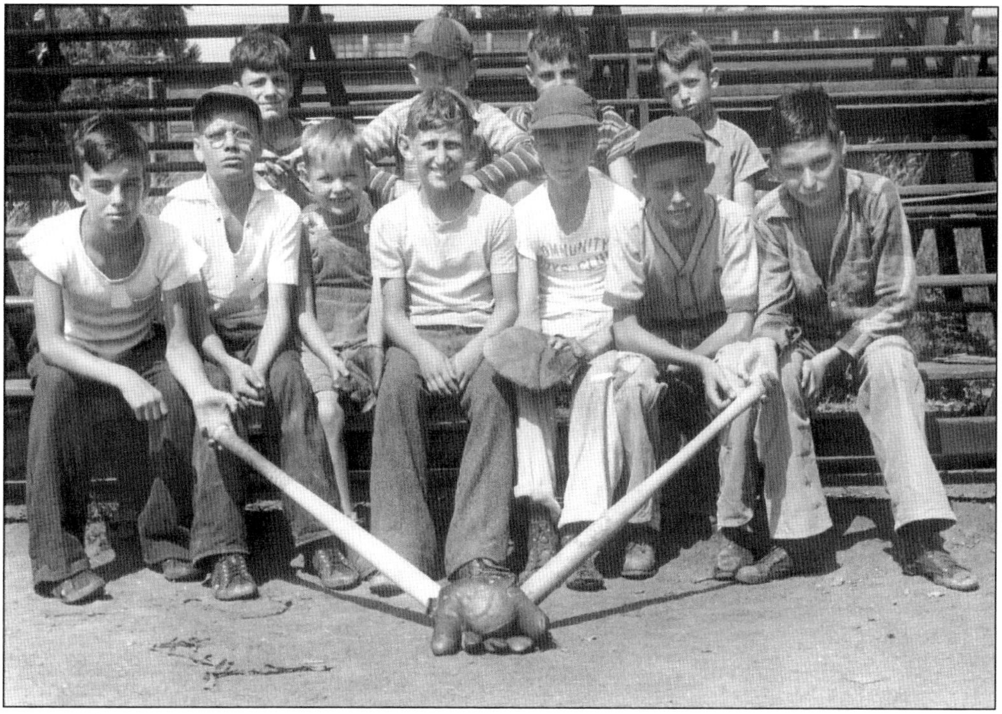

Baseball has always been a favorite pastime for the young and old in Whiting-Robertsdale, dating as far back as 1891, when the Whiting Greys were formed. (Vrabel family.)

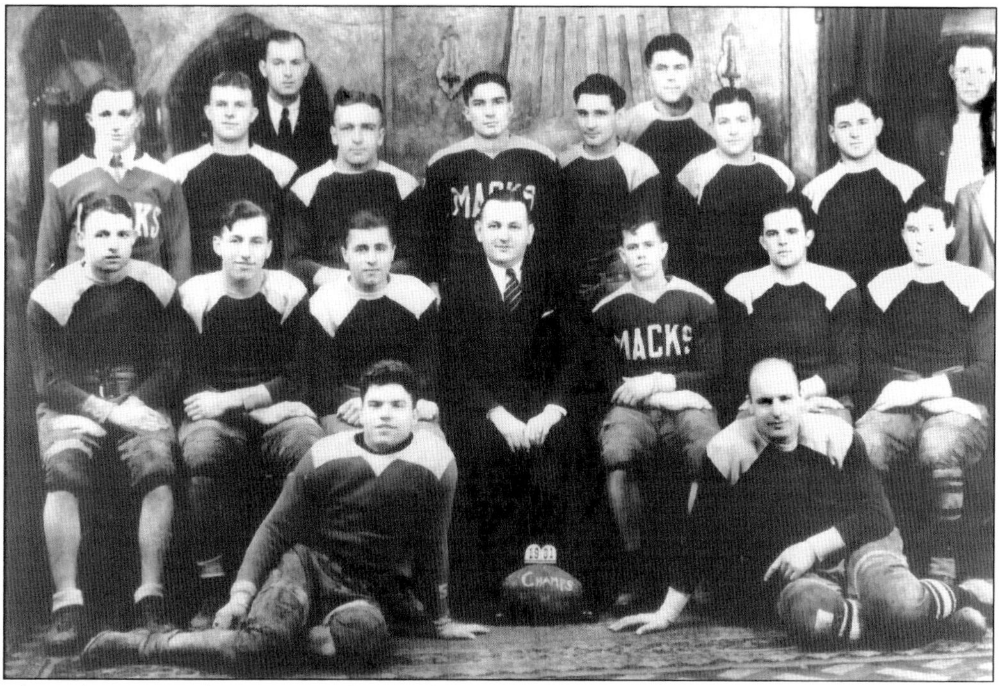

The Whiting Macks, a semiprofessional football team, won a championship in 1931. James McNamara (center) owned the team. He was a sports promoter and the mayor of Whiting from 1935 to 1948. (Whiting Public Library.)

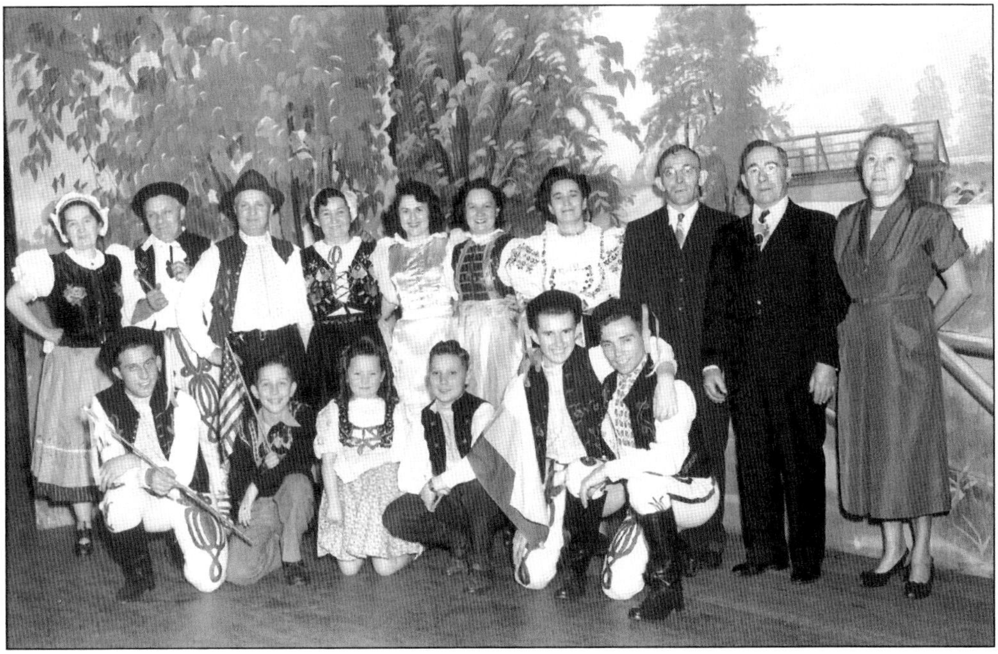

The American Slovak Ladies, the Zivenas, sponsored the dramatic production *Kamenný Chodnicek* in 1950 in the Slovak Dom auditorium. From left to right are (first row) John Hrabovsky, John Ciesar Jr., Diane Matis, Milan Matuska, George Knezo, and Joseph Macak; (second row) Emilia Pakan, John Figuly, Stephen Cutka, Margaret Kalapach, Ruth Luptak, Susan Mudrak, Ellen Matuska, Mike Kacer, assistant director John Kacer, and director Mary Ciesar, who was also president of the Zivena Society. (Joseph Macak and Milan Matuska.)

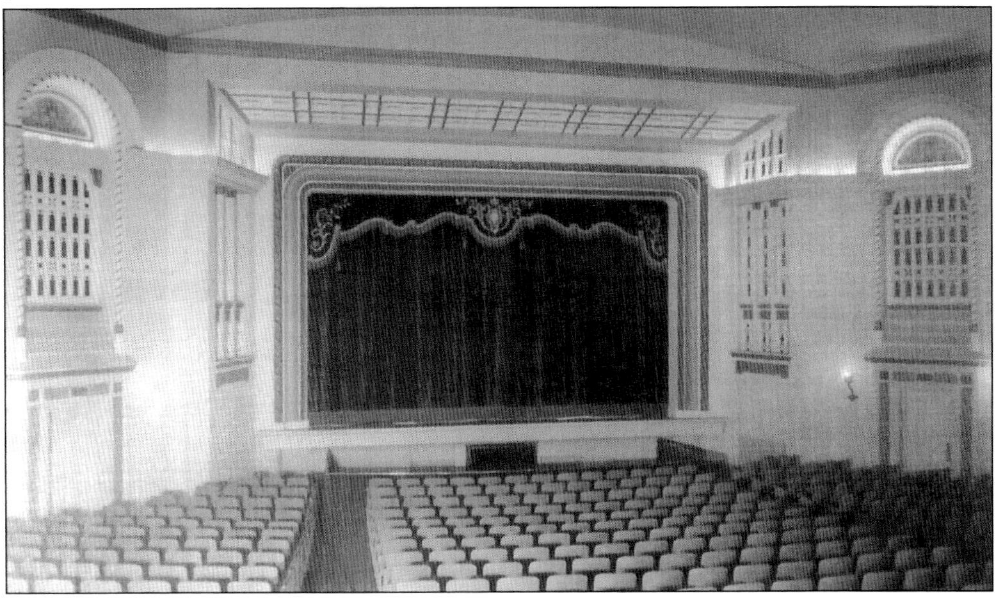

Dramatic productions were a popular form of entertainment throughout much of the 1900s, and the Whiting-Robertsdale community boasted an abundance of auditoriums, such as this one in the Whiting Community Center. There were also four theaters, the Slovak Dom, church halls, and school auditoriums. (Sandrick family.)

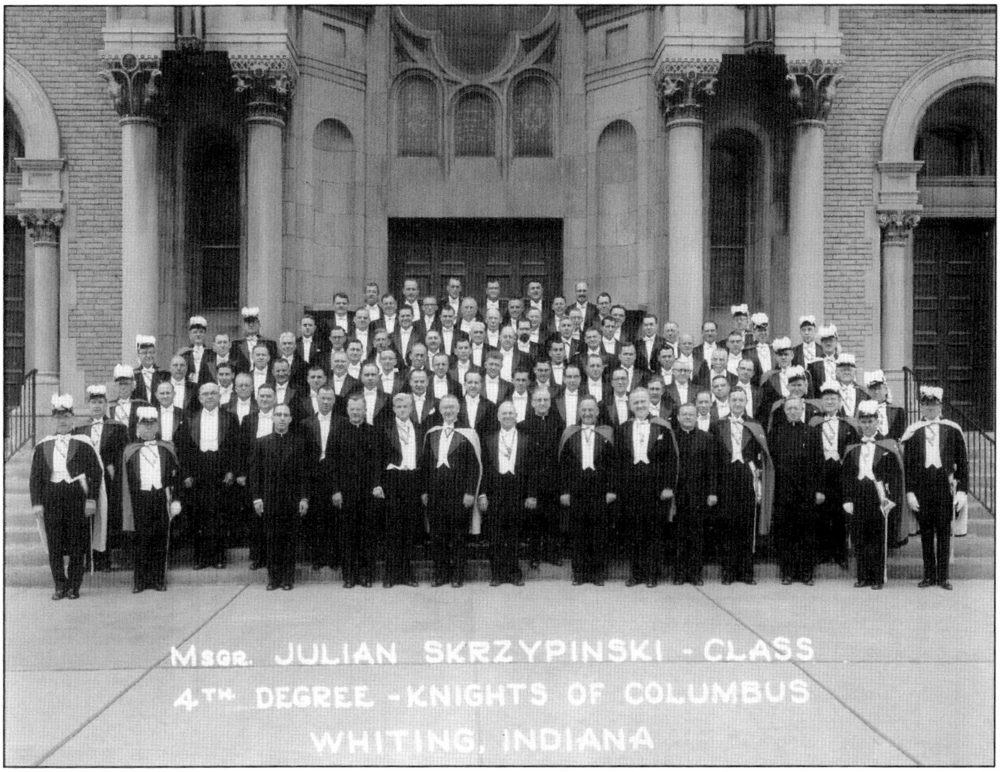

Fourth-degree Knights of Columbus gather in their full regalia for a group photograph in front of St. John the Baptist Church in 1956. The fourth degree is the highest within the Knights of Columbus organization. The Knights' primary purposes are to foster a spirit of patriotism and to encourage active Catholic citizenship. (Saliga family.)

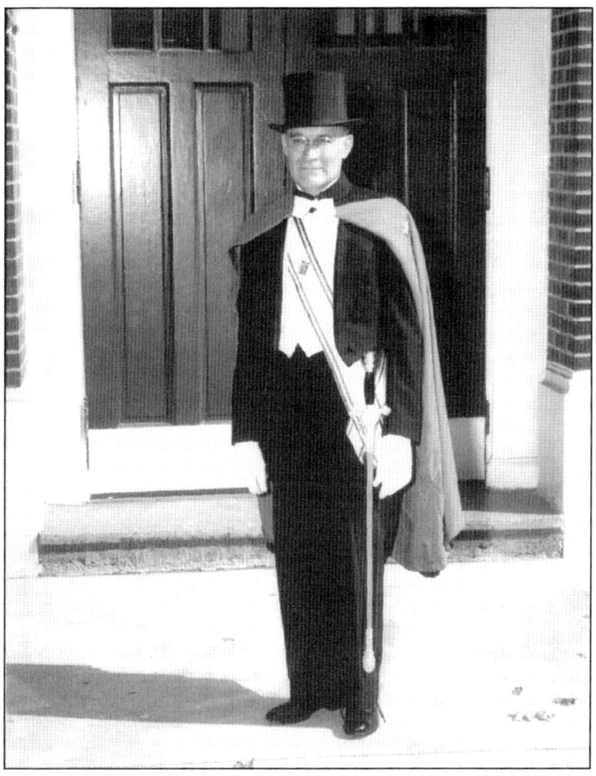

Joseph Kubayko was a proud member of the Knights of Columbus, Whiting Council No. 1696. An employee at Standard Oil and a parishioner at St. John the Baptist Parish, he also operated Joe's O.K. Service out of the basement of his home on Stanton Avenue. He enjoyed fixing radios and televisions and was proud to say that he installed the first television antenna in the Whiting-Robertsdale area. (Saliga family.)

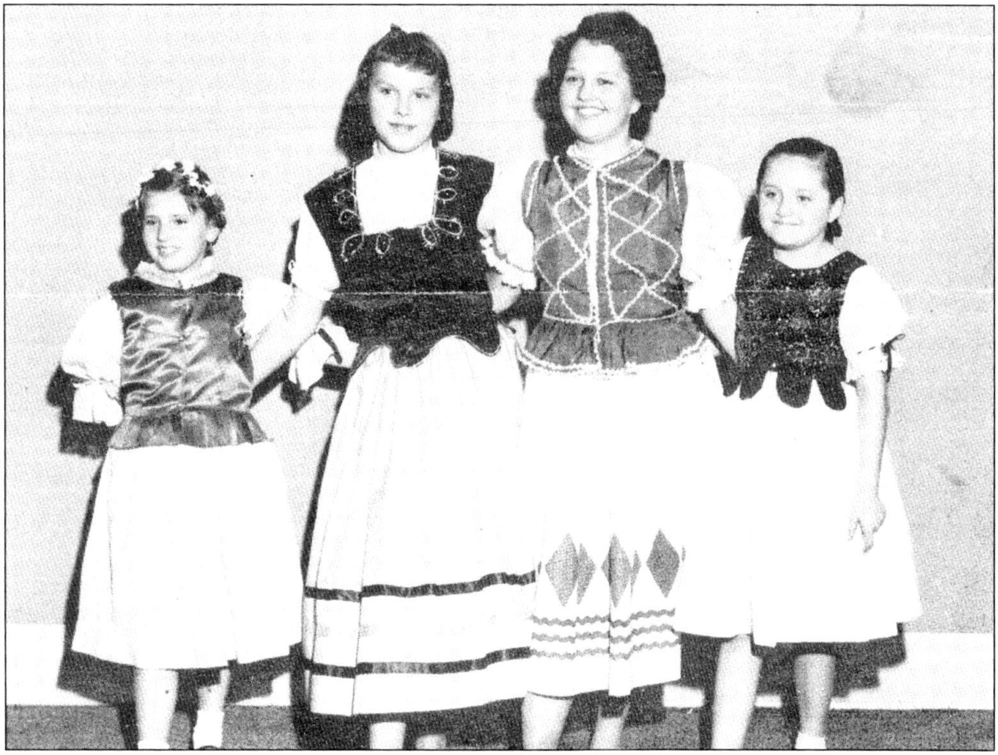

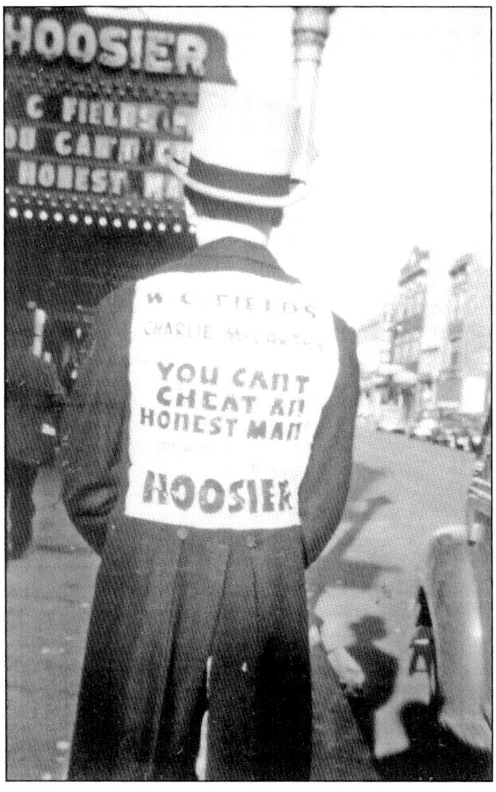

These young girls kept Slovak traditions alive in the Calumet Region by performing authentic folk dances at special events. Seen here in traditional Slovak dance attire are, from left to right, Betsy Dedinsky, Carol Mikula, Dolores Gallo, and Karen Zabrecky. (Carol Mikula Jacobson.)

The Hoosier Theatre on 119th Street was one of four theaters that provided entertainment in Whiting over the years. All of them except for the Hoosier have since closed and been converted into other types of businesses. The Hoosier was renovated and reopened as a contemporary theater in 1997. (Sandrick family.)

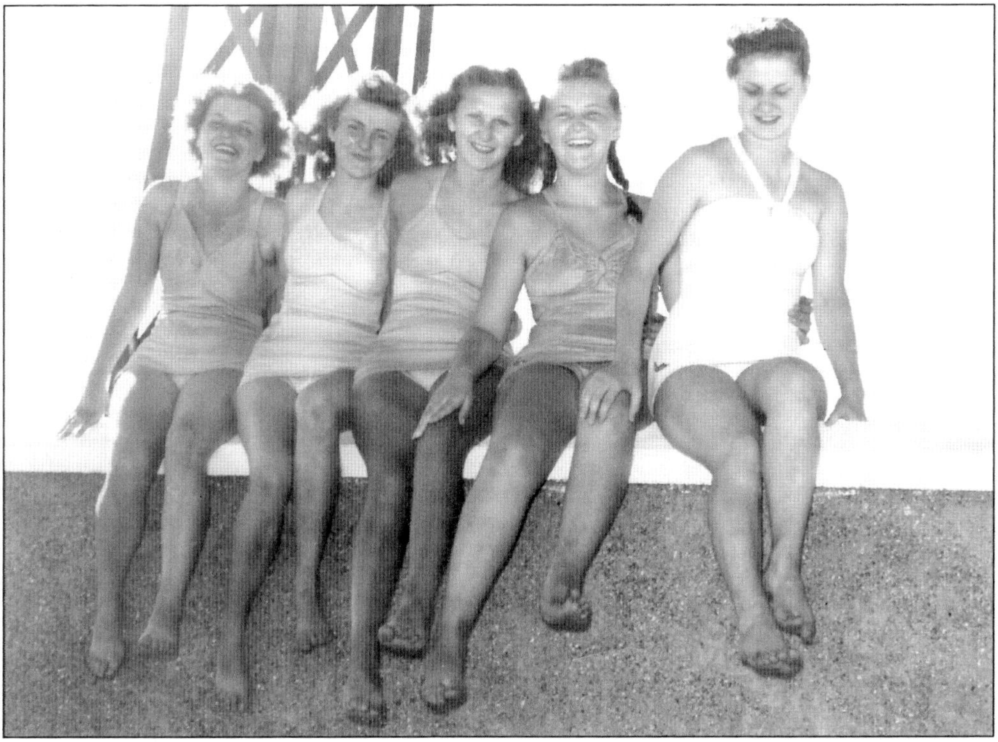

Irene Svitko (far left) and friends pose on the beach wall while having fun in the sun at Whiting Park. (Svitko family.)

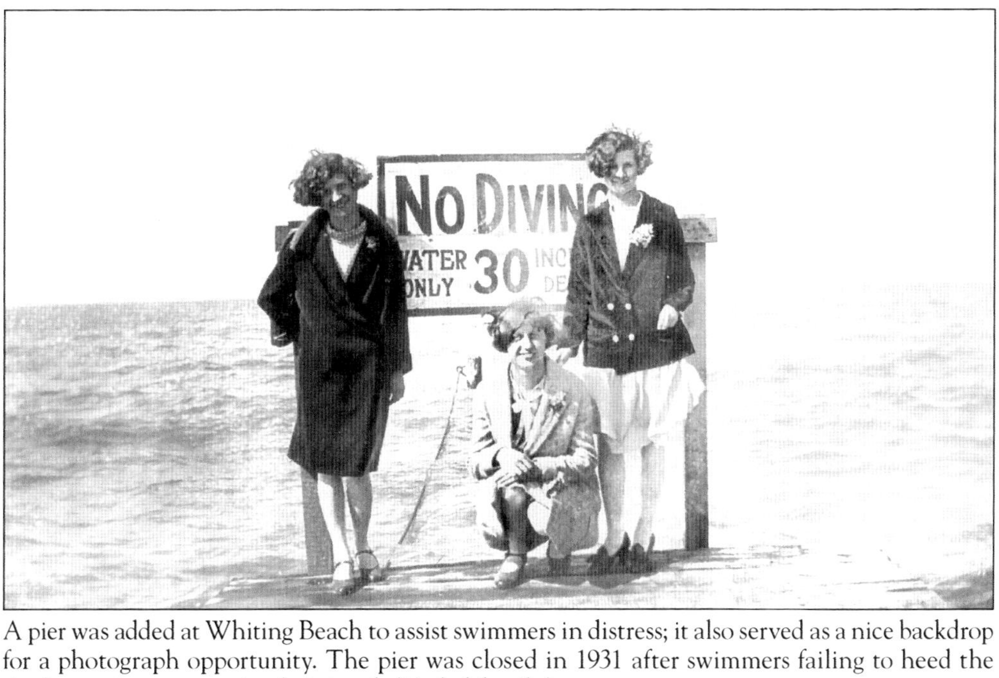

A pier was added at Whiting Beach to assist swimmers in distress; it also served as a nice backdrop for a photograph opportunity. The pier was closed in 1931 after swimmers failing to heed the sign's warning were seriously injured. (Vrabel family.)

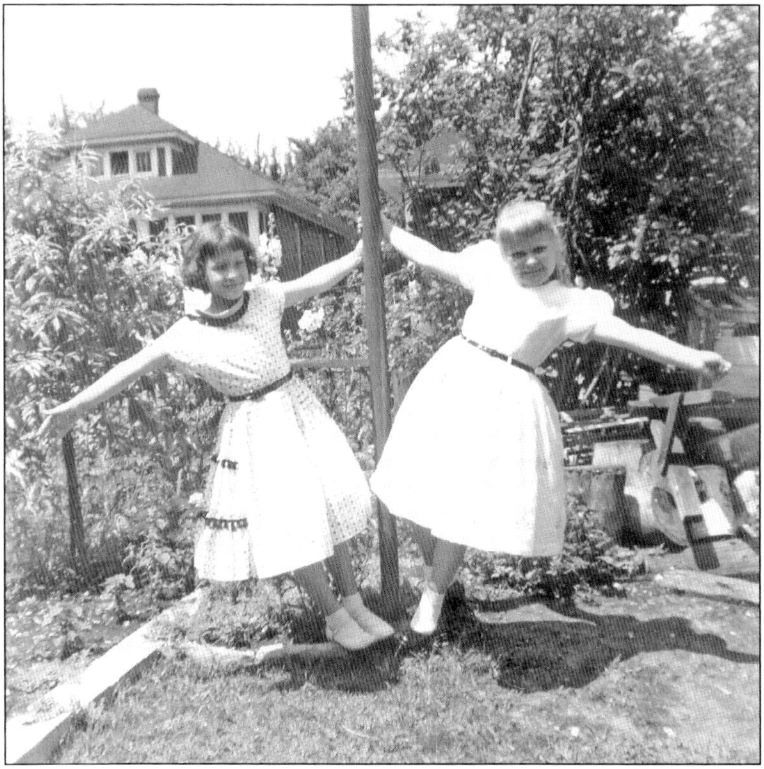

Best friends Janice Michalak (left) and Ruth Tkach swing from a clothesline pole, a common prop in many backyards. (Tkach family.)

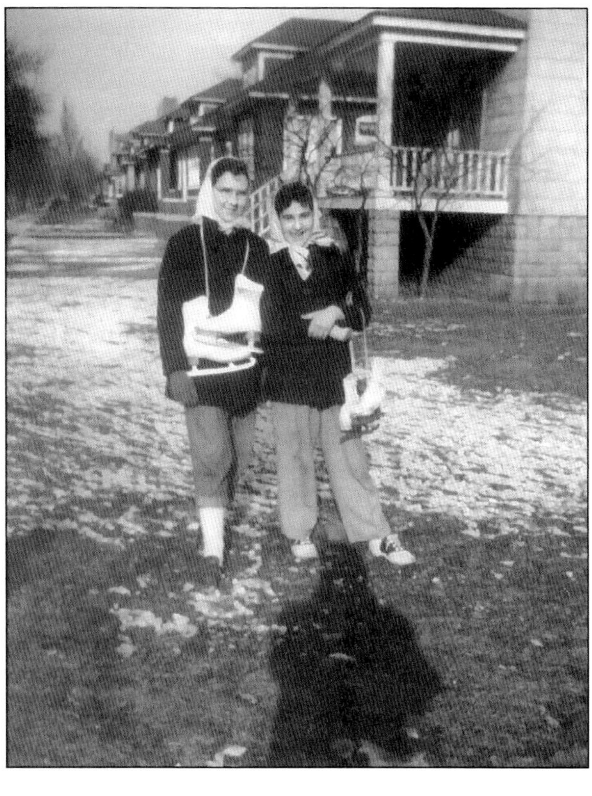

Two young ladies head out for some ice skating, one of the most popular winter activities in the area. Local parks provided a safe skating environment on man-made rinks and lagoons, while inland lakes provided an option for the more adventurous. (Tkach family.)

In the days before air conditioners, local residents sought the cool waters of Lake Michigan during the heat of the summer. For bathing beauties Gerri Kacer (left), Nancy Tkach (center), and Dodie Kacer (right), the beach was also a popular place for socializing with their friends. (Tkach family.)

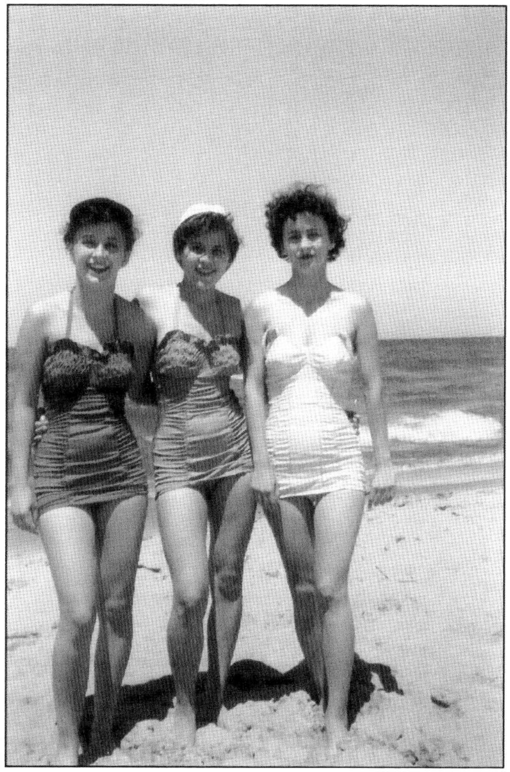

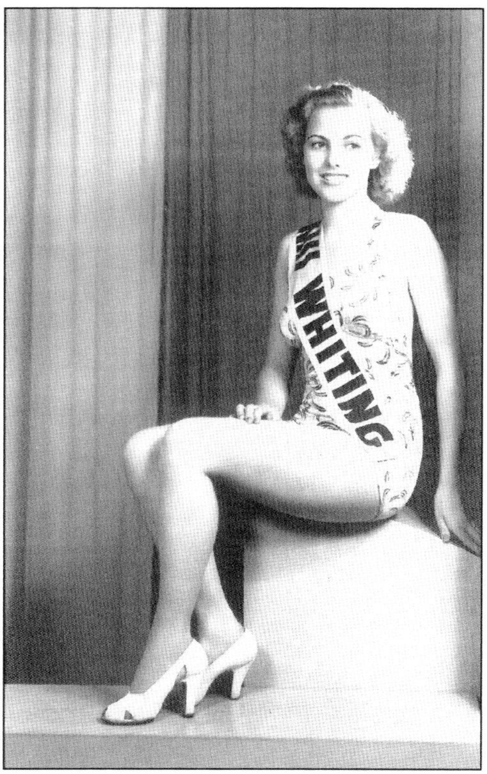

More bathing beauties could also be spotted at the annual Fourth of July Bathing Beauty Contest, which was held at the Hoosier Theatre in the 1930s. In 1938, Rosemary Downey Wonnacott, seen here, won the contest and was given the honor of being Miss Whiting. She went on to be the runner-up in the Miss Indiana pageant. (Vrabel family.)

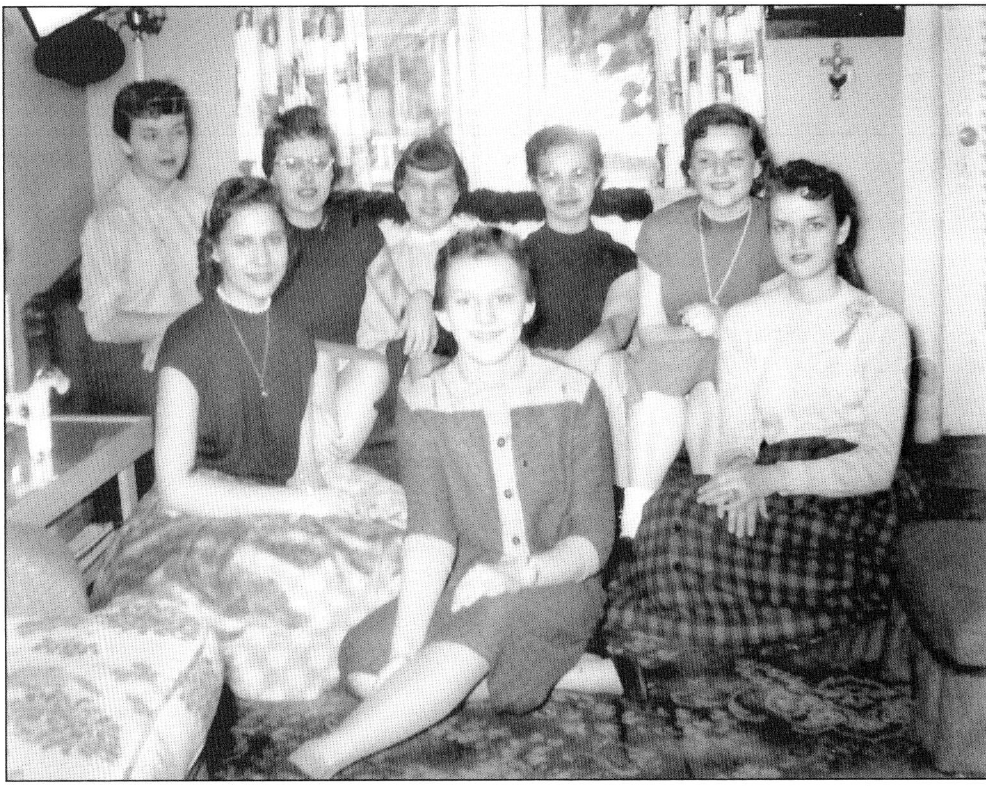

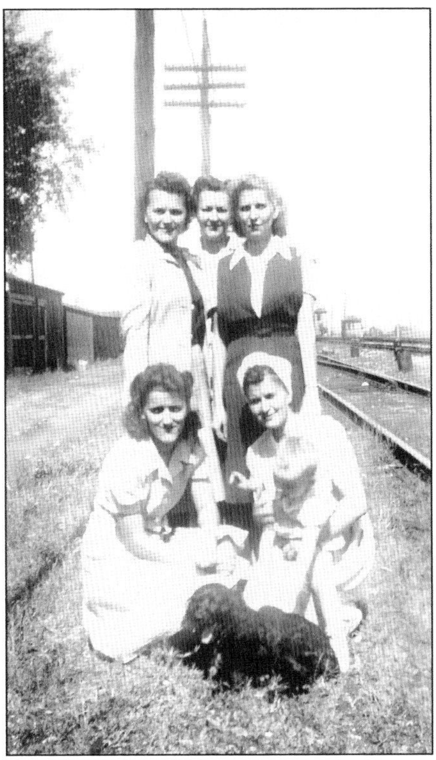

These young ladies enjoyed gathering for parties and get-togethers in formal and informal settings. Seen here from left to right are (first row) Kay Adamcik, Pat Brenkus, and Lydia Walczak; (second row) Rosalind Anton, Suzanne Vater, Judy Kalina, Carol Ayers, and Christine Lakatos. (Tkach family.)

Posing alongside the railways near Whiting Park are the Svitko family girls with youngster Barbara Kostanczyk, the first grandchild and the beginning of the next generation. (Svitko family.)

Five

WORKING

With its abundance of railroads, the Calumet Region was a magnet for industry. Following Standard Oil's lead, many other industries began to set up production in the area, providing residents with many options for employment.

Companies that settled in Whiting-Robertsdale included Petrolene Company, Westrumite Company, Carbide and Carbon Plant, American Smelting and Refining Company, Amaizo, and Lever Brothers Soap. Other large companies, such as Inland Steel and Youngstown Sheet and Tube, were located in nearby communities and offered additional employment opportunities.

Family-owned businesses became an important part of the community, and as a result, Whiting-Robertsdale became a full-service community. Businesses ranging from banks to restaurants to retail stores thrived and were passed on from one generation to the next.

Common family names that are associated with local businesses and evoke fond memories include Sherman, Geffert, Reicht, Winsberg, Smidt, Spiccia, and Madura. Businesses such as the Whiting News Company, Whiting Flower Shop, and Poppen's Service Station became long-standing institutions in the community.

During the Great Depression, while many neighboring communities struggled to make ends meet, Whiting experienced steady employment. Production at the refinery gradually fell as low as 50 percent, and to avoid layoffs, the company transferred employees to work in construction and repairs whenever possible. Eventually, however, several hundred employees were laid off and wages were reduced for a short time. Although the oil industry suffered briefly, Whiting was generally thought of as a depression-proof city.

In the 1940s, the entire community dedicated itself to World War II efforts. Standard Oil switched to war production under government direction, and by 1941, the company devoted all of its resources to filling the demand for oil products in support of the war effort. It also began to modernize and expand its facilities to meet the growing demand for gasoline.

Other industries in the area also adjusted their operations to support the war efforts. Lever Brothers generated cleaning products for the armed forces to help prevent the spread of disease, and Amaizo transformed corn into food products to provide food resources to the troops. By 1949, Standard Oil employed 9,000 people, and the community continued to prosper.

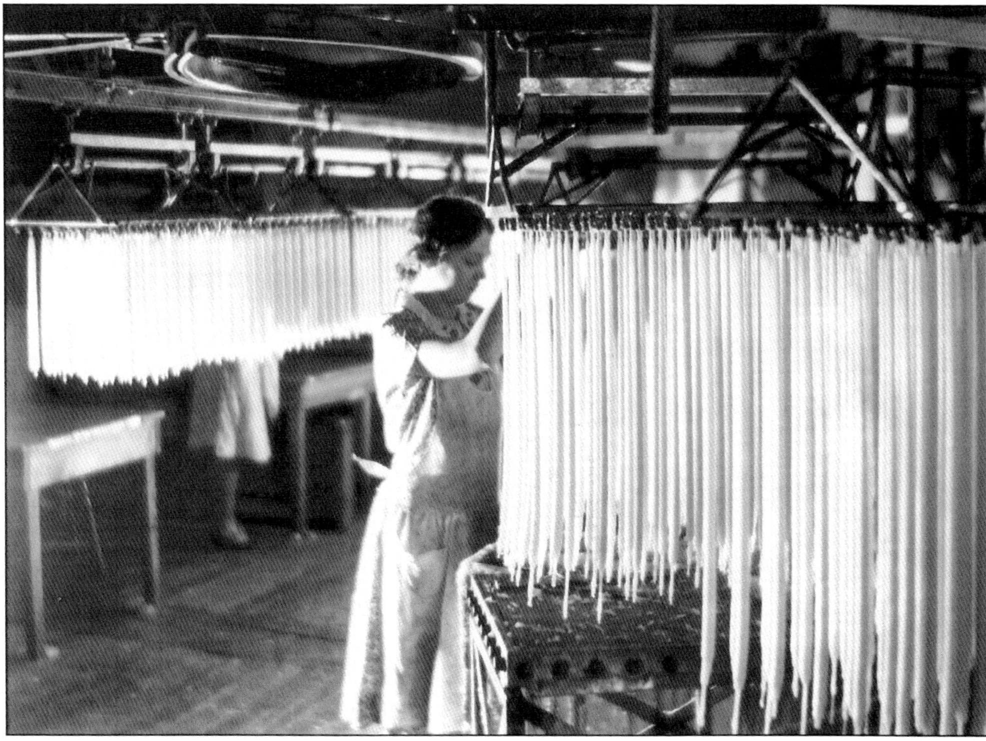

Whiting's refinery operated a candle factory from 1893 to 1956 to utilize the paraffin wax that is a by-product of the oil refining process. The factory employed mostly women and manufactured products ranging from plain white candles to cakes of paraffin for canning to novelty candles. During both World Wars, the factory operated around the clock and shipped out millions of candles to troops around the world. (Whiting Public Library.)

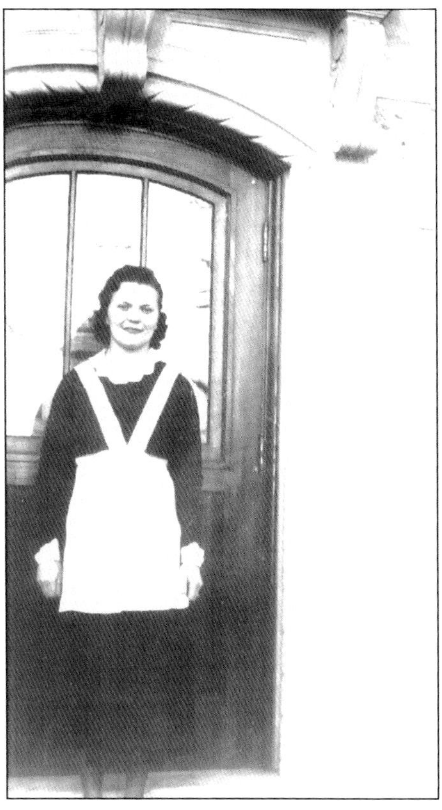

Margaret Kmetz is seen here in her uniform outside the home of Harry and Hortense Glair, where she worked for the family as their maid. Harry Glair was an executive with Standard Oil Company of Indiana. (Svitko family.)

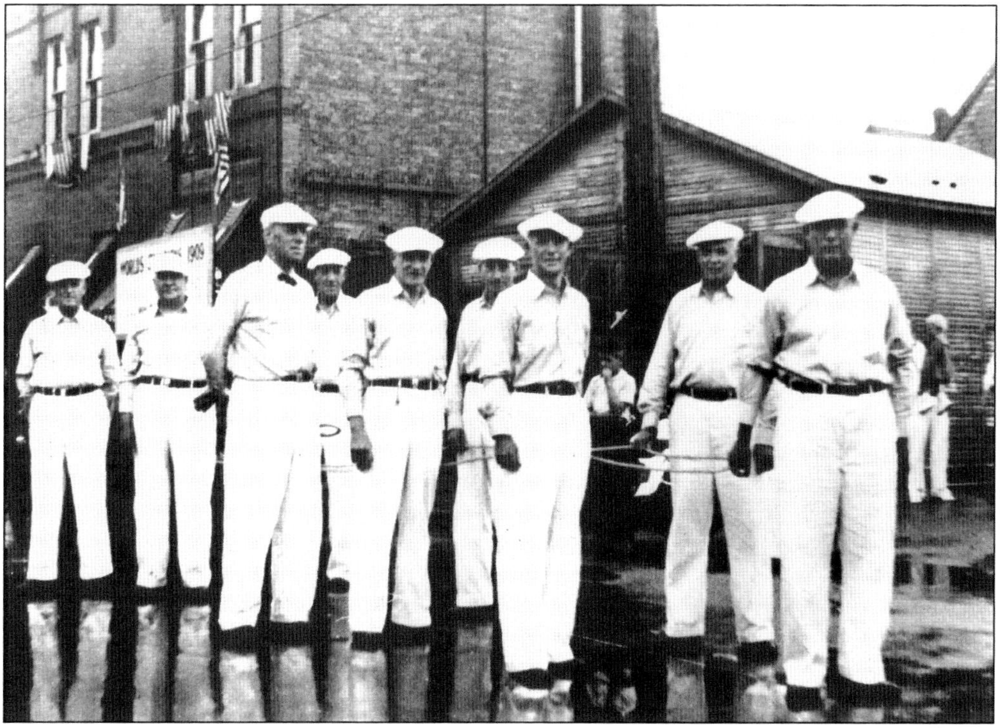

Whiting's local fire department is seen here after winning the 1909 World Championship firefighter competition. This photograph was taken near the corner of White Oak and Fischrupp Streets. In the background are city hall, the fire and police building, and the horse barn. (Whiting Historical Society.)

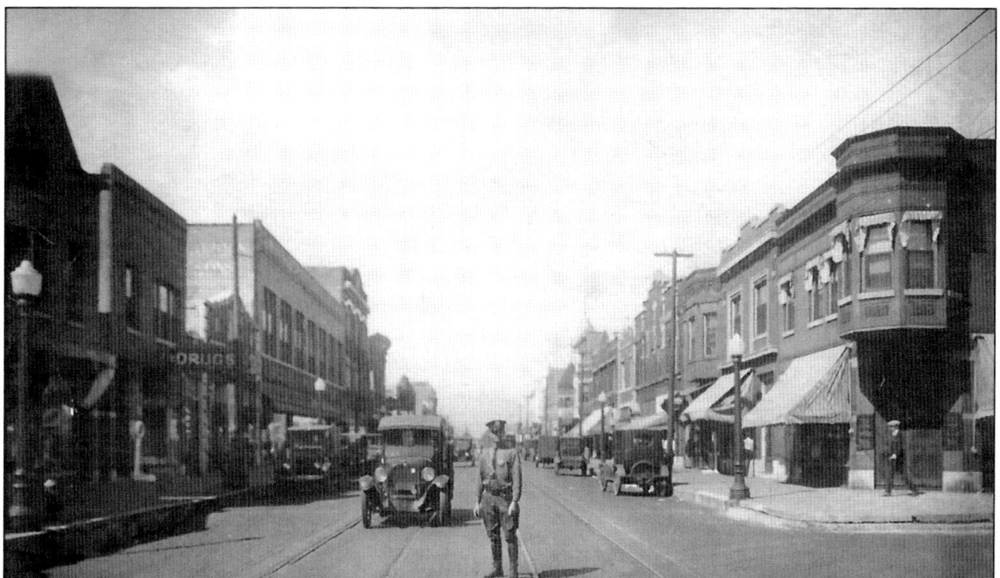

This police officer is prepared to direct traffic and help schoolchildren cross the street at the corner of 119th and Oliver Streets. Behind him, looking to the west, are the many shops and businesses lining the community's main street. (Sandrick family.)

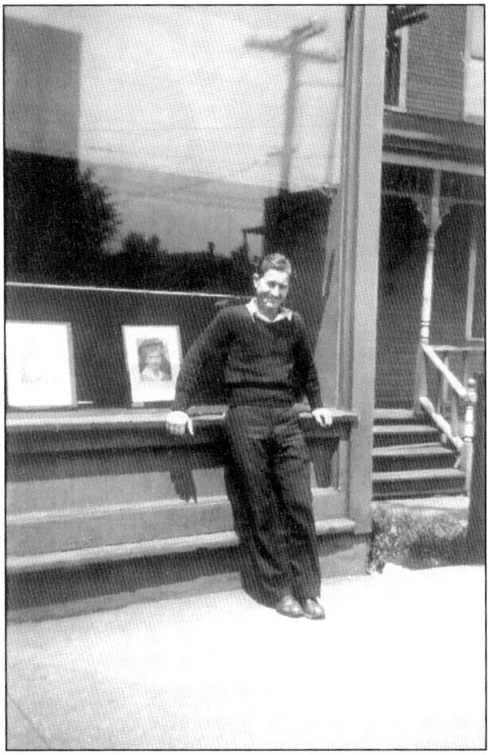

George Vrabel became one of the community's top studio photographers. His photographs are a treasured record of the community's historical events, weddings, sports teams, and theatrical productions, and many of them are included in this book. Vrabel's first studio was in the basement of his apartment building, but he later moved to a 119th Street studio near where St. John's gymnasium now stands. He eventually moved to a studio on Indianapolis Boulevard. (Vrabel family.)

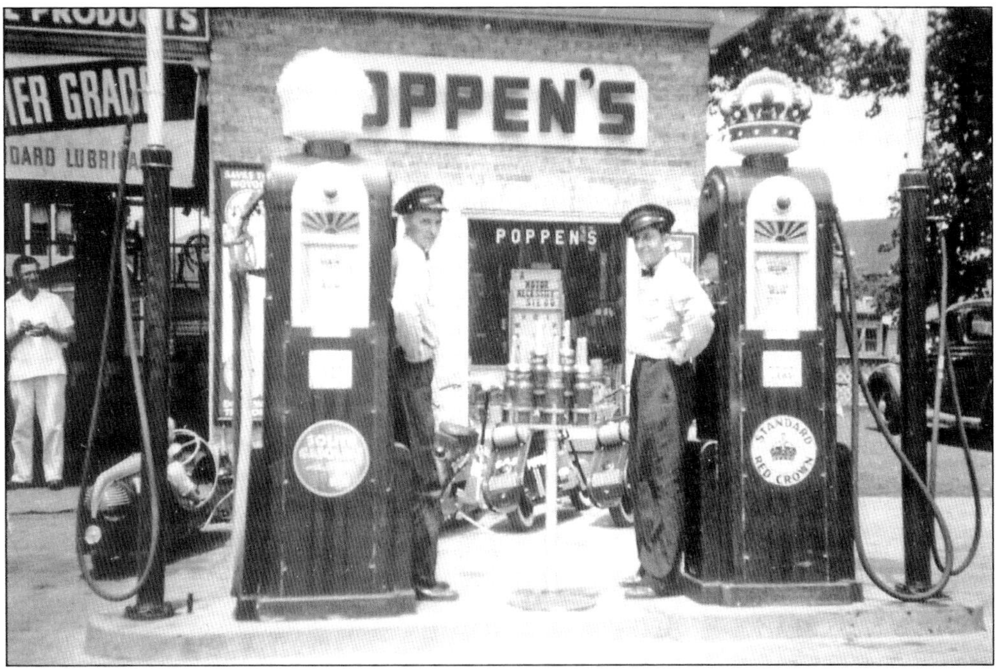

Fred Poppen opened his service station on 119th Street in 1936. To this day, the business emulates the same honesty and integrity upon which the landmark business was built more than 75 years ago. Station attendants from an early era are seen here wearing clean, crisp uniforms and ready to pump gas, wash windshields, and check oil. (Poppen family.)

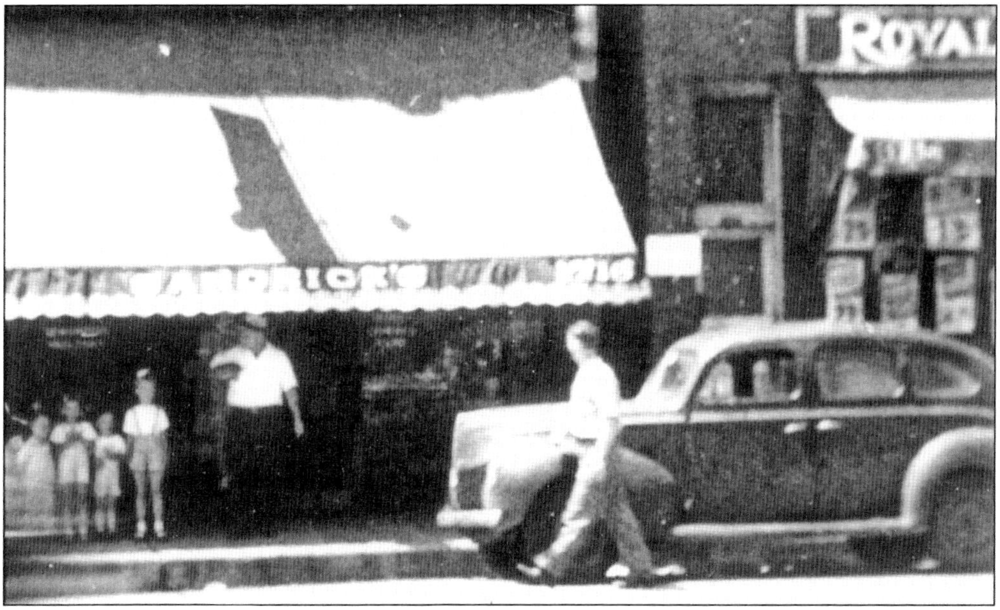

In 1945, Frank Sandrick opened Sandrick Toys and Confections, expanding a few years later to the location seen here at 1716 Indianapolis Boulevard, where it was known as Sandrick's Sundries. Two doors west of this store was the Sandrick Brothers Hardware Store. Sandrick businesses have been a longtime tradition in the community; Jim and Norma Sandrick currently operate the eighth family business venture, Sandrick Financial Group. (Sandrick family.)

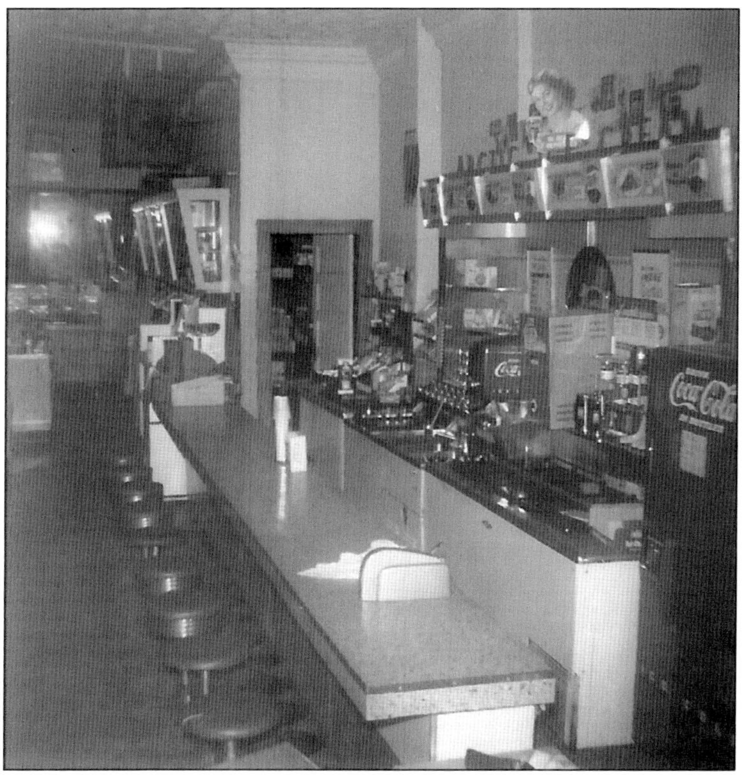

Sandrick's Sundries, well known for its soda fountain, Green River dispenser, and 12 different flavors of hard-packed ice cream, was a popular stop for locals as well as visitors traveling to and from Chicago on Indianapolis Boulevard. Famous patrons included Bing Crosby, Bob Hope, Jim Thorpe, and hometown legend Johnny Mostil. The store sold a variety of other items ranging from American Flyer trains to bowling balls to baseball cards. (Sandrick family.)

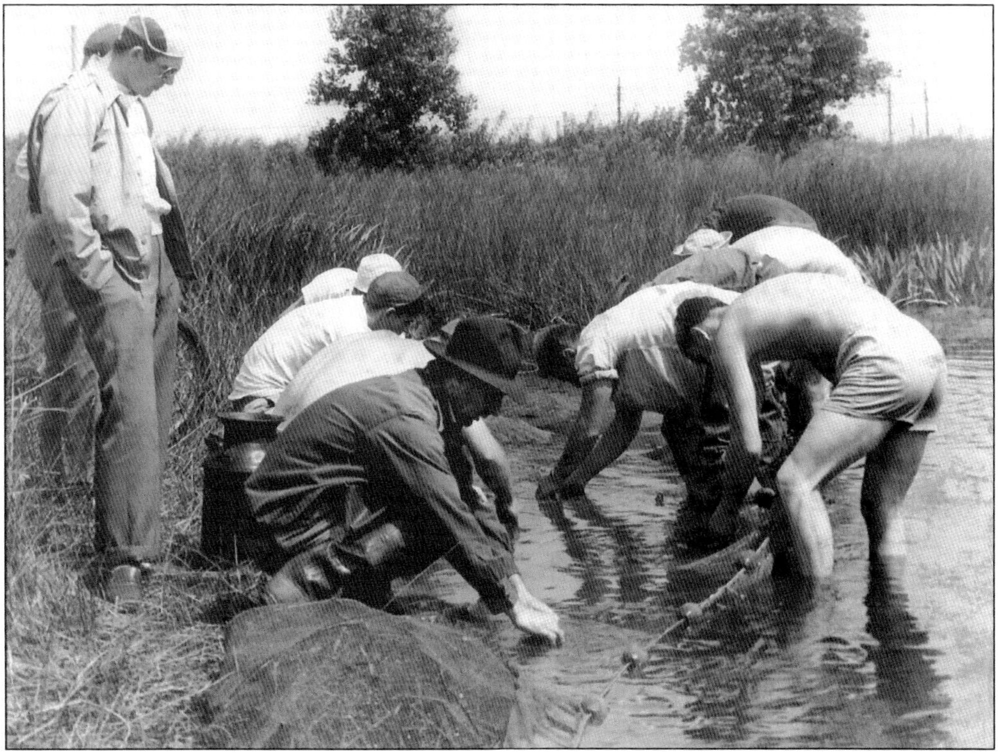

Most of northwest Indiana was sandy marshland before it was transformed into a booming industrial center. By 1910, most of the sand ridges were gone and the swamps were drained, replaced by steel mills, oil refineries, railroad car manufacturers, and other factories. Through the work of groups like the Whiting Conservation Club, seen here at George Lake in 1937, some natural habitats have been preserved. (Whiting Historical Society.)

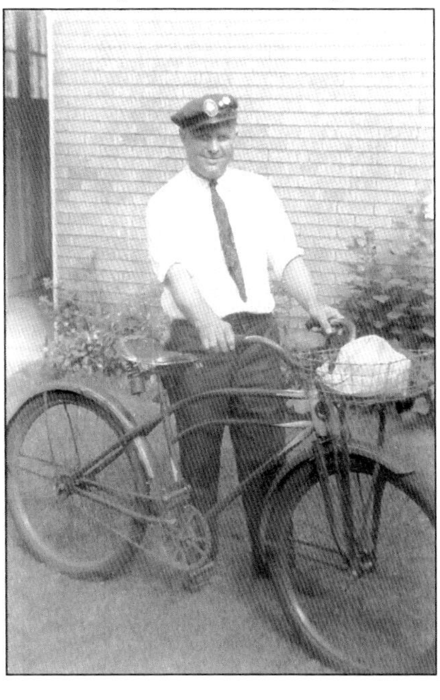

Bicycles are a common form of transportation in the Whiting-Robertsdale area. John Tkach, seen here, rode his bike to work every day at Standard Oil. One of the nicest features of the community is that nearly everything is within easy walking or riding distance. Ironically, while the area was responsible for producing much of the nation's gasoline supply, many Standard Oil refinery employees never had the need to own a car. (Tkach family.)

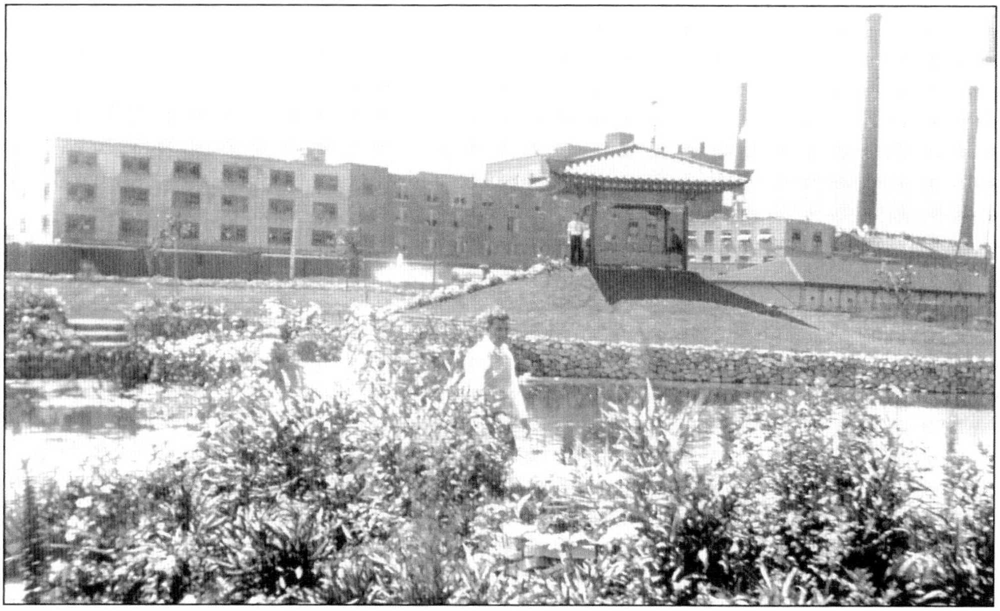

Amaizo, located on the north side of Wolf Lake in Robertsdale, produced corn syrup and other corn products. The Western Glucose Company built the original plant in 1905, and it became part of the American Maize Products Company in 1908. Raymond Daly took over the plant in 1910, and it grew rapidly during his 30-year tenure. Daly's focus was not just on production but also on creating an aesthetically pleasing and family-oriented environment. The plant became Cargill in 2001. (Vrabel family.)

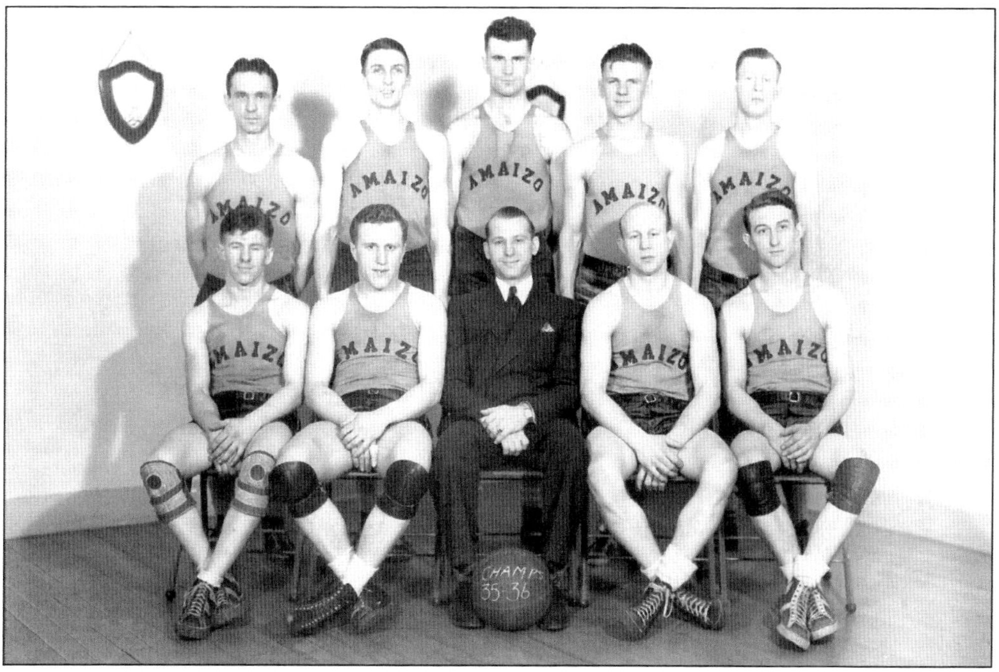

In addition to providing a favorable place to work, Amaizo was well known for the special events, picnics, and recreational activities it sponsored for its employees, including golf, bowling, baseball, and basketball. Amaizo's 1935–1936 championship basketball team is seen here. (Vrabel family.)

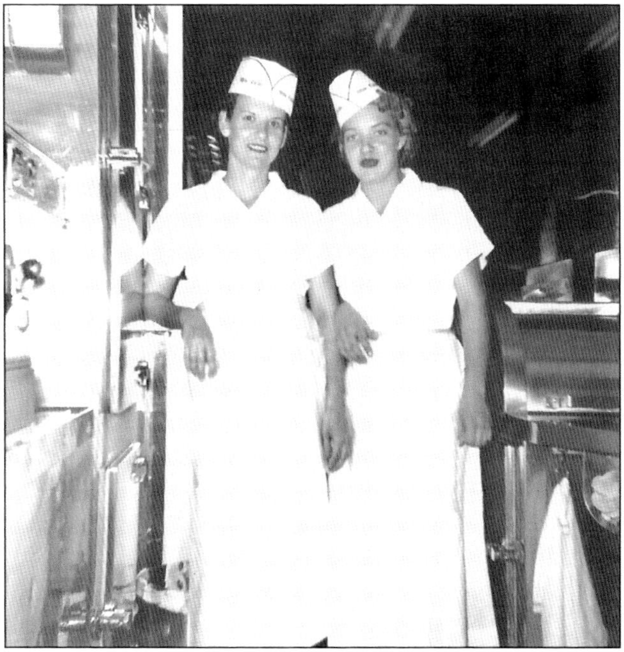

White Castle is a familiar landmark at the corner of Indianapolis Boulevard and 119th Street. It had record sales in its first week of business in Whiting and has continued to be a high-sale location for the company. Here, employees Jean Johnson (left) and Goldie Faulkner are wearing the famous White Castle paper hats. This is the oldest existing White Castle building still in operation. (Whiting Historical Society.)

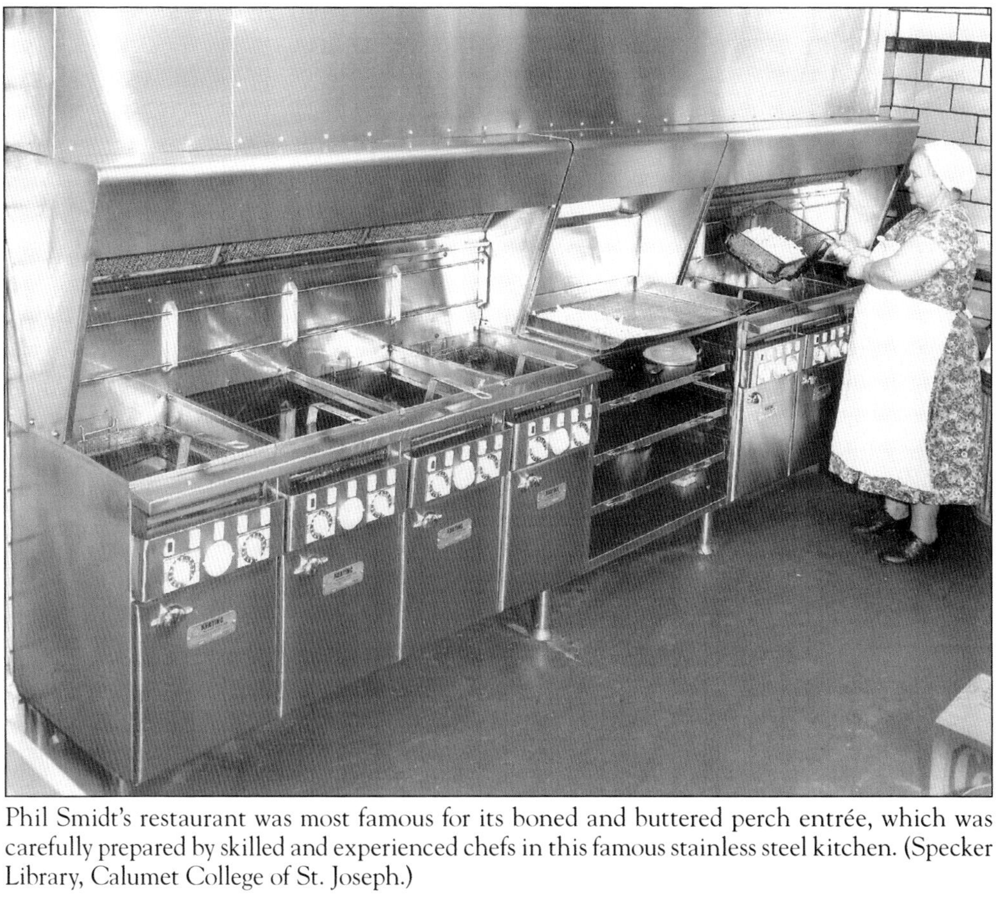

Phil Smidt's restaurant was most famous for its boned and buttered perch entrée, which was carefully prepared by skilled and experienced chefs in this famous stainless steel kitchen. (Specker Library, Calumet College of St. Joseph.)

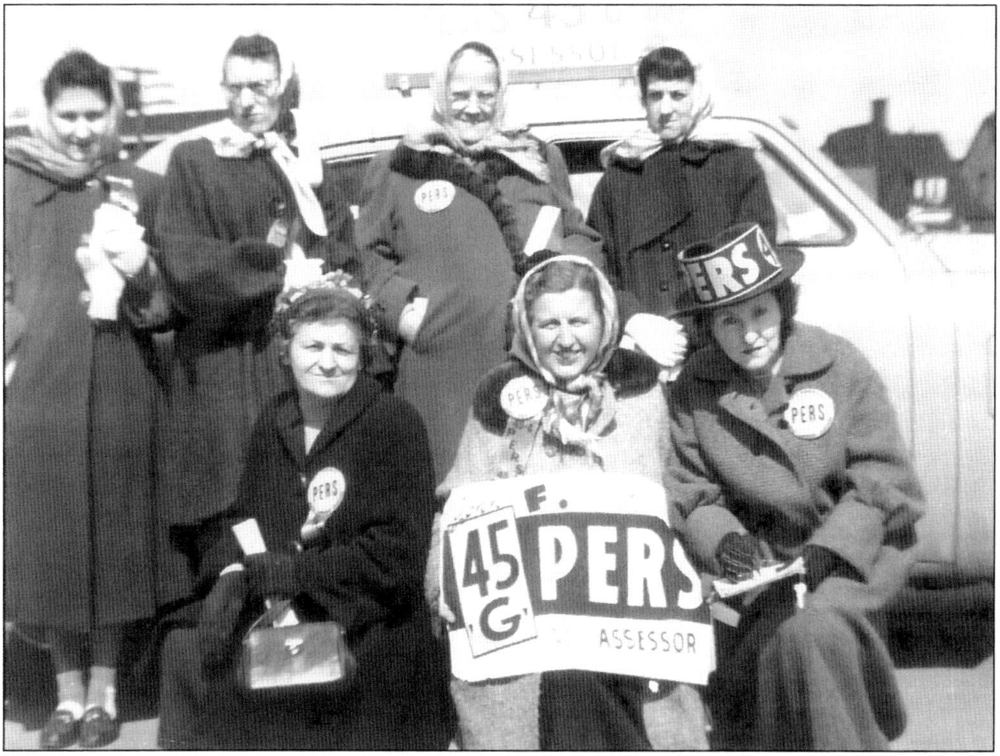

After obtaining the right to vote in 1920, women were quick to become more involved in local politics. (Vrabel family.)

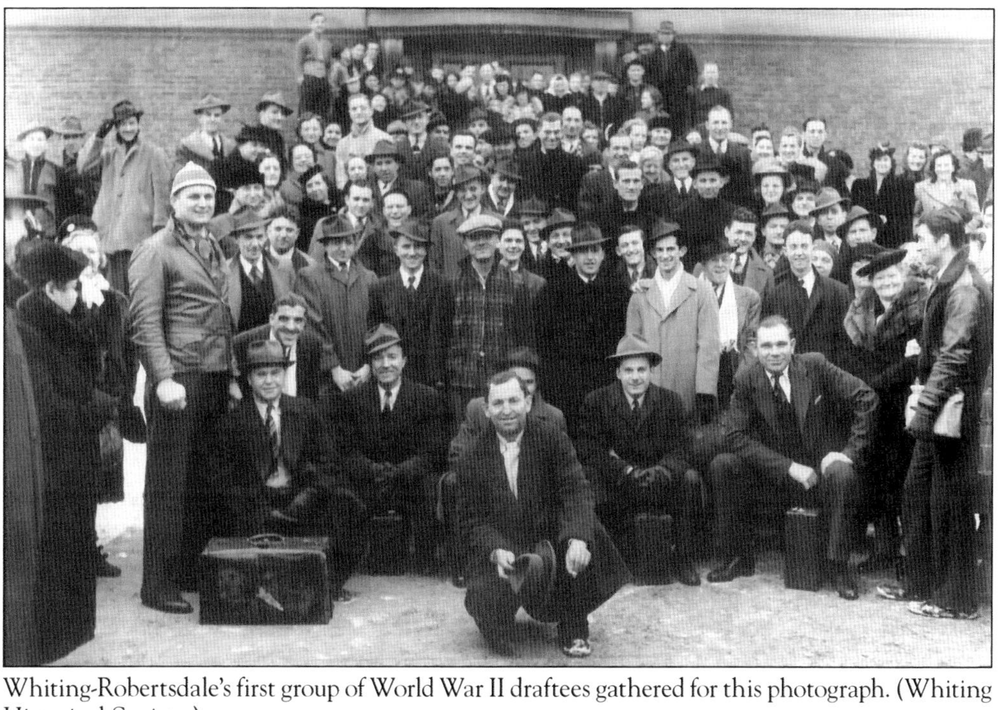
Whiting-Robertsdale's first group of World War II draftees gathered for this photograph. (Whiting Historical Society.)

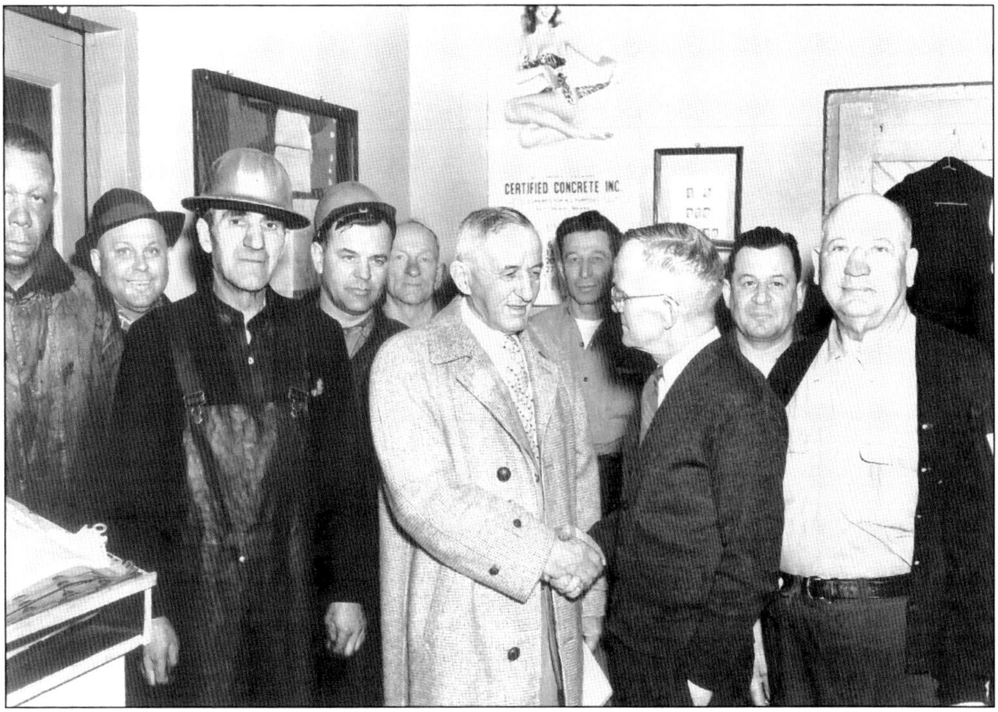

Promotions, retirements, and visits by special guests brought work teams together in support of one another in the Standard Oil offices. (Tkach family.)

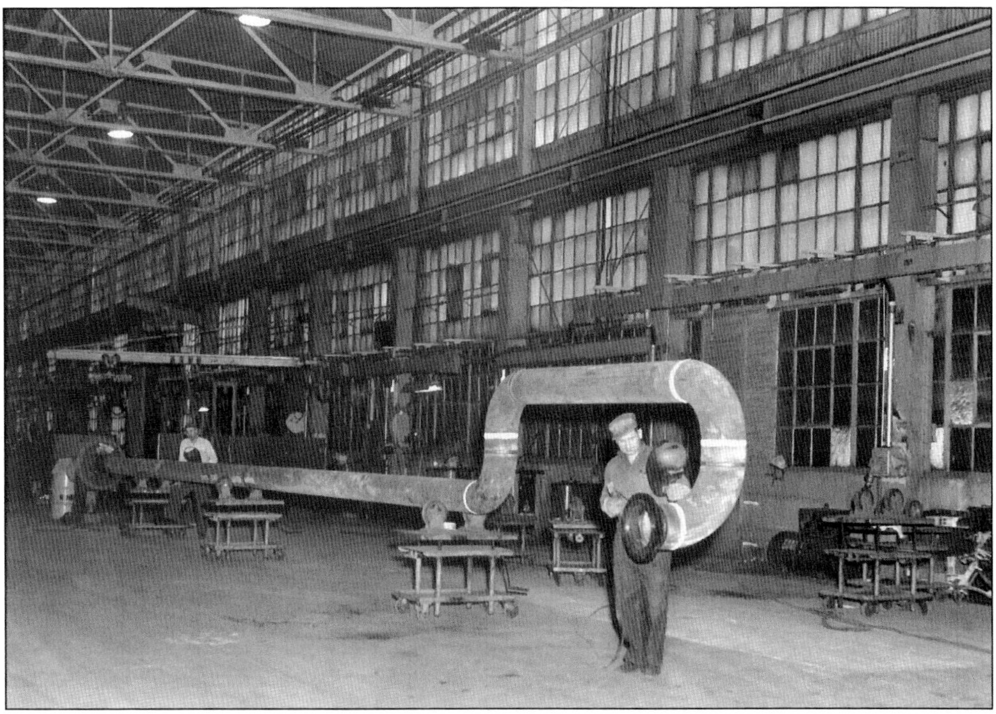

Stanley Boncela is seen here in November 1959 in the expansive welding shop at the Standard Oil refinery as he removes his safety helmet to examine his weld. (Boncela family.)

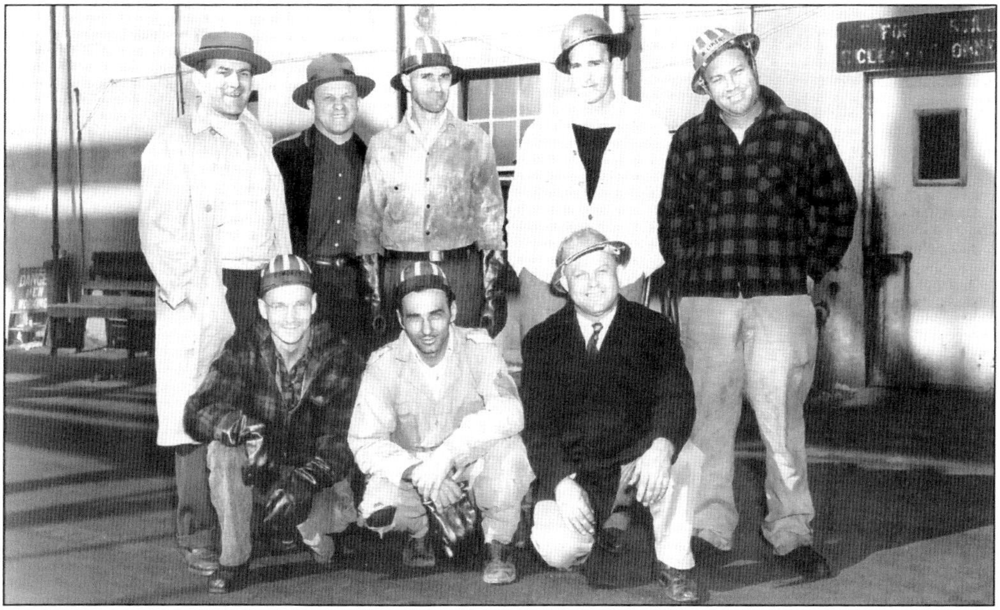

These men operated hydraulic decoking equipment for pipe stills at the Standard Oil refinery. They are, from left to right, (first row) Rudolph Moery, Paul Runcik, and John Tkach; (second row) George Stimac, Edward Rzonca, Clifford Galloway, Jim Frank, and Willis Likens. This photograph was featured in the company's employee newsletter, *Standard Torch*, in January 1952. (Tkach family.)

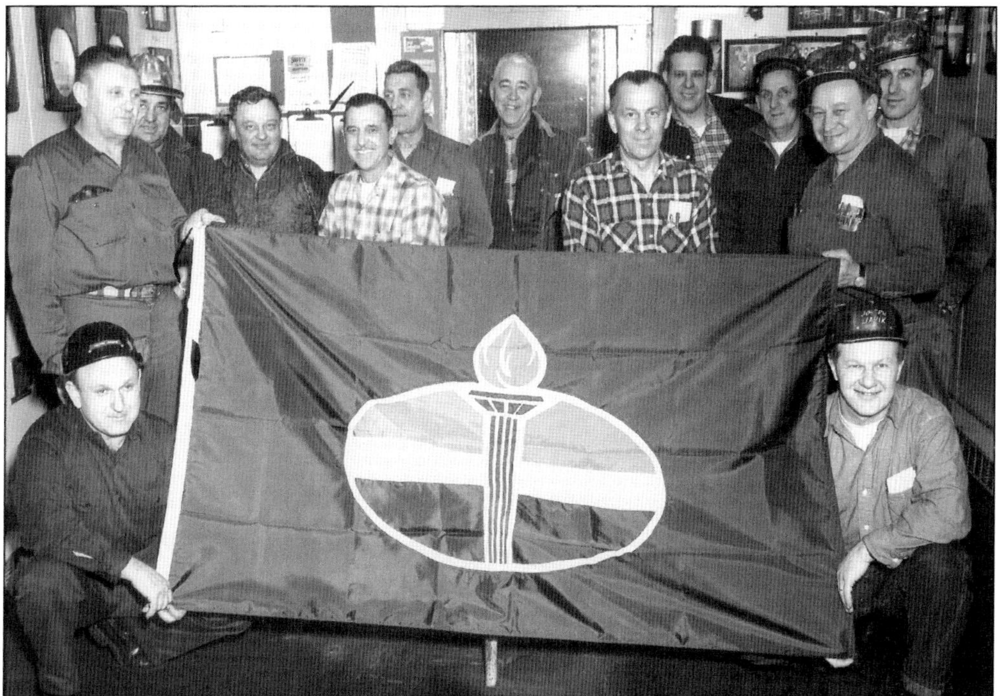

A group of Standard Oil employees who had a record production run on March 20, 1967, holds the flag bearing the Standard Oil oval and torch logo. (Whiting Historical Society.)

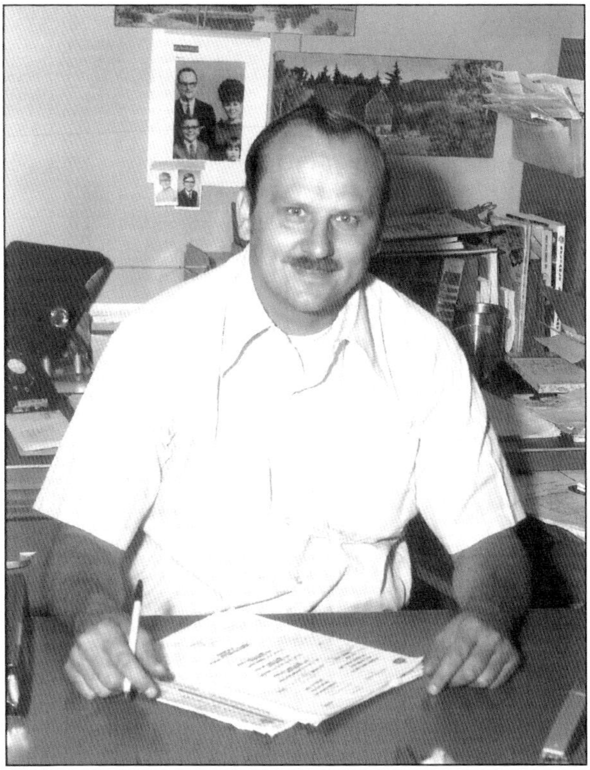

A first-generation American who was always proud to call Whiting home, Edward Domasica worked at Standard Oil for many years. He is seen here in the early 1970s in his office at the research lab at what is now Calumet College of St. Joseph. (Domasica family.)

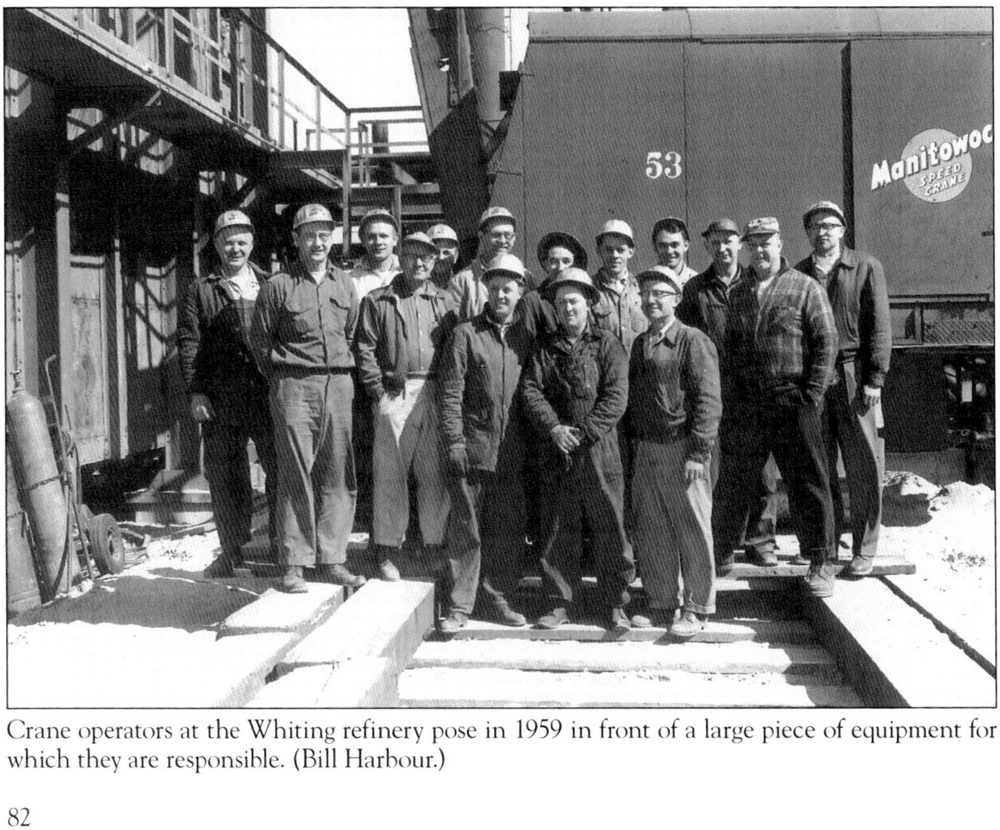

Crane operators at the Whiting refinery pose in 1959 in front of a large piece of equipment for which they are responsible. (Bill Harbour.)

Standard Oil Company has offered steady employment and favorable employee benefits since it first established the Whiting refinery in 1889. (Whiting Historical Society.)

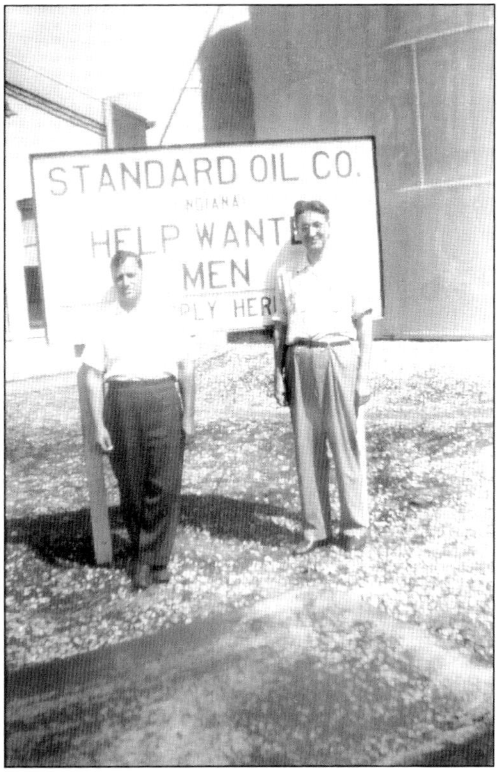

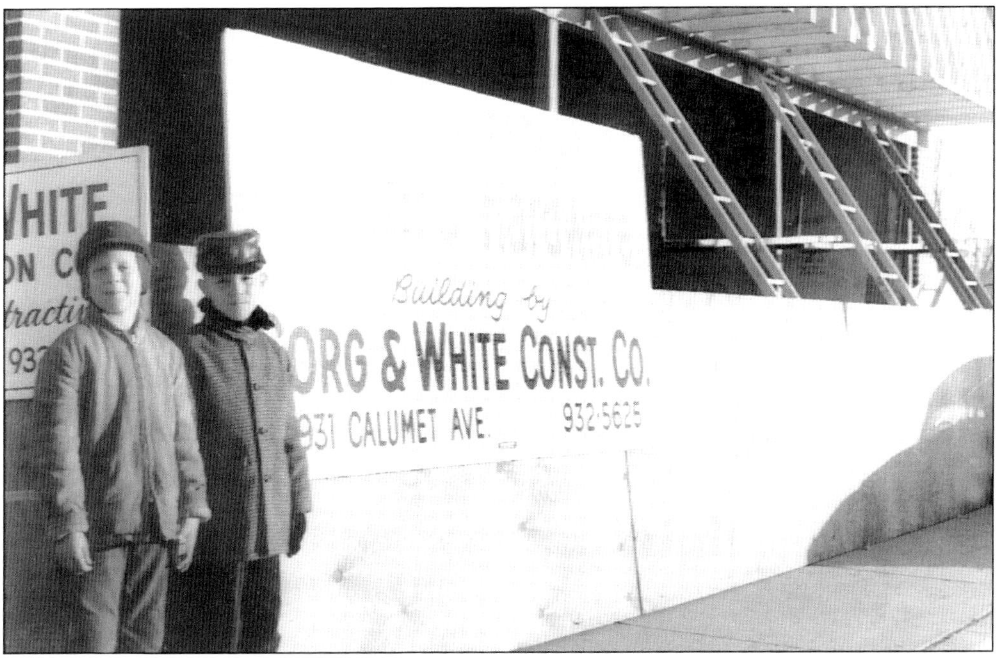

Geffert Hardware was a favorite location for men and women in search of just the right part or special tool. It is likely that nearly every home in Whiting and Robertsdale has something from Geffert's holding it together. After more than 60 years in business, the store began the closing process in 2011. (Geffert family.)

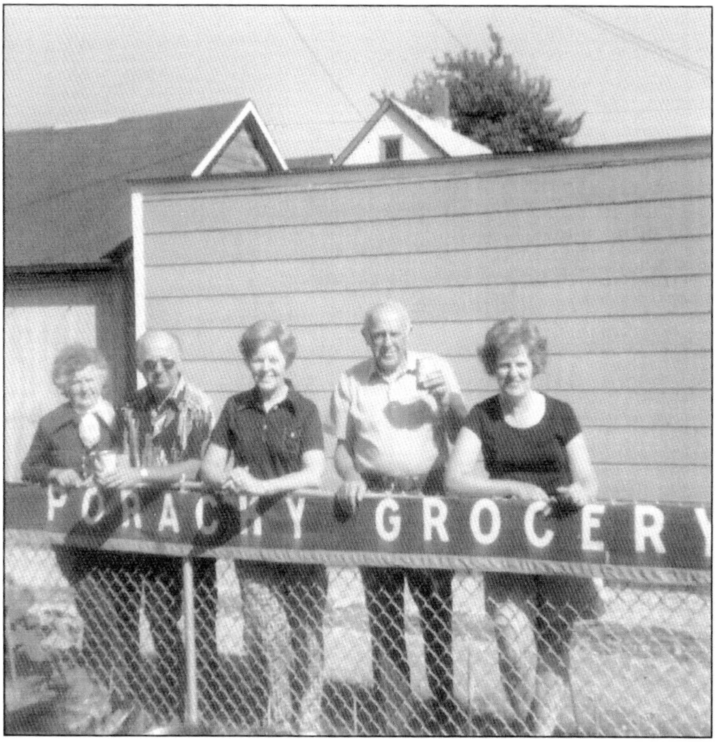

The Poracky family was one of the many families who owned and operated a local grocery store. Their store was on Indianapolis Boulevard. (Vrabel family.)

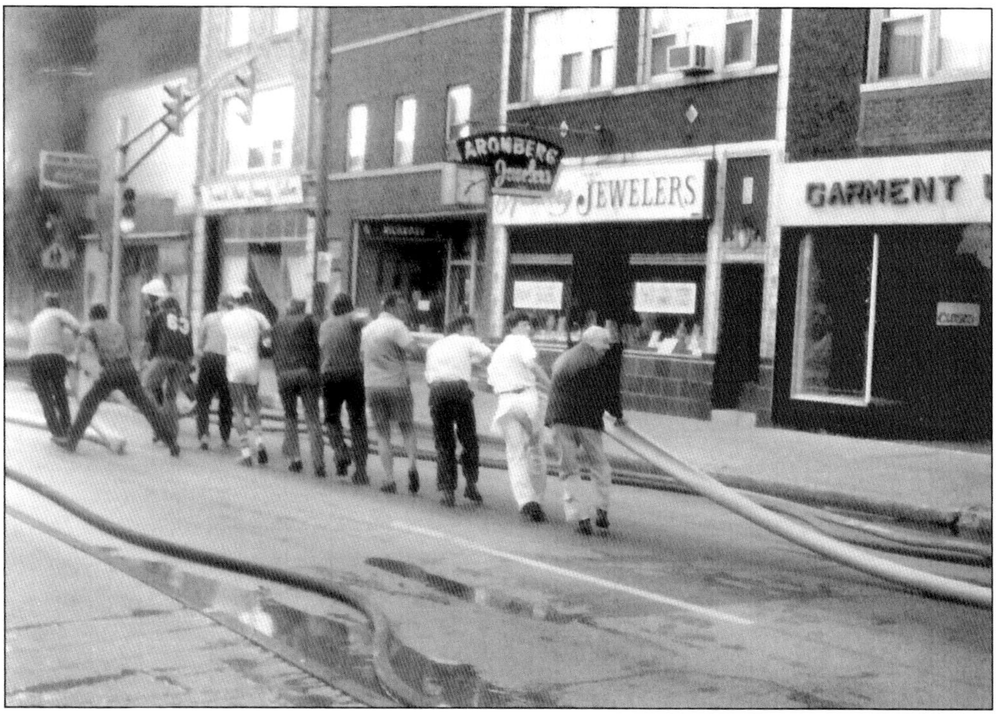

In 1980, a fire destroyed several businesses in the heart of Whiting's business district. As is typical in the Whiting-Robertsdale community, neighbors came from all over to help in the time of need. (Kacer-Householder family.)

Six

WORSHIPPING

Whiting-Robertsdale is home to numerous churches of various denominations, all of which have had a significant impact on the community.

St. John's Evangelical Lutheran Church was organized in June 1891. The first church was destroyed by fire in 1912, and a new church was built at the corner of Cleveland Avenue and 117th Street in 1915. St. Paul Evangelical Lutheran Church was established in 1904 and became well known for making its own *oblatky* for Christmas. The original irons used to make them were made by John Ciesar Sr. St. Paul's new church was dedicated on June 30, 1957.

The Plymouth Congregational Church was founded in 1890 on Center Street. It constructed a new building in 1894 and eventually moved to its current location at 119th Street and Stanton Avenue. Whiting's first Methodist church, Epworth Methodist Episcopal Church, was dedicated in 1895. A new church was built in 1923, and it later became known as Whiting United Methodist Church.

The oldest Catholic parish in the community is Sacred Heart, which was established in 1889. The parish's first church was on Center Street, and the parish school, St. Michael's, opened in 1895. The cornerstone for the present church was laid in 1926. St. John the Baptist Parish was founded in 1897, and the current church was dedicated in 1931. St. John's has operated a parish school since 1901. St. Adalbert Parish was formed in 1900. A small wooden church was built in 1902, and a new church was constructed in 1953. The parish operated a school from 1906 to 1979.

Immaculate Conception Parish was founded in 1922, the church was built in 1924, and its school opened in 1926. St. Mary's Assumption Byzantine Catholic Church was established in 1899. Its present church was built in 1918, the social hall was added in 1940, and a grade school operated from 1952 to 1972. SS. Peter and Paul Catholic Church was formed in 1910 and closed in 2003. Our Lady of the Rosary Shrine, a traditional Roman Catholic shrine, was dedicated in 1982.

Whiting's Hungarian Reformed Church was established in 1918. Other houses of worship include New Life Christian Church, Assembly of God, St. Nicholas Greek Orthodox Church, Church of the Nazarene, Whiting Baptist Church, Community Bible Church, and Congregation Bnai Judah.

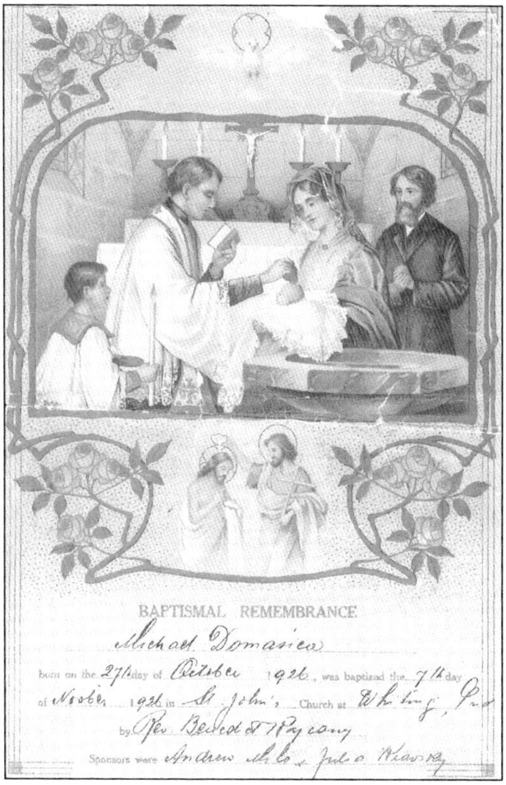

This elaborate certificate documents the holy sacrament of baptism in the Catholic Church. (Michael Domasica.)

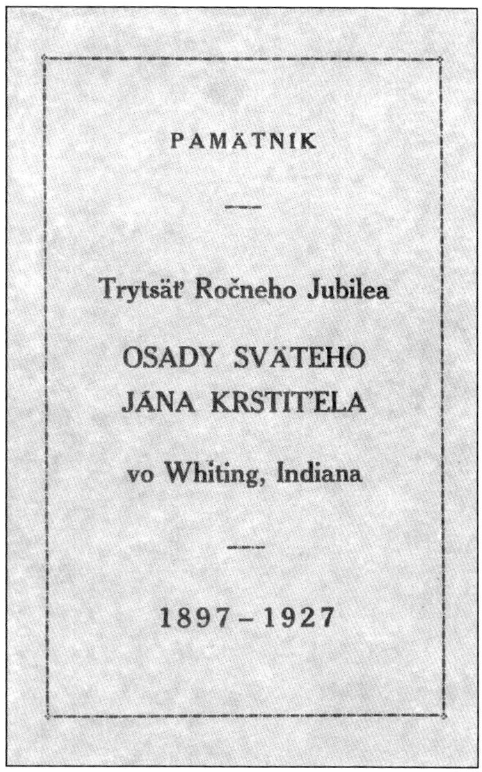
PAMÄTNIK

Trytsäť Ročneho Jubilea

OSADY SVÄTEHO
JÁNA KRSTITEĽA

vo Whiting, Indiana

1897 – 1927

Fr. Benedict Rajcany arrived in Whiting-Robertsdale in 1897 and was charged with serving the growing immigrant population, many of whom were Slovak and in need of someone who could minister to them in their Slovak language. He dedicated the new parish to St. John the Baptist because he felt like "one crying in the wilderness." This booklet commemorated the 30th anniversary of the parish. (Specker Library, Calumet College of St. Joseph.)

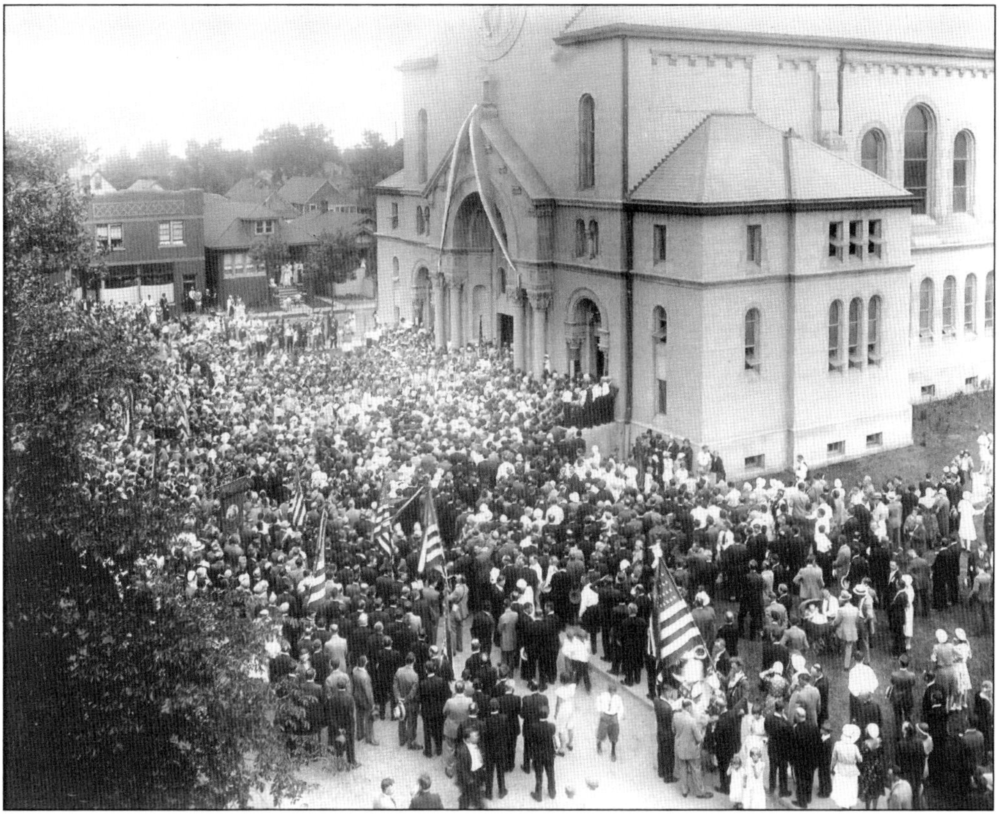

Established in 1897, St. John the Baptist Parish had 1,500 members by 1910. Although the church was located in Robertsdale, 1,300 members of the congregation were Whiting residents. By 1924, the parish had a membership of 3,250 and a need for a much larger church. Ground was broken in 1930 for the new church, and on June 21, 1931, hundreds gathered for the dedication of the beautiful new structure. The church's steeple can be seen from miles around and has become one of the most significant and recognizable landmarks in the Whiting-Robertsdale community. (Both, St. John the Baptist Parish.)

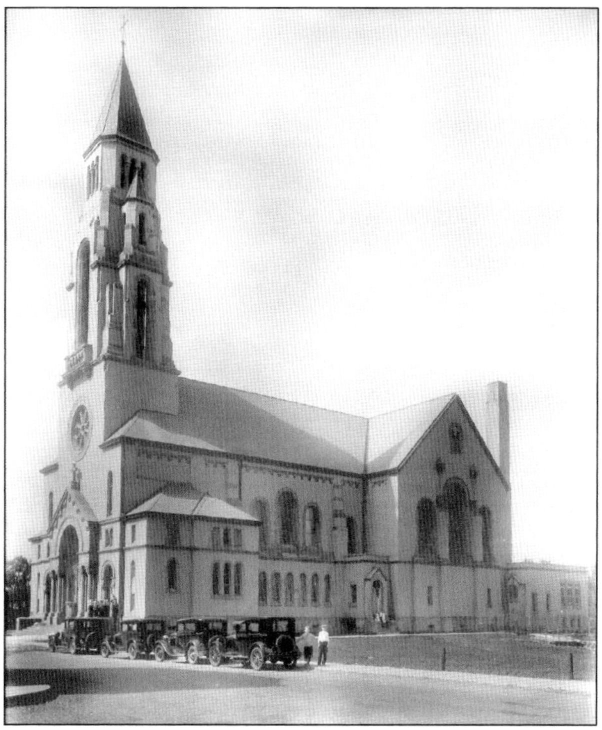

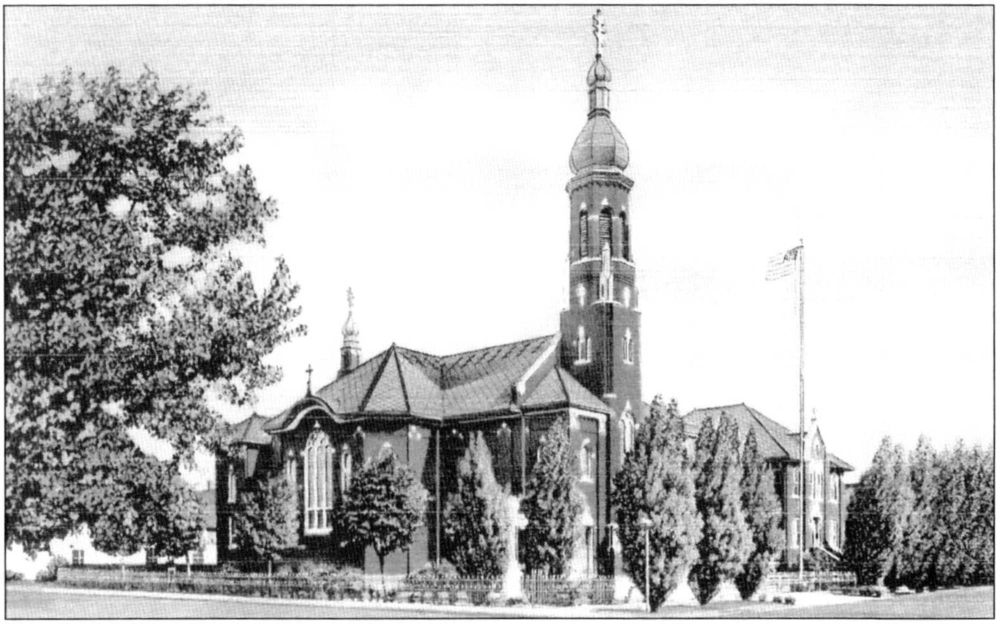

Many of the Slovak immigrants who settled in Whiting brought with them beliefs and traditions associated with the Byzantine Catholic rite and established St. Mary's Assumption Byzantine Rite Catholic Church in 1899. The original church building was on Davidson Place, and the present church was built in 1918, with a social hall added in 1940. In 1952, the parish added a grade school, which operated until 1972. (Tkach family.)

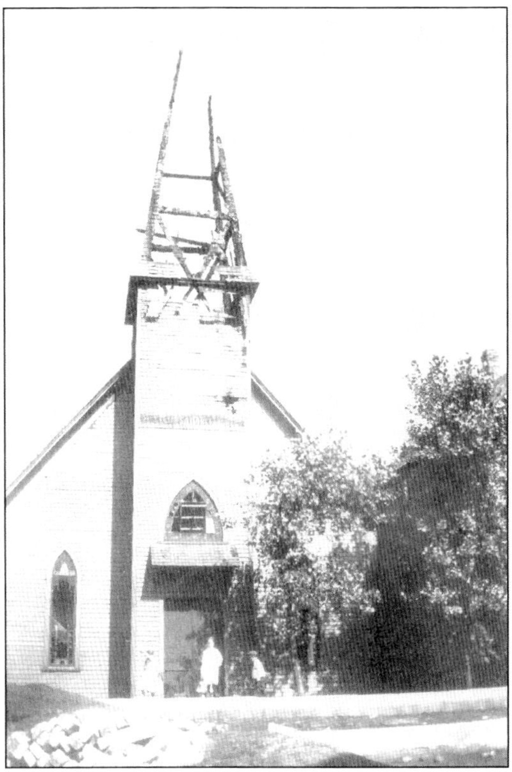

The first sermon at St. John's Evangelical Lutheran Church on Clark Street was delivered on New Year's Day, 1892. It was initially a German Lutheran church, but Slovaks who settled in the area were allowed to use it until they formed their own in 1903. After it was destroyed by a lightning strike in 1912, a new church was constructed at 117th Street and Cleveland Avenue in 1915. (Whiting Historical Society.)

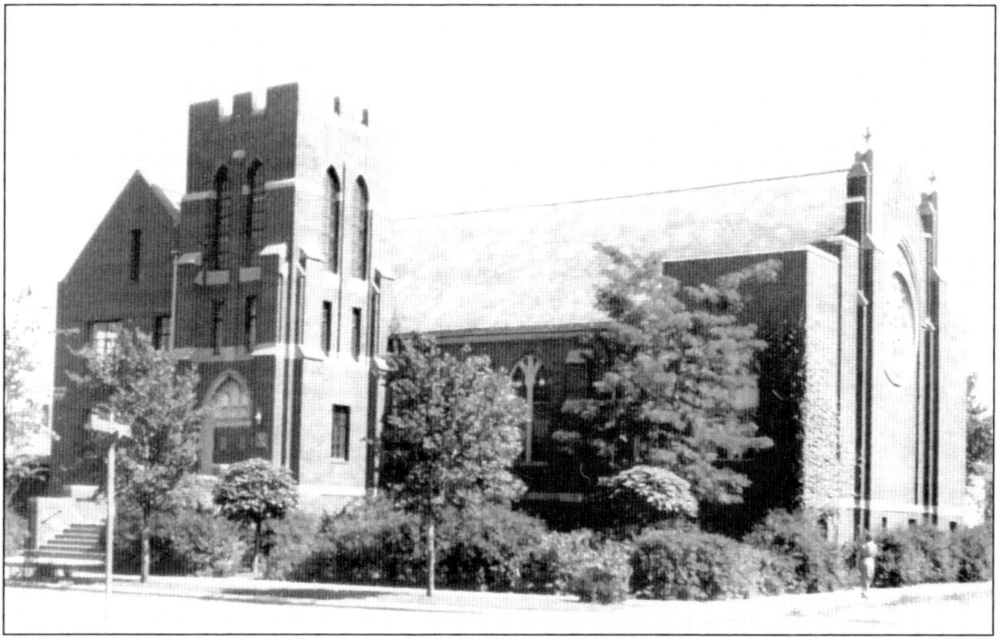

Plymouth Congregational's original church was on 119th Street in what is now city hall. The church seen here is its third and current location at the corner of 119th Street and Stanton Avenue in Robertsdale. The church graciously shared its facilities with the Hungarian Reformed Church when the latter was forced to close its own sanctuary after 87 years. (Whiting Historical Society.)

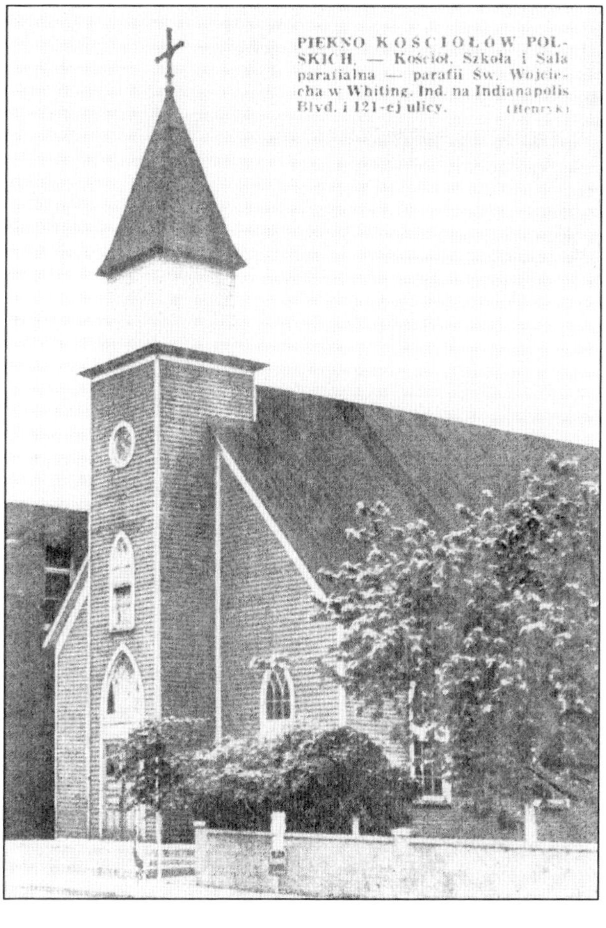

St. Adalbert Parish was established in 1900 by 35 Polish families who settled in the Whiting-Robertsdale area. A wooden church was completed in the spring of 1902 and was briefly named St. Peter's. In 1904, parishioners formed St. Hedwig's Society to foster and preserve Polish customs and traditions. In 1951, ground was broken for a new church, and the cornerstone was laid in 1952. (St. Adalbert Parish.)

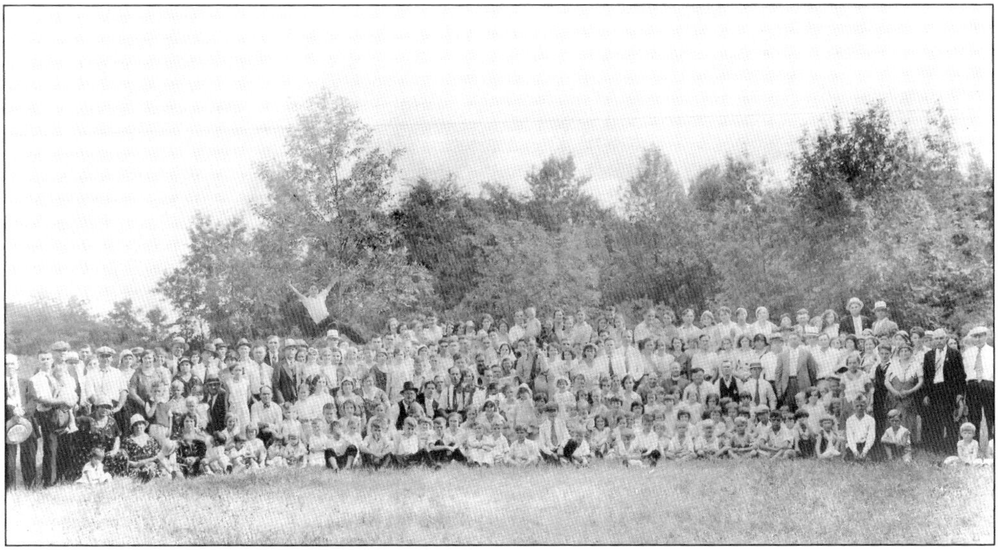

The families of St. Mary's Assumption Church posed for this photograph at their annual picnic. One particularly exuberant young man is leaping up in the background to make sure he makes it into the picture. In addition to serving the spiritual needs of their parishioners, churches provided social activities so people with common backgrounds and traditions could come together and feel a sense of belonging and security. (Tkach family.)

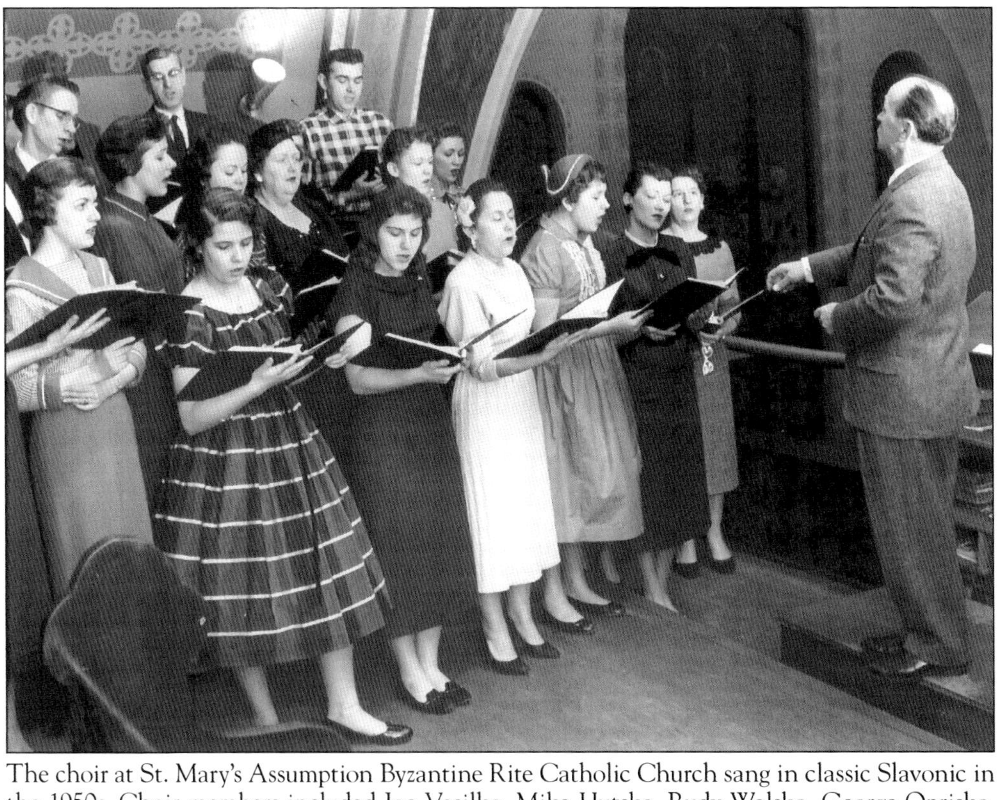

The choir at St. Mary's Assumption Byzantine Rite Catholic Church sang in classic Slavonic in the 1950s. Choir members included Joe Vasilko, Mike Hutsko, Rudy Walsko, George Oprisko, Nick Vischak, Betty Zehme, and Irene Horvat. (Whiting Historical Society.)

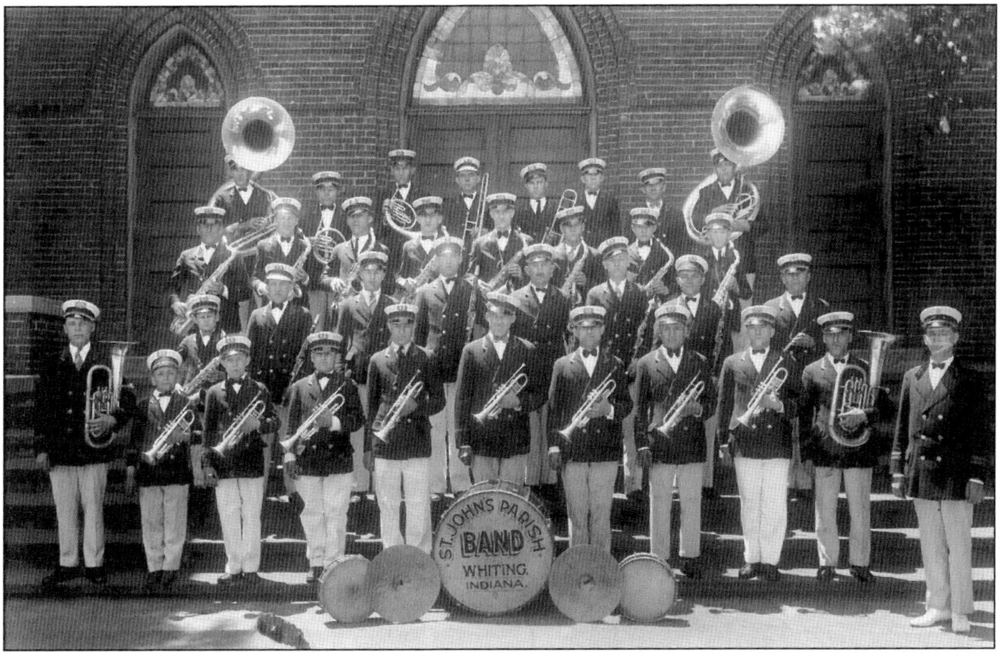

In addition to providing religious services and ministries, parishes provided an outlet for musical, athletic, and social skills. There were numerous parish bands, sports teams, clubs, societies, fraternal organizations, and theatrical groups. St. John the Baptist's parish band is seen here in the 1930s in front of its first church. (St. John the Baptist Parish.)

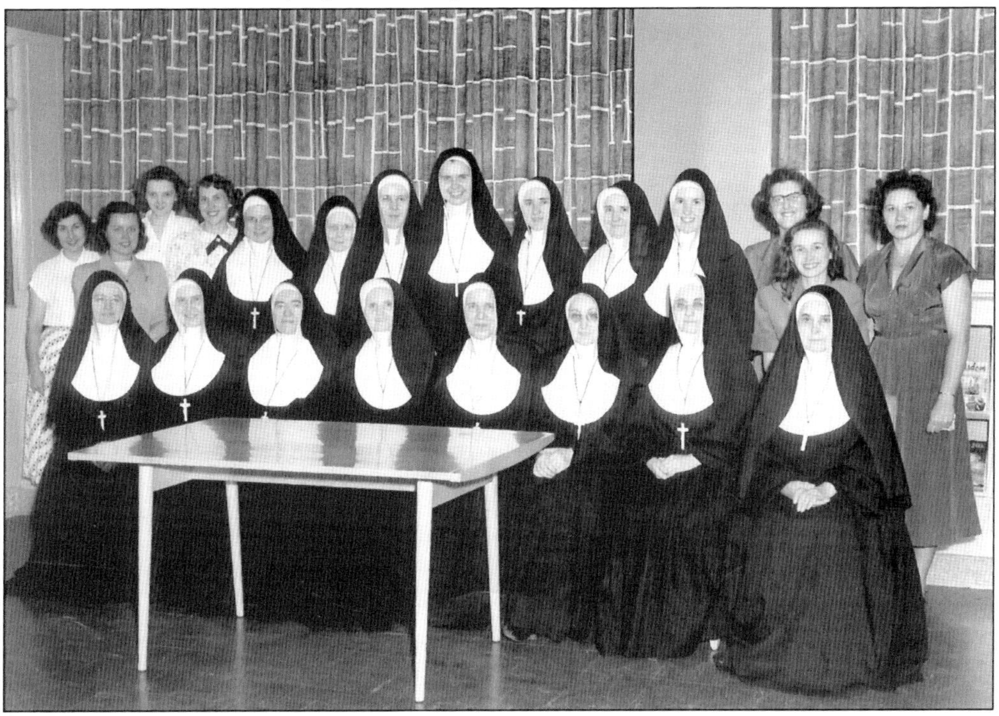

In the parochial schools, nuns were charged with teaching the parish schoolchildren not only academics but also religion, morality, discipline, and etiquette. (Vrabel family.)

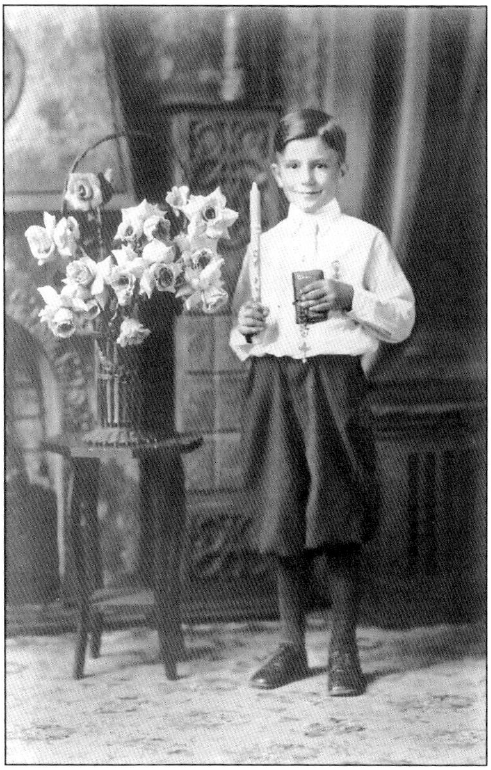

Ben Saliga poses in his First Communion attire in the early 1930s. In the 1920s and early 1930s, it was typical for young boys to wear knickers until they graduated from grammar school. (Saliga family.)

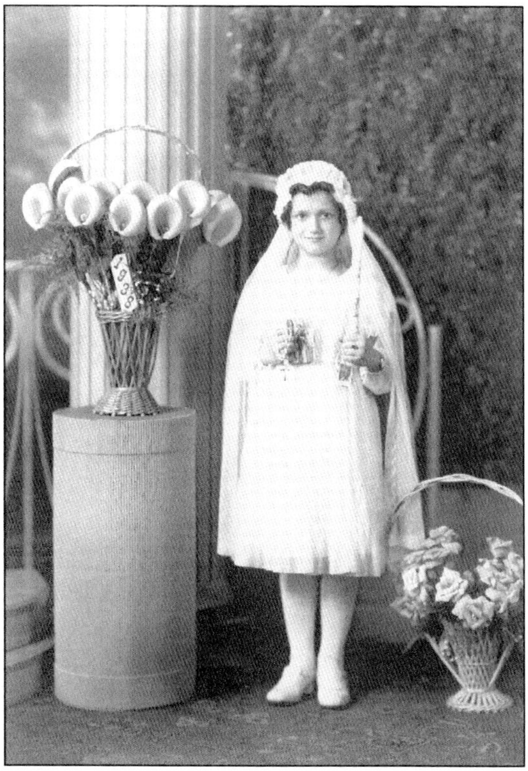

Maryann Palikan poses for a traditional First Communion picture in 1938. (Mores family.)

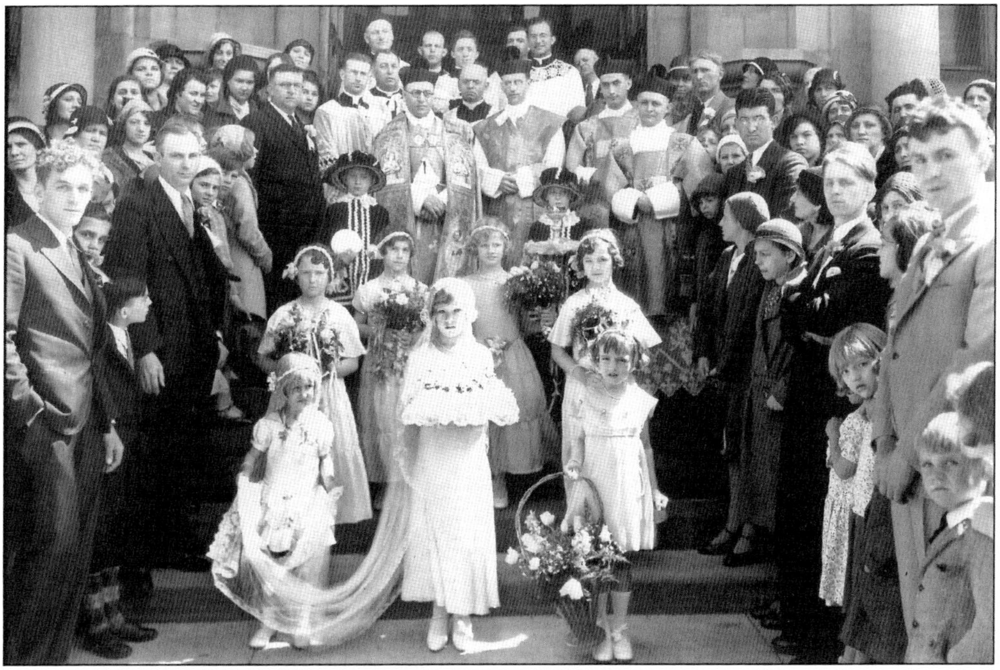

Among the most pleasant childhood memories of those who grew up in the Catholic schools of Whiting and Robertsdale was the annual May crowing of the Blessed Mother, seen here. Other fond memories include Mother's Day plays and selling Holy Childhood stamps to "save the pagan babies." (St. John the Baptist Parish.)

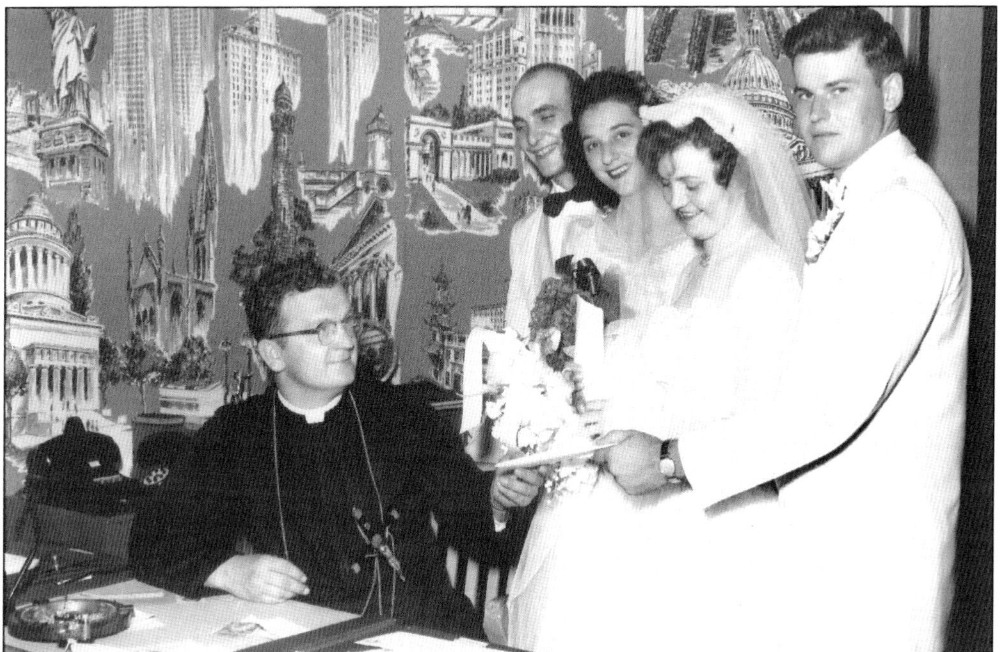

Fr. Edward Homco (left), a lifelong member of St. John's Parish and the pastor for 31 years, officiates the signing of a wedding certificate for Irene Svitko and Tom Morgan. Witnesses Bernie Svitko and Rose Svitko are in the background. (Svitko family.)

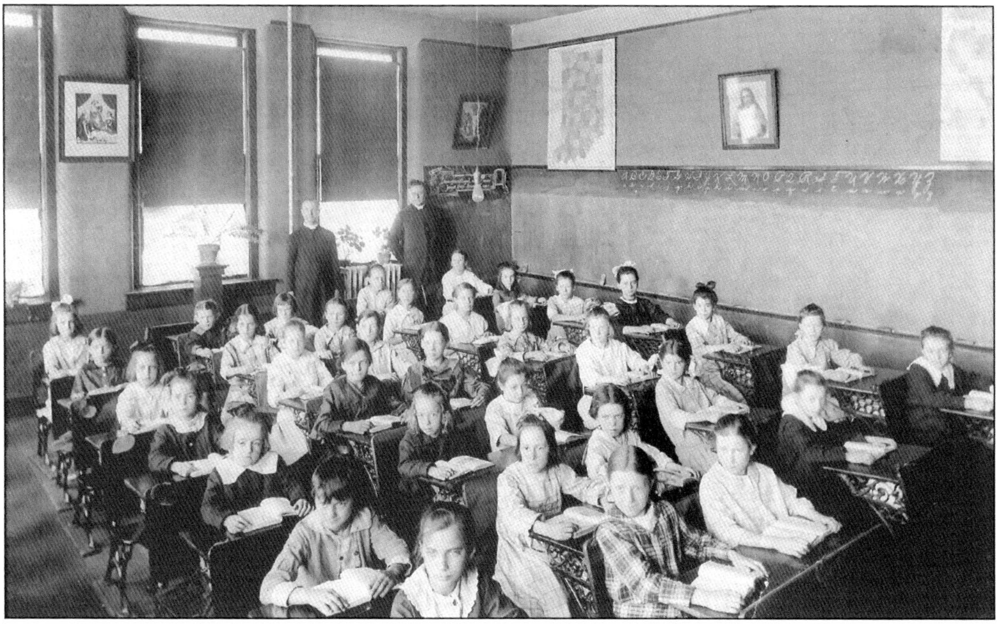

Most of the parochial schools in Whiting-Robertsdale have closed due to low enrollments. In the community's early years, however, several of the parishes had grade schools associated with them. Seen here is a young class at Immaculate Conception's grade school. (Whiting Historical Society.)

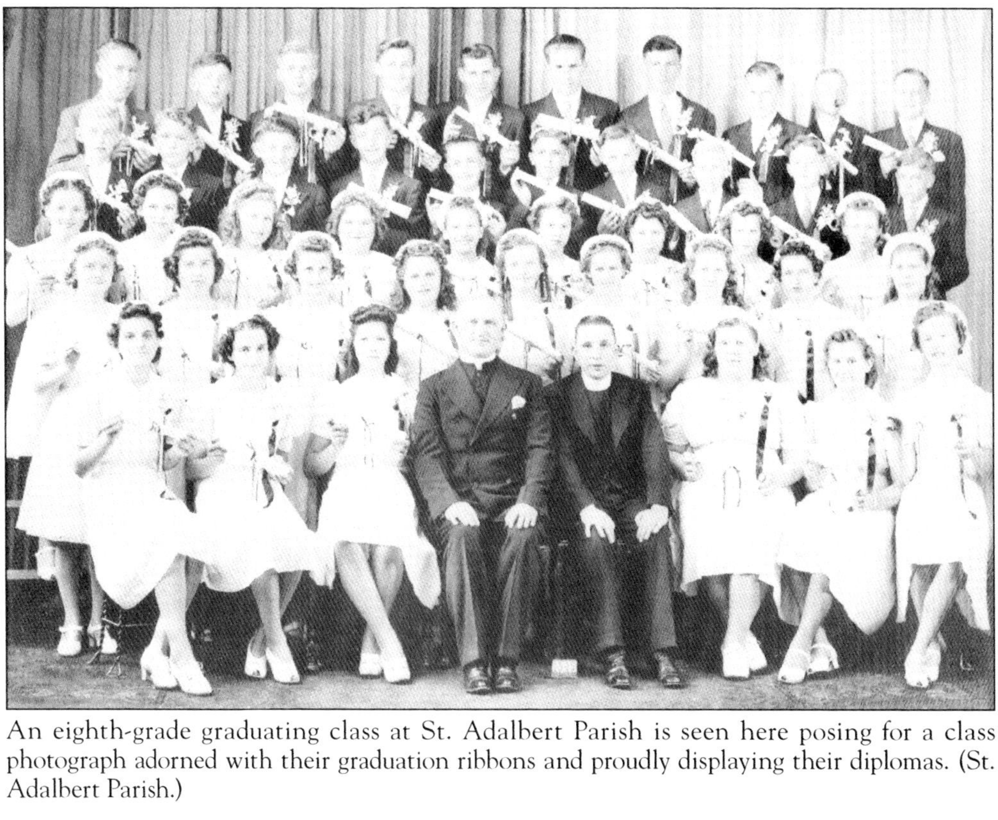

An eighth-grade graduating class at St. Adalbert Parish is seen here posing for a class photograph adorned with their graduation ribbons and proudly displaying their diplomas. (St. Adalbert Parish.)

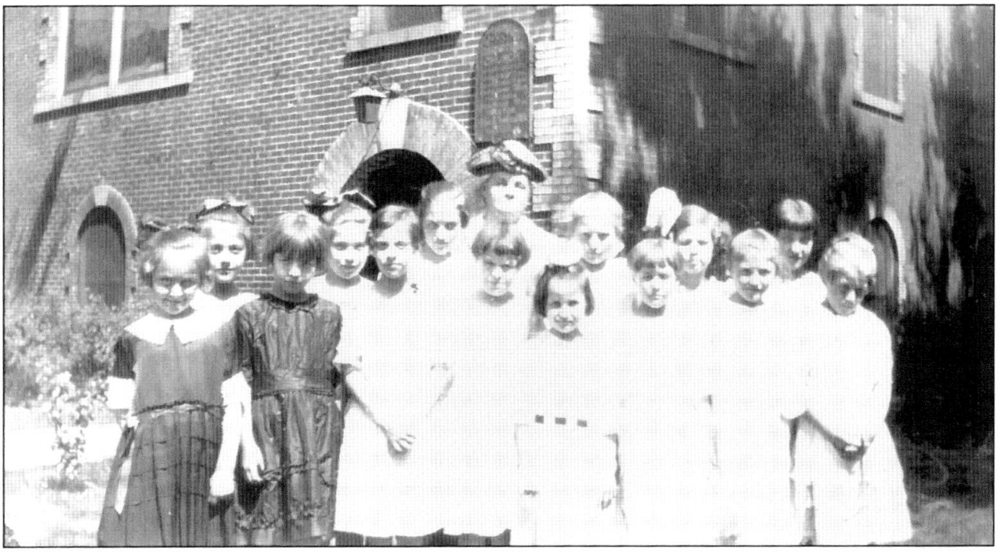

Plymouth Congregational's Crusaders Sunday school class gathered outside the church on 119th Street, at what is now city hall. In the background is the teacher, Mrs. Shelley. The students, in no particular order, are Estelle Abbot, Daisy Nedjl, Vivian Rowe, Billie Klose, Bonnie Jean Davidson, Ann Harris, Mary Elizabeth Judson, Virginia Kyle, Rose Paryos, Margaret Seto, Doris Matson, Margaret Paryos, Elizabeth Long, and Sophie Gabor. (Whiting Historical Society.)

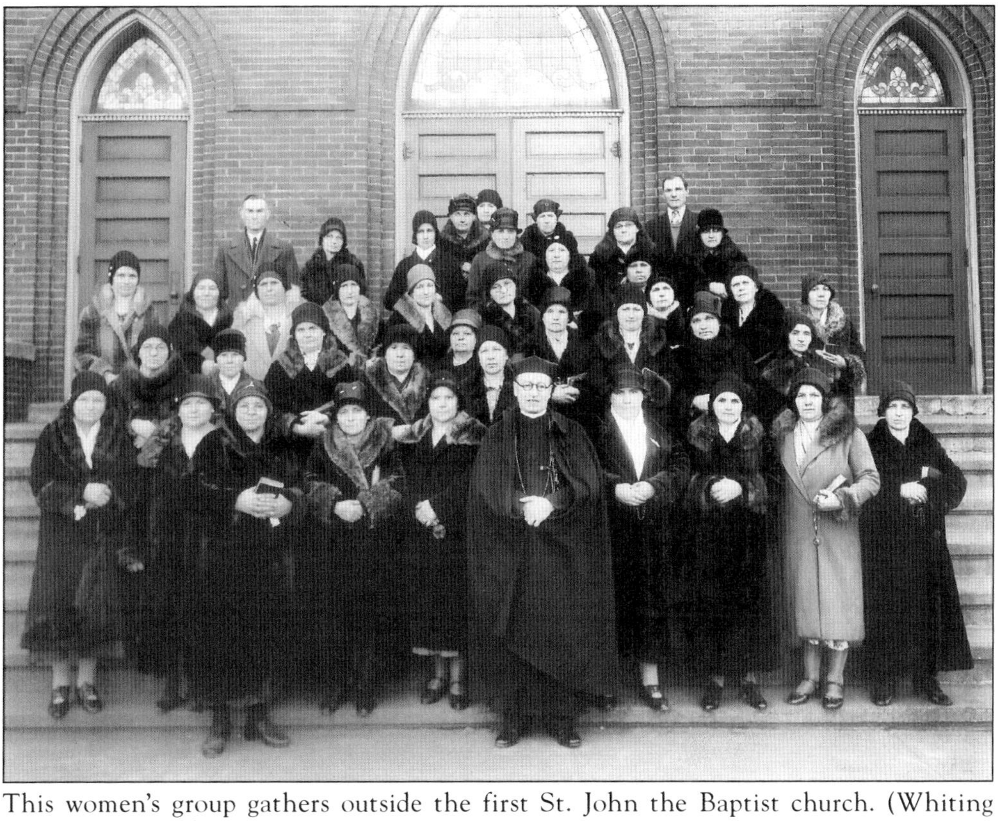

This women's group gathers outside the first St. John the Baptist church. (Whiting Historical Society.)

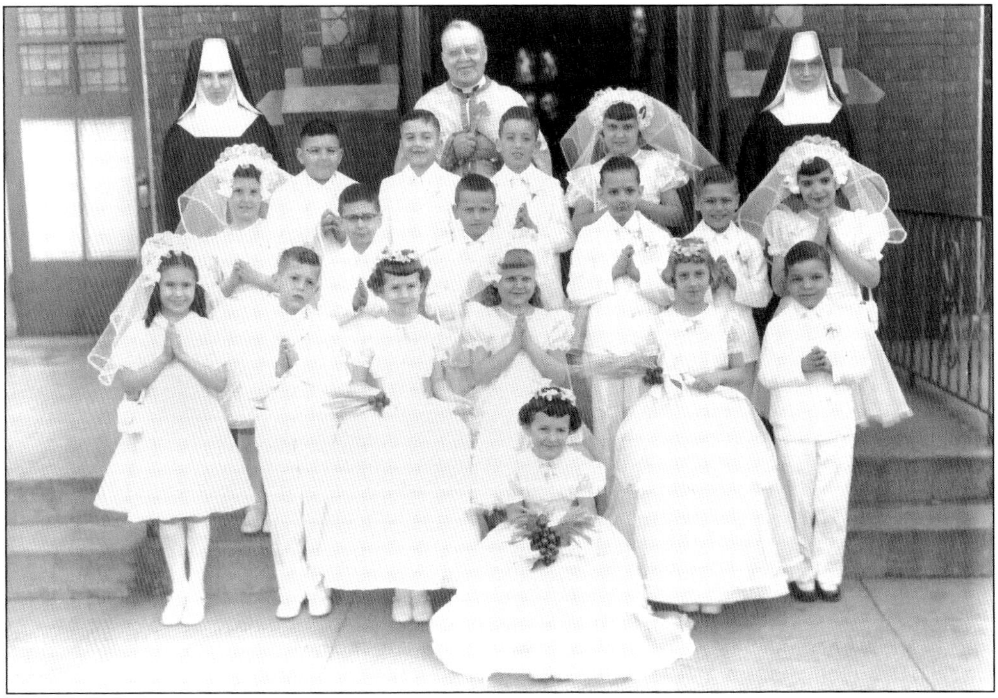

The 1955 communion class at St. Mary's Church poses with Rev. John Slivka and Sisters Athanasius and Hilaria. The three girls in the center wearing bell-shaped dresses and wreaths are a year younger than the communicants and were chosen to be the "angels" who led the procession into church. The angels are holding bouquets of wheat and grapes to signify the body and blood of Christ. (Tkach family.)

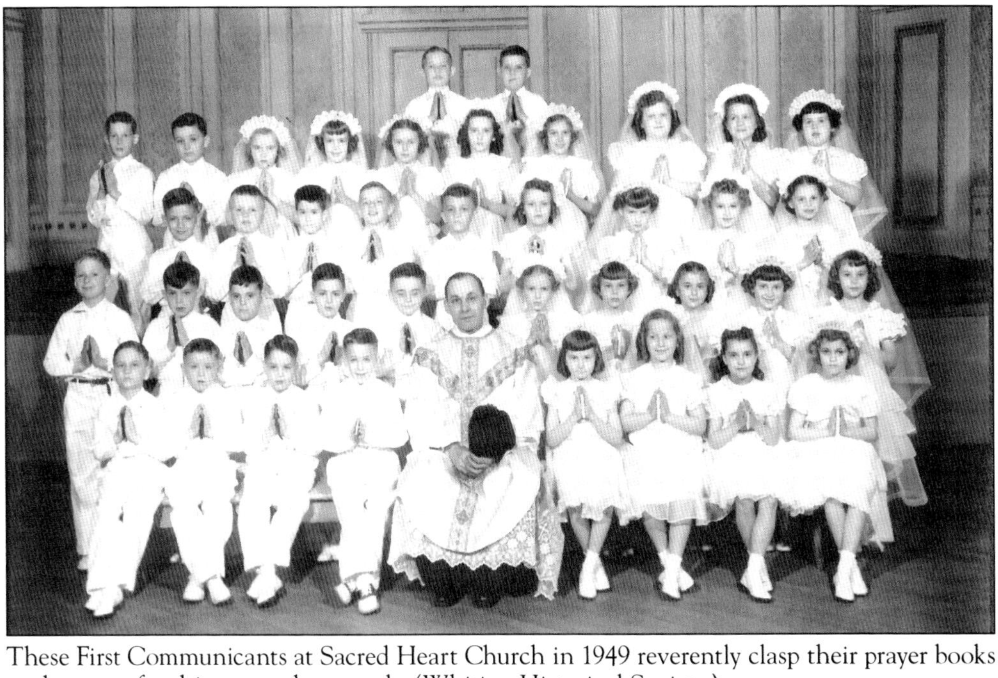

These First Communicants at Sacred Heart Church in 1949 reverently clasp their prayer books as they pose for this group photograph. (Whiting Historical Society.)

Rev. John Bradac was the first resident pastor at St. Paul Evangelical Lutheran Church. He was born and educated in Europe and was one of the signers of Czechoslovakia's constitution. He also served as Whiting's air-raid warden during World War II. He retired in 1963 after serving for 51 years. Reverend Bradac is seen here with his wife, Dorothy, in 1962. (Kacer-Householder family.)

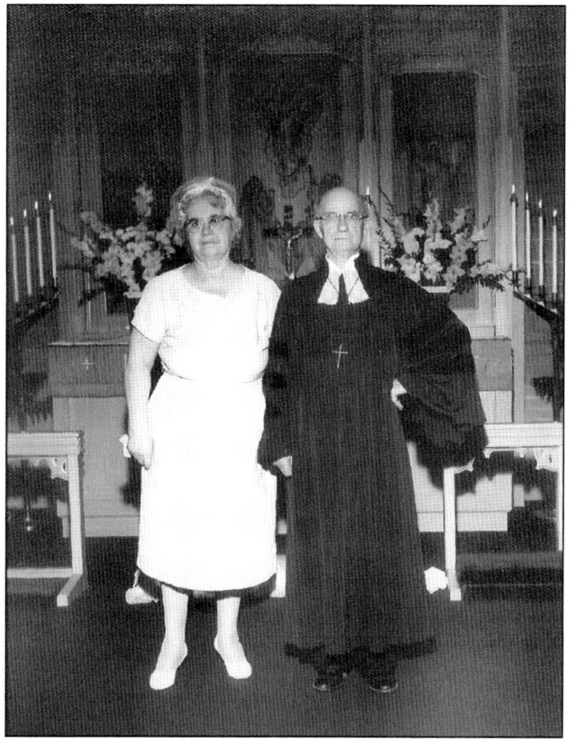

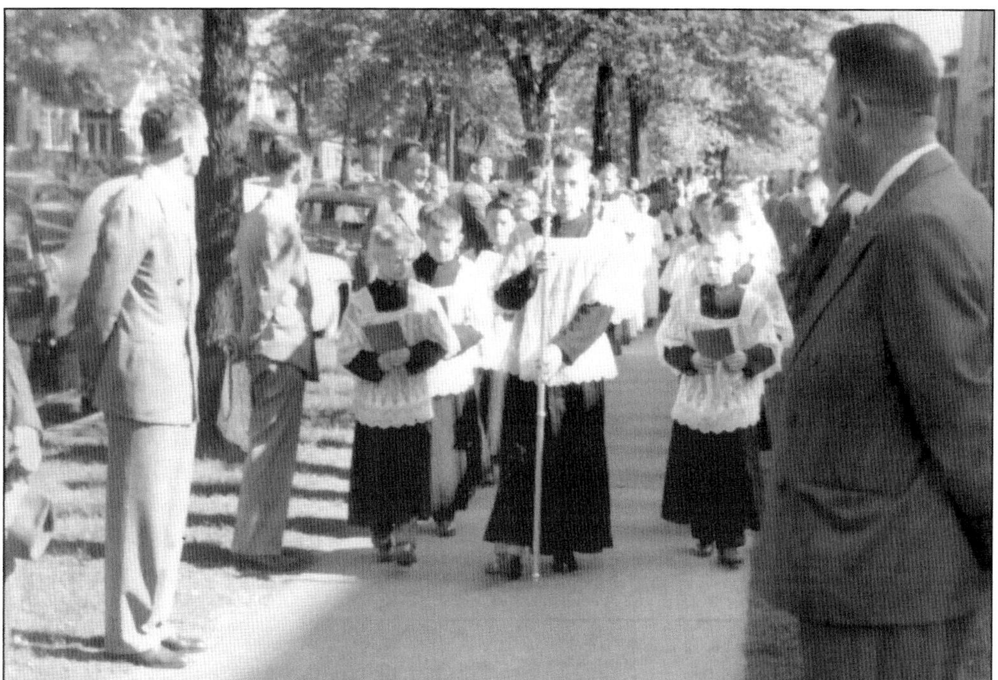

Many church ceremonies included formal processions both inside and outside the church. Here, altar boy Francis Lentvorsky (center) leads a group of altar boys, priests, and congregation members outside of Sacred Heart Church. (Lentvorsky family.)

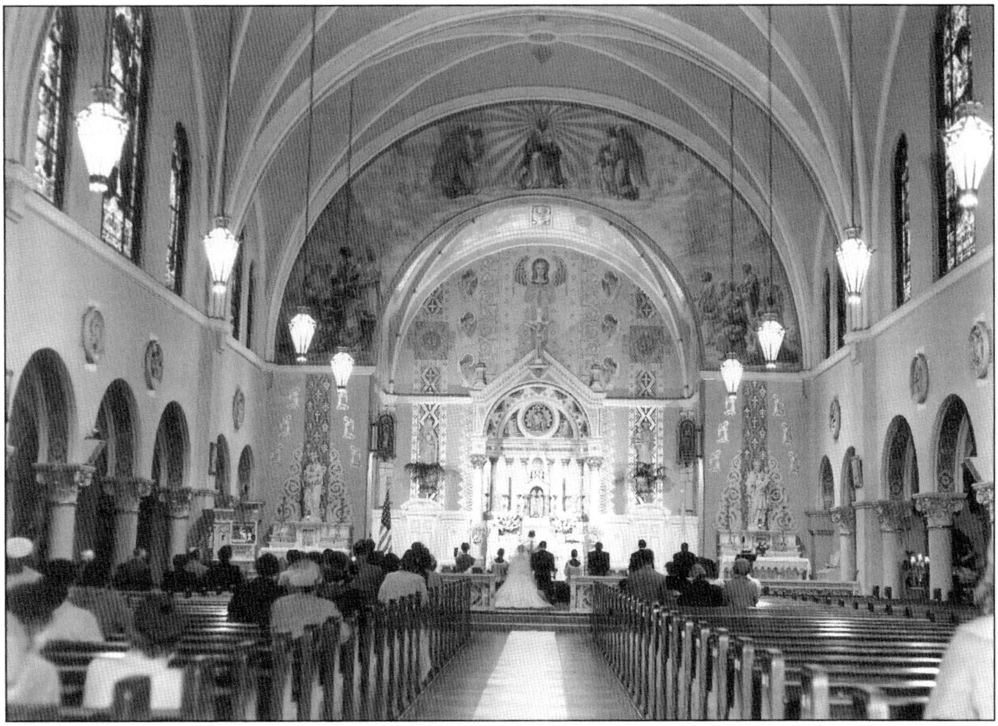

Sacred Heart is one of the oldest parishes in Whiting and has seen many changes over the years. This photograph from the 1950s highlights the church's beautiful archways and intricate artwork. (Saliga family.)

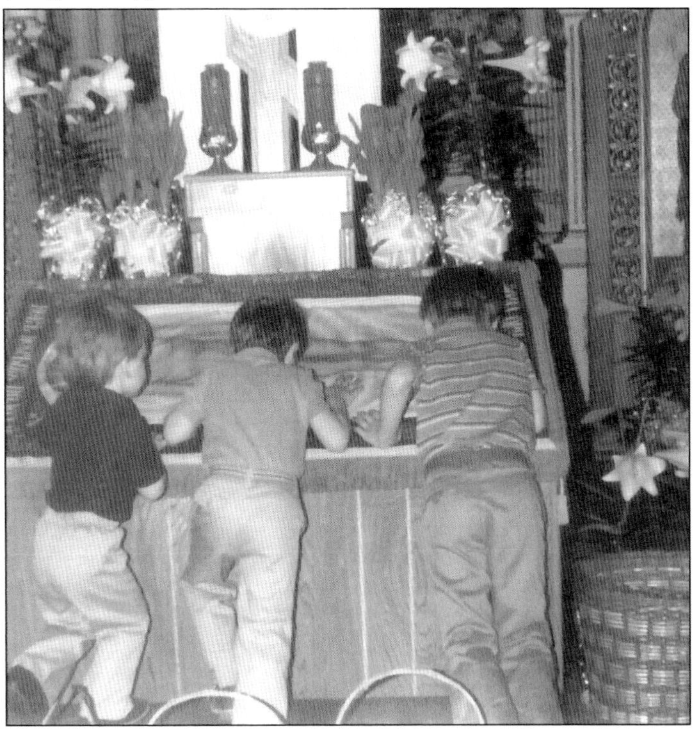

Faith and traditions run deep with St. Mary's parishioners and are passed on to new generations in the hopes that they will not be lost. Here, the great-grandchildren of an early parishioner kiss the *Epitaphios*, an icon of "Jesus in His Shroud" on Holy Saturday, following the blessing of the children's Easter baskets. Epitaphion icons are traditionally found in Catholic churches that follow the Byzantine Rite. (Eck family.)

Seven

Celebrating Everything

The Whiting-Robertsdale community has become well known in the Calumet Region for its year-round celebrations. Residents of Byzantine heritage celebrate St. Nicholas Day in early December with banquets and rituals once practiced in Europe. As the month of December progresses, there are parades, cookie bakes, and a community tree-lighting ceremony. Parishes host a *vilija*, the traditional Slovak Christmas Eve dinner. To conclude the Christmas season, a Twelfth Night celebration is held on January 6 where Christmas trees and wreaths are set ablaze and wishes are exchanged for health and prosperity in the new year.

The Easter season features parades, an Easter bonnet-decorating contest, and visits from Easter bunnies. The Hungarian Reformed Church makes and sells its special Easter sausage, and St. John the Baptist sells *pirohis*, the Slovak version of pierogies. Those of Eastern European heritage prepare their traditional Easter foods for the blessing of baskets on Holy Saturday, and congregations participate in the Sacred Triduum.

Whiting-Robertsdale's largest celebration has traditionally been its annual Fourth of July parade and picnic at Whiting Park. Over the years, the picnic has featured activities such as sack races, horseshoe tournaments, variety shows, dancing, and carnival rides. In the early 1920s, the program consisted of folk dancing as well as the playing of Polish, Russian, Slovak, Greek, and Hungarian national anthems, followed by dancing groups in native costumes. The celebration has evolved as times have changed, but the popularity, the patriotism, and the spectacular firework show remain unchanged.

Whiting weddings are typically large, lavish occasions. Beautiful churches provide sacred settings, and numerous halls and restaurants provide practical as well as elegant settings for the receptions. In years past, some of the most common locations for large wedding receptions were the halls at the Slovak Dom, St. Mary's, and St. John the Baptist.

Other celebrations unique to the Whiting community are house blessings that offer protection against harm; the blessing of pets to coincide with the feast of St. Francis of Assisi; the blessing of fruit; and the blessing of flowers. As a whole, the community of Whiting-Robertsdale tends to celebrate more enthusiastically and fervently than any other community in the Calumet Region.

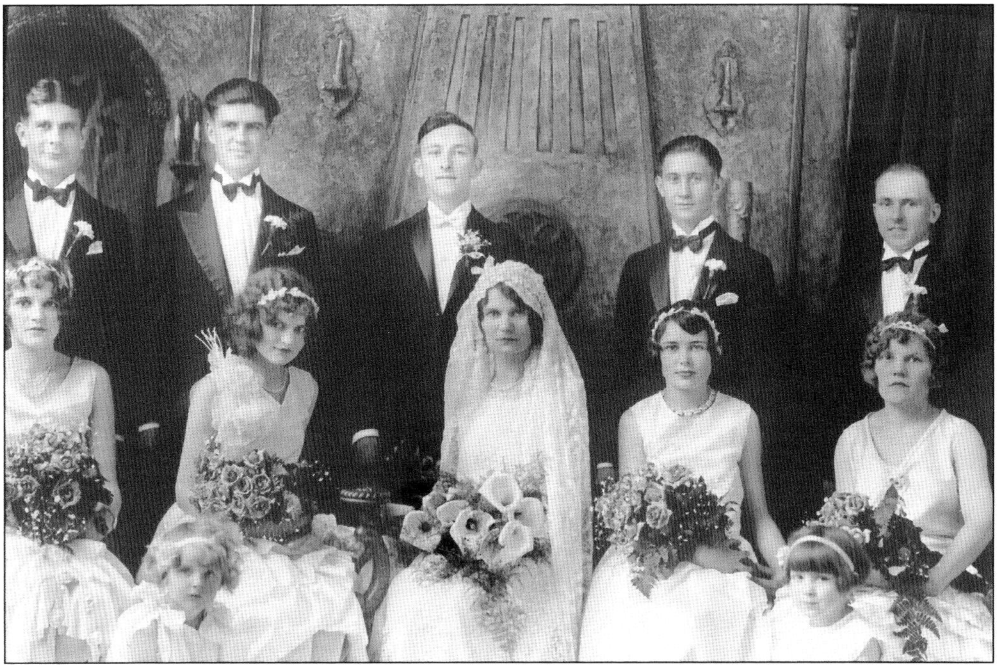

John Kaminsky and his bride, Mary Cvaniga, pose with their wedding party in June 1929. (Vrabel family.)

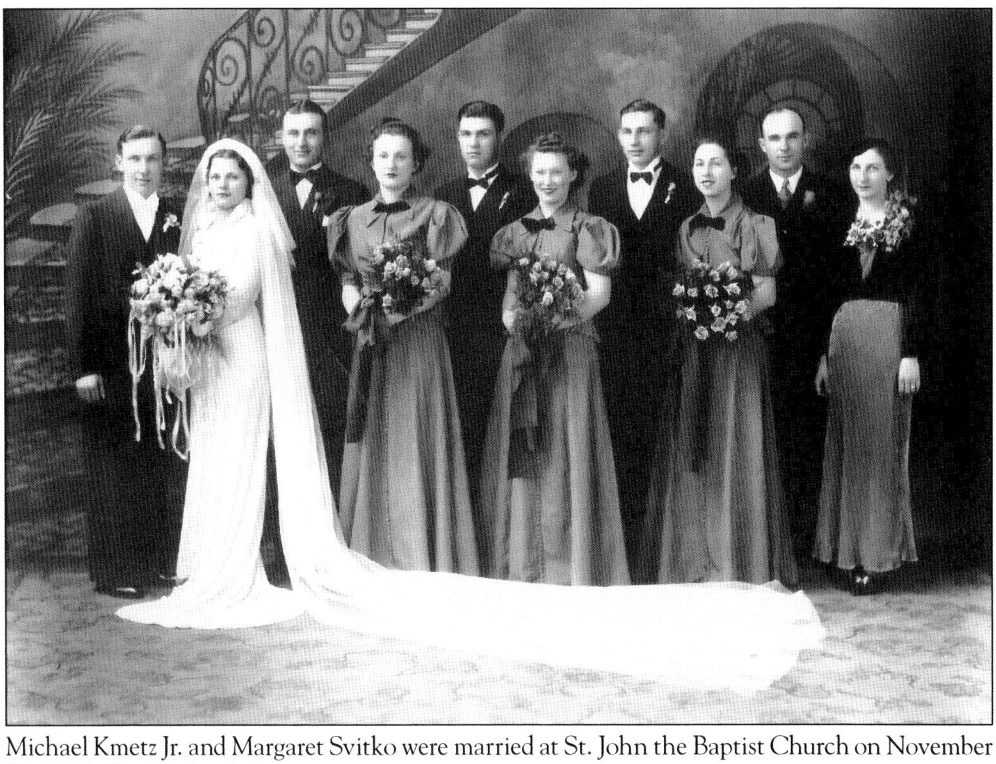

Michael Kmetz Jr. and Margaret Svitko were married at St. John the Baptist Church on November 28, 1936. (Svitko family.)

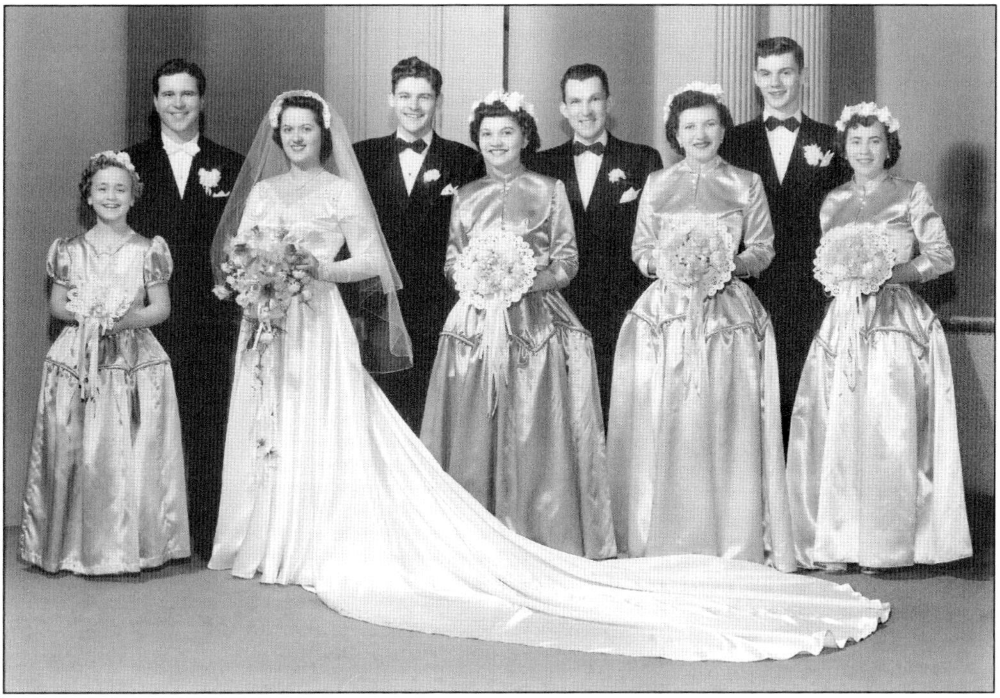

Florian Mores and his bride, Mary Ann Palikan, were married in 1951. (Mores family.)

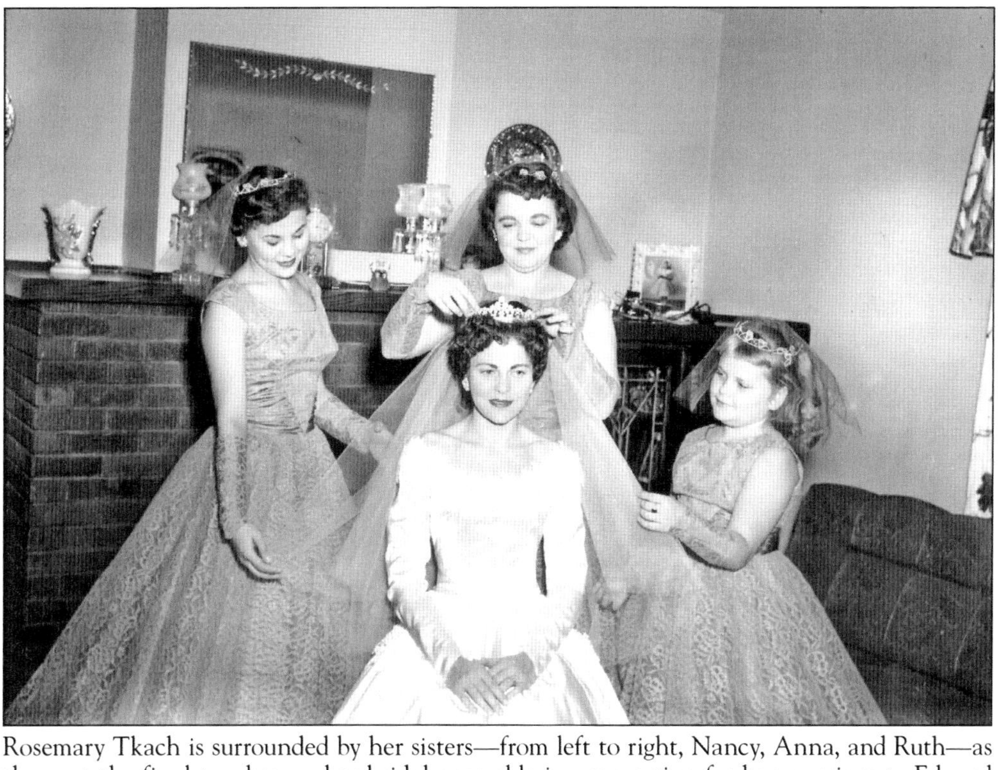

Rosemary Tkach is surrounded by her sisters—from left to right, Nancy, Anna, and Ruth—as they put the final touches on her bridal ensemble in preparation for her marriage to Edward Domasica on October 20, 1956. (Domasica family.)

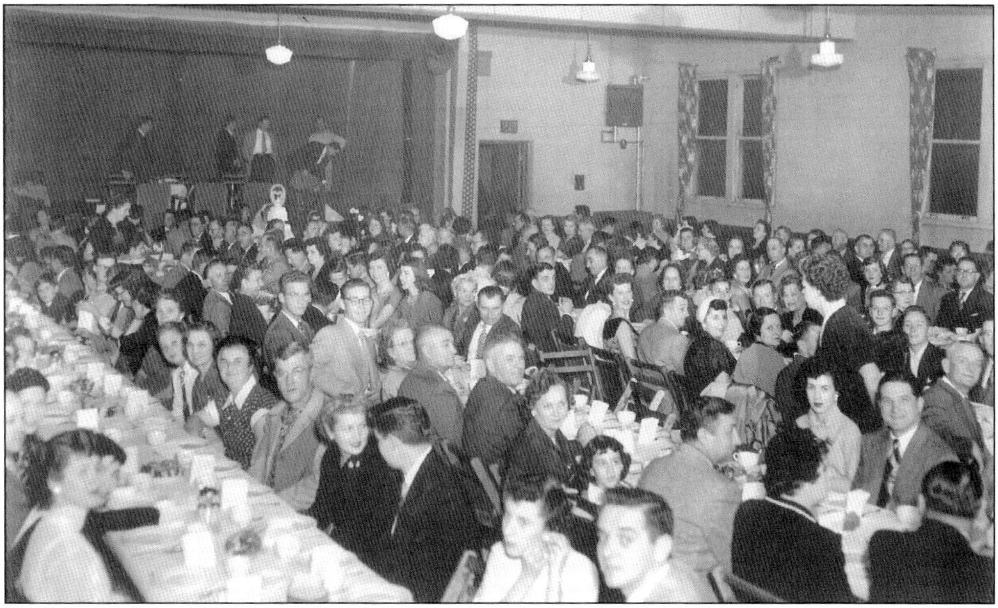

This wedding reception for Joann and Ben Saliga was held at St. Mary's Hall in 1953. At that time, the focus was on food and dancing rather than fancy tablecloths and centerpieces, and it was typical to have 400 to 500 people in attendance. Families hired a cook and brought in their own food, making it much more economical to feed a large crowd. A typical reception like this cost around $500. (Saliga family.)

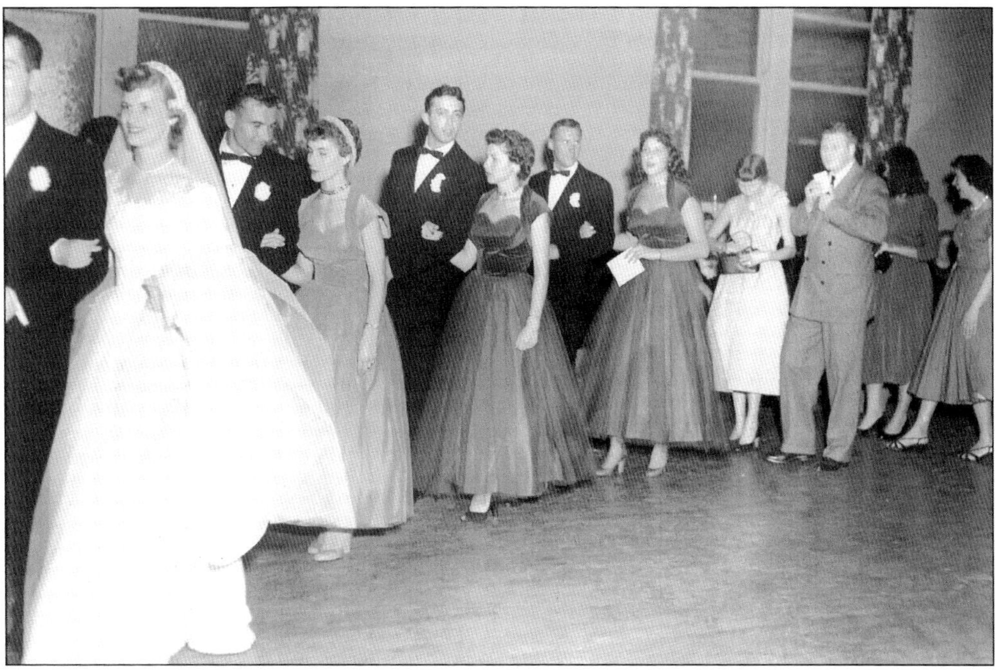

The Grand March is an Eastern European tradition and was the highlight of the ethnic wedding reception. The bride and groom led the march and were followed by their attendants. After the march, the wedding party lined up to form a receiving line so that guests could congratulate the bride and groom and present them with cards and monetary gifts. (Saliga family.)

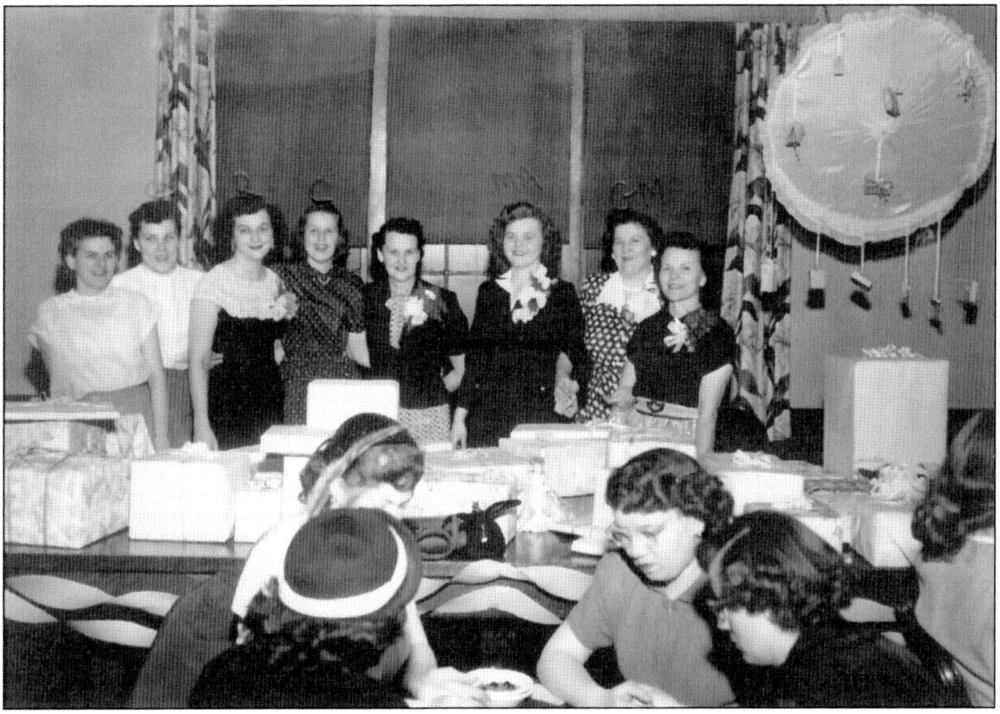

The Whiting Community Center was a common location for bridal showers such as this one. (Svitko family.)

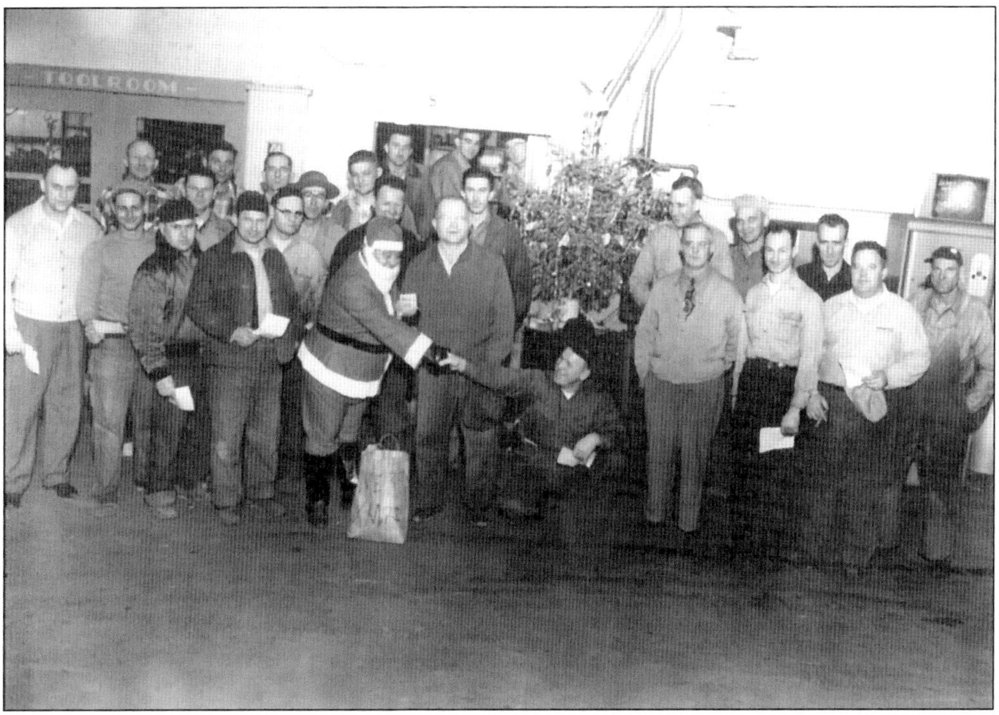

To liven up their holiday spirits, Santa Claus paid a visit to the employees at the Standard Oil refinery. (Boncela family.)

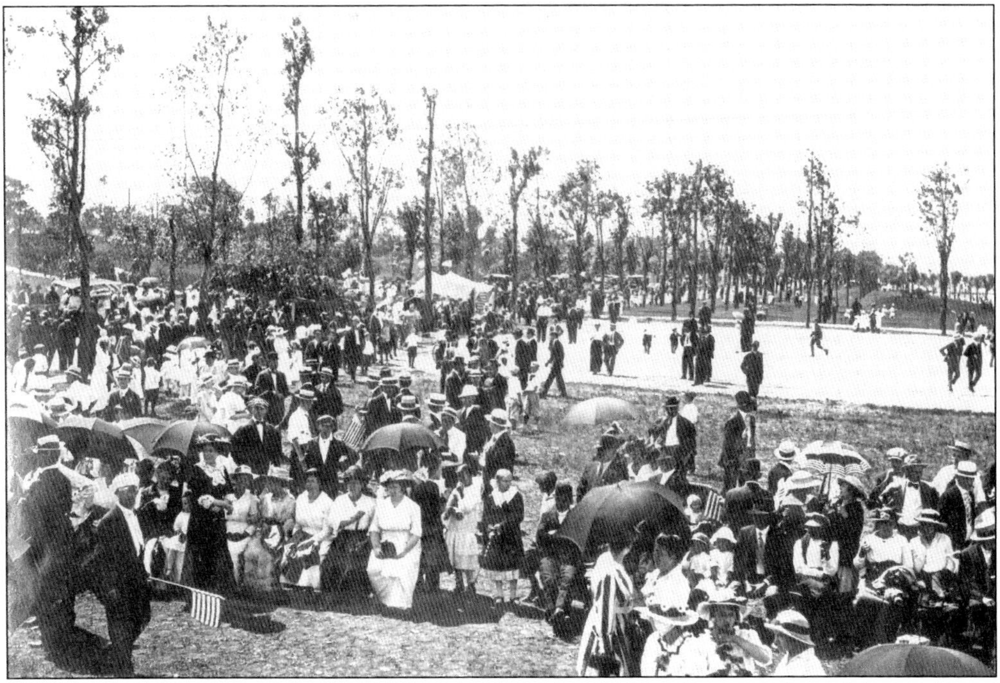

The Fourth of July was a particularly memorable occasion for Whiting-Robertsdale families in the 1920s. After the annual parade, hundreds would gather at the park for family picnics and to watch or participate in various events and activities, such as trap shooting, canoe races, tennis matches, swimming contests, boxing matches, bicycle races, and ball games. The day concluded with fireworks over Lake Michigan. (Whiting Historical Society.)

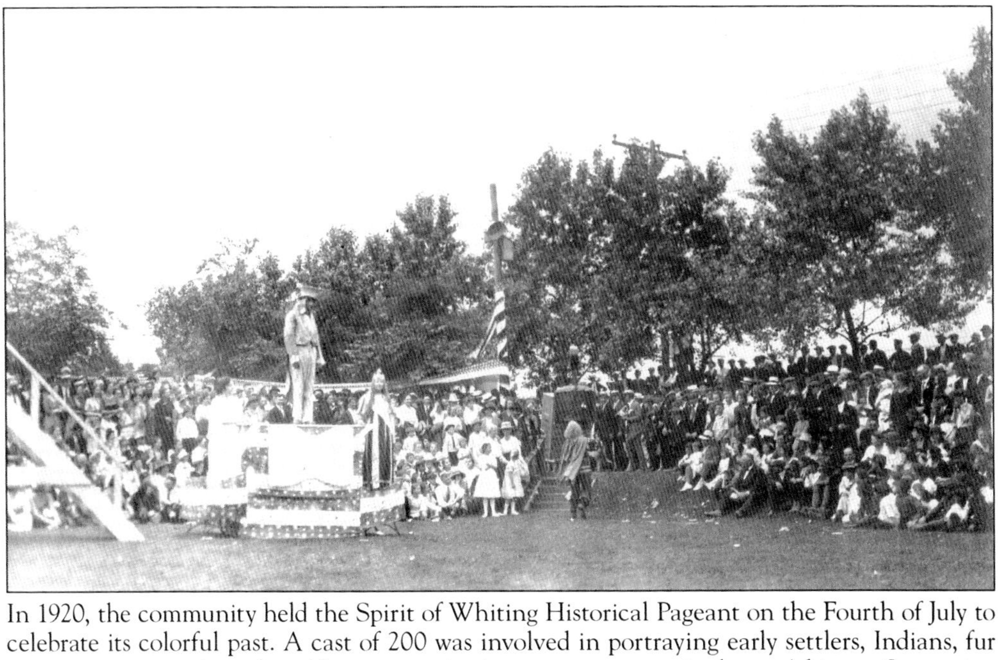

In 1920, the community held the Spirit of Whiting Historical Pageant on the Fourth of July to celebrate its colorful past. A cast of 200 was involved in portraying early settlers, Indians, fur trappers, war generals, and presidents, recreating important moments in the area's history. Supporting players were the Spirits of Industry, Opportunity, and Unity. (Whiting Historical Society.)

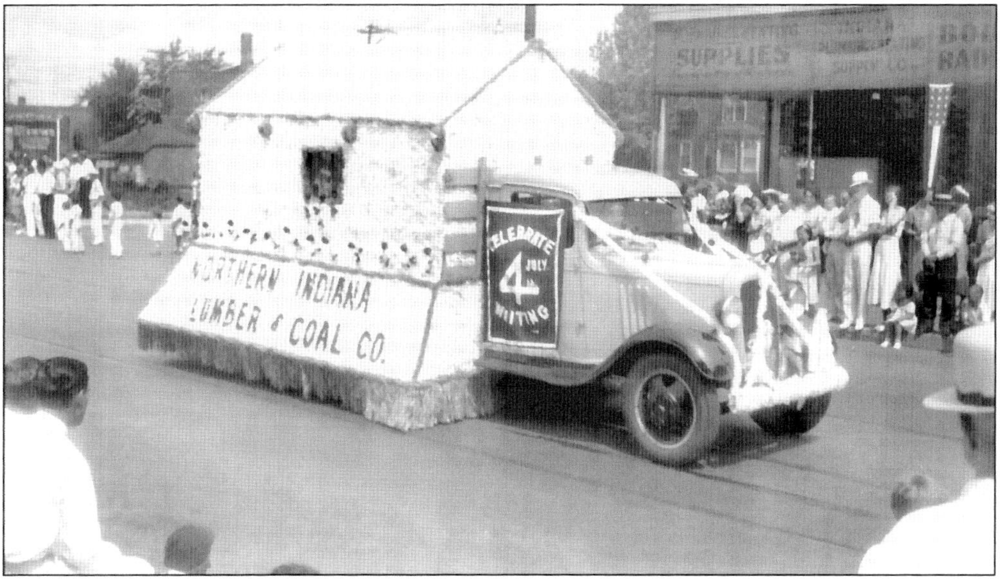

The annual Fourth of July parade is one of the oldest and most popular traditions in the Whiting-Robertsdale community. Large crowds gather along Indianapolis Boulevard and 119th Street every year to watch the marching bands, majorettes, floats, and other parade entries pay tribute to America. (Whiting Historical Society.)

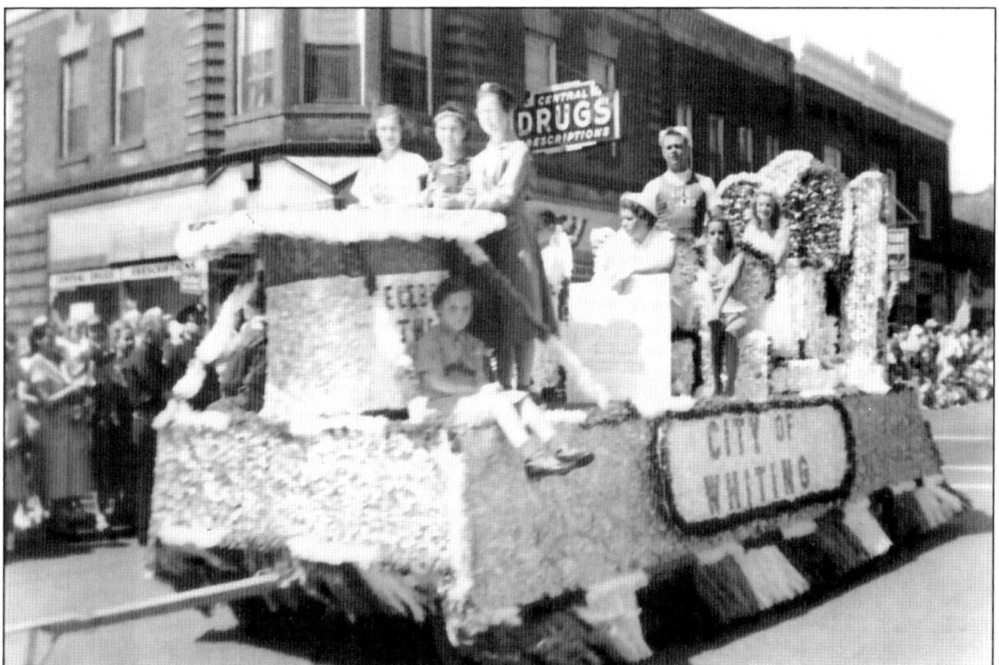

The annual Fourth of July parade makes its way down 119th Street. Note the businesses of days gone by in the background. (Whiting Historical Society.)

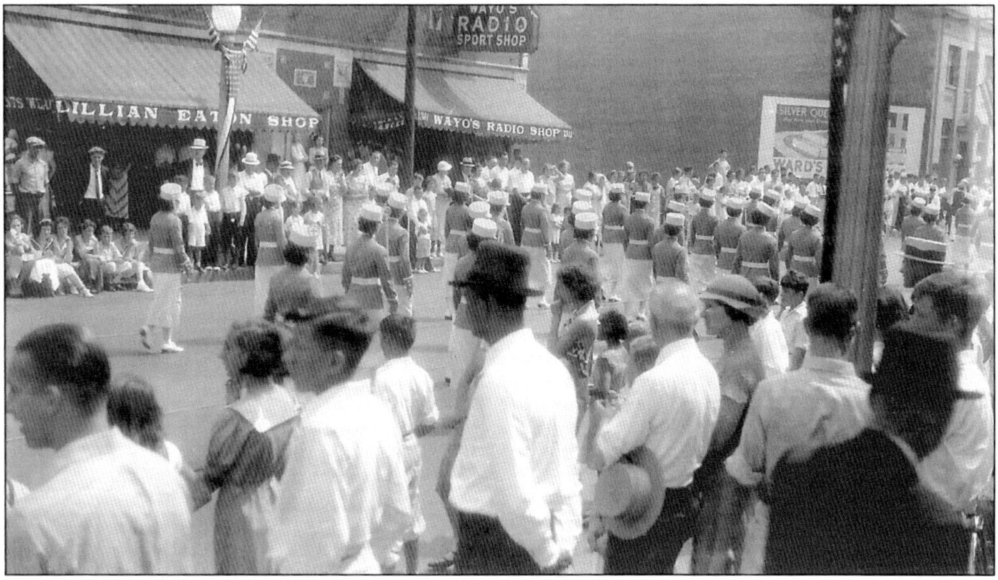

Whiting's Fourth of July parade is credited with being the oldest annual parade in the state of Indiana. (Vrabel family.)

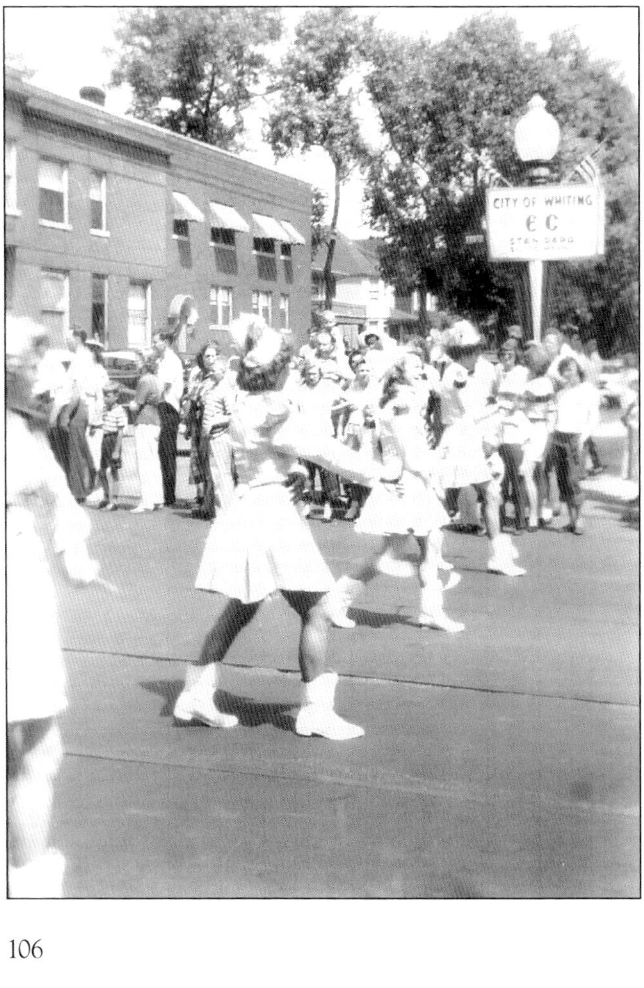

Majorettes march in unison in the Fourth of July parade. Note the "City of Whiting" sign and lamppost in the background. (Tkach family.)

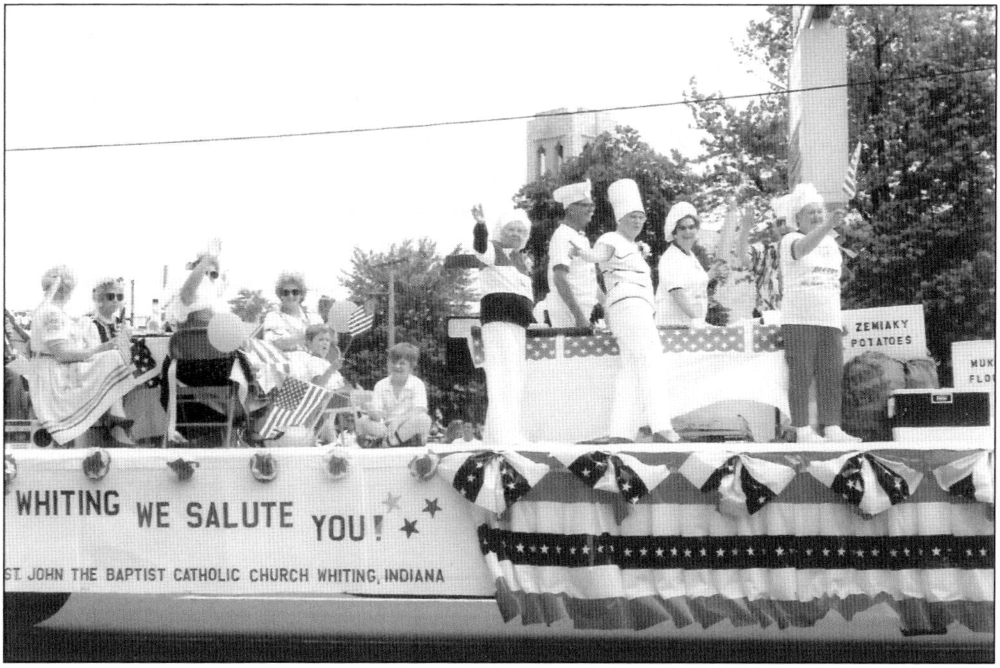

Community churches, organizations, and businesses put forth extra effort in decorating their floats in 1989, when the annual Fourth of July parade celebrated Whiting's 100th anniversary. (Saliga family.)

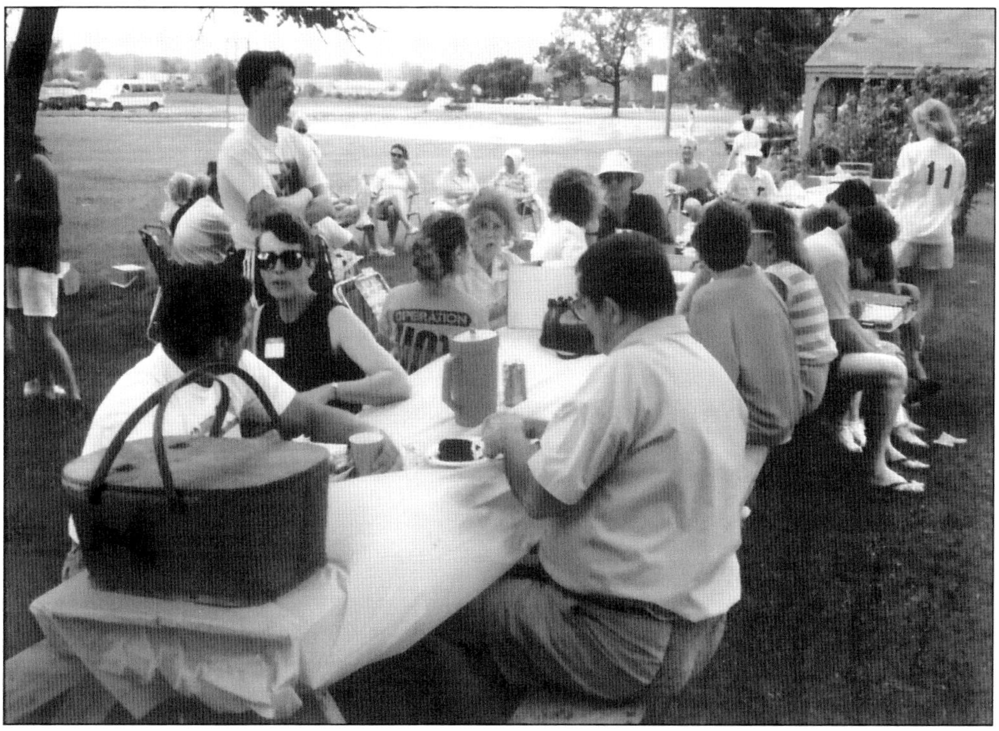

Family picnics and reunions are common occurrences at Forsythe Park, located on the north side of Wolf Lake in Robertsdale. (Vrabel family.)

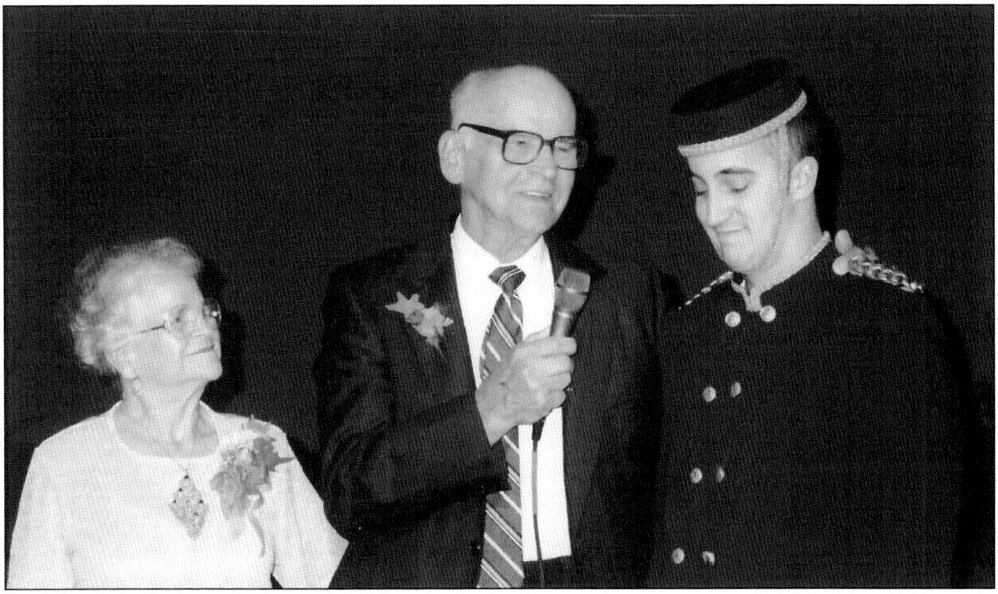

A special ceremony was held for the grand reopening of the Hoosier Theatre in 1997. Gert and Frank Sandrick pose here with their nephew John Sandrick, who wears the original usher suit used when the theater first opened. Frank and Gert met at the theater when he was working there as a young man. He ushered on the right side of the theater, so at the grand opening, John sat them on the right side of the theater and asked them to share how they met with the crowd. (Sandrick family.)

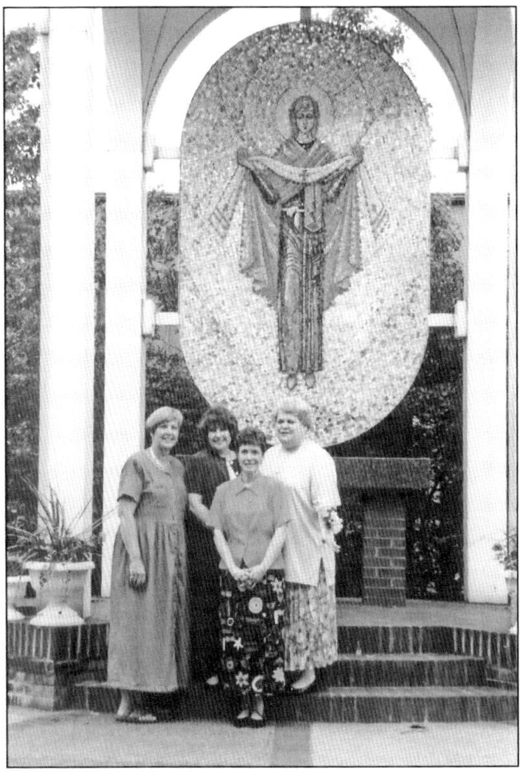

Gathered together to celebrate a milestone birthday, these lifelong friends pose in front of the Marian Shrine on Clark Street after mass at St. Mary's Church. They are, from left to right, Diane Tegosik Toth, Barbara Boncela Devitt, Janice Michalak Blandford, and Ruth Tkach. (Eck family.)

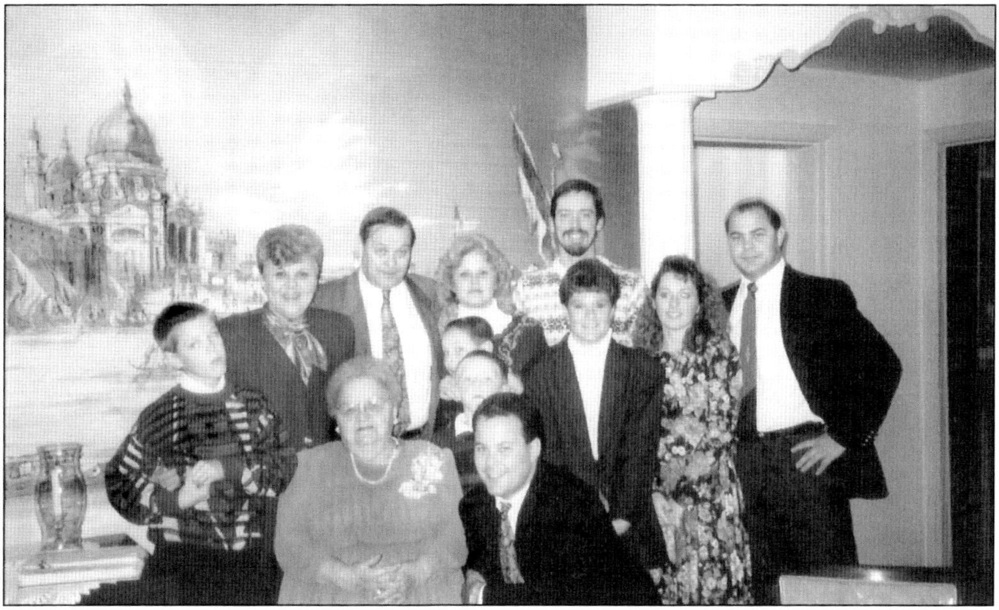

Anna Tkach is surrounded by family members at her 80th birthday party at Spiccia's Restaurant on Calumet Avenue. Spiccia's served the Whiting-Robertsdale area for 61 years and was a common destination for special celebrations such as this one. Note the lovely mural in the background. (Tkach family.)

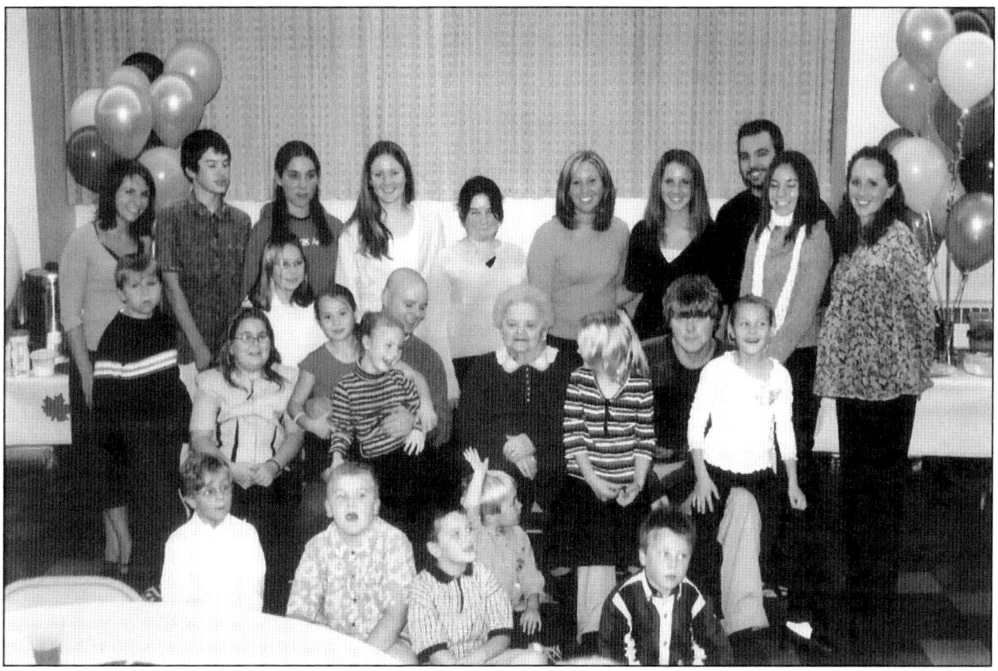

Family parties are also often held at the facilities at St. John's School. Here, Anna Tkach is surrounded by several of her great-grandchildren at her 93rd birthday celebration in the Mural Room. Along with many other Whiting and Robertsdale residents, she left behind family and friends in Slovakia to start a new life in America. She remained a lifelong resident of Robertsdale and taught her family quite a lot about faith, love, pride, and tradition. (Eck family.)

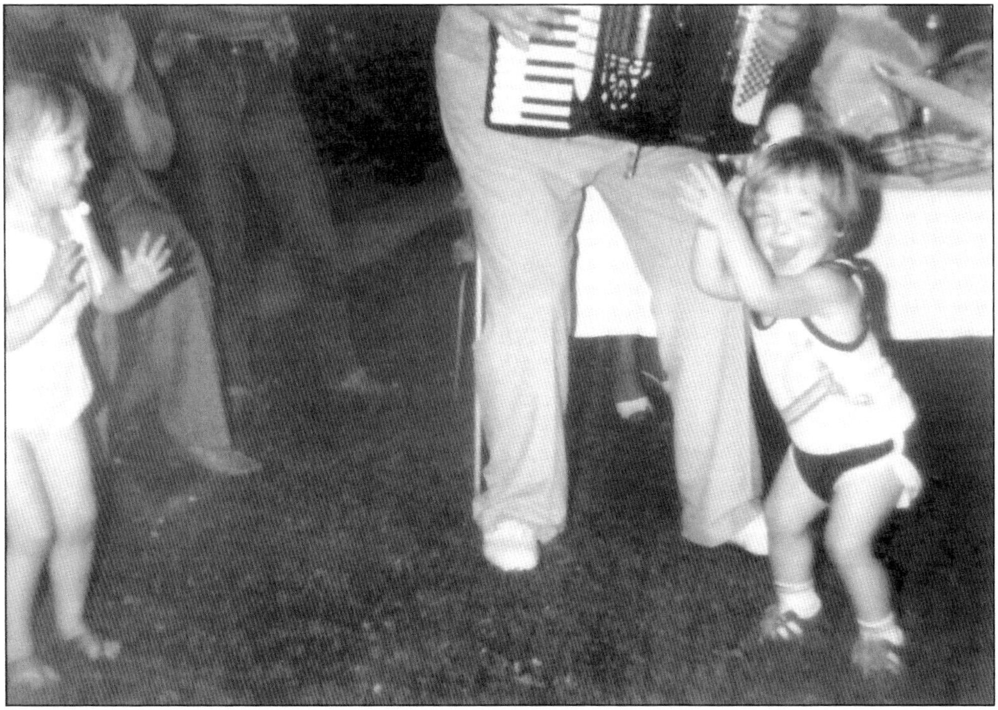

In true Slovak tradition, singing and dancing are always a part of family gatherings and are enjoyed by young and old alike. (Eck family.)

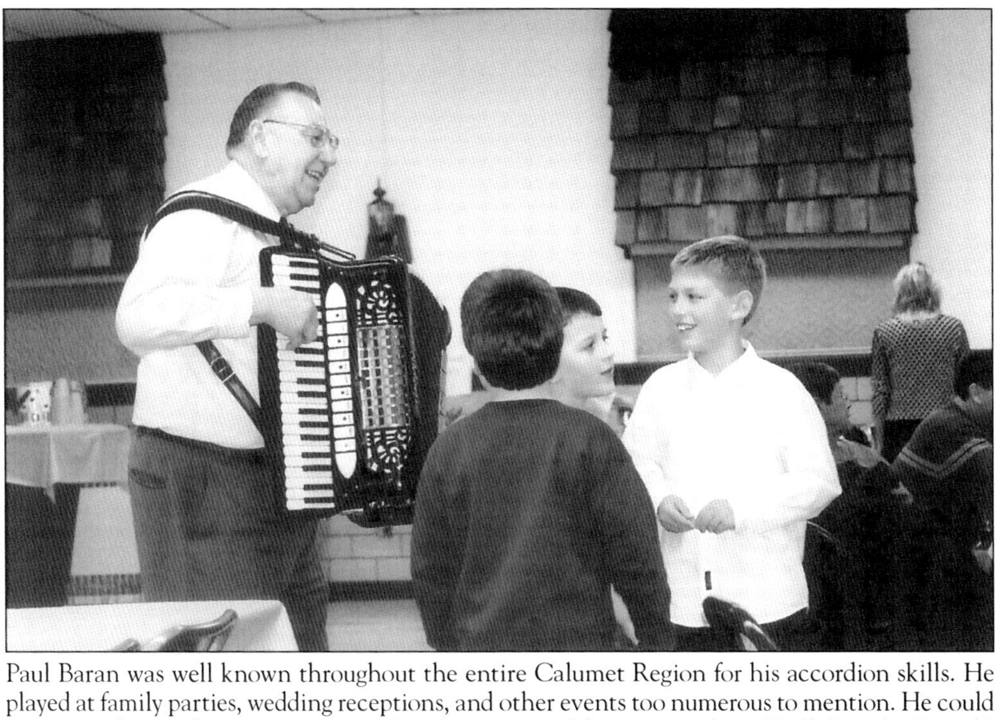

Paul Baran was well known throughout the entire Calumet Region for his accordion skills. He played at family parties, wedding receptions, and other events too numerous to mention. He could be counted on to liven up any event by playing crowd favorites such as "Roll Out the Barrel," "Take Me Out to the Ballgame," and "Let Me Call You Sweetheart." (Eck family.)

Eight

Evolving Yet Staying the Same

One of the most memorable events in the history of the Whiting-Robertsdale community was the fire at the Standard Oil refinery on August 27, 1955. It happened at 6:00 a.m. on a Saturday morning, startling many residents out of their beds. Oil tanks near the initial explosion caught fire and also began to explode. It was reported that the pillar of smoke rose four miles high. The fire was quickly contained but continued to burn for more than a week. Like other major tragedies, Whiting and Robertsdale residents will always remember where they were when the explosion happened and how it changed the community.

In 1985, Standard Oil changed its name to Amoco, and in 1998, it merged with British Petroleum (BP). The refinery is still the community's main employer and recently embarked on a multibillion-dollar project that created thousands of jobs during the construction phase and several permanent positions.

The Whiting-Robertsdale community has experienced many successes and challenges throughout its history, and it continues to build on those successes in a multiphase plan that is launching it into the future. The initiative, Whiting: Refining the Heart of Community, focuses on revitalizing and enhancing the key assets of the community, including the lakefront, small businesses, industry, neighborhoods, and events. Much change is underway, yet the past is still honored and preserved. Additionally, Whiting's Historic Preservation Commission is working to maintain the historical aspects of 119th Street with lighting, awnings, and color schemes consistent with how the main street looked years ago. The Whiting Community Center continues to offer many activities for residents, and the chamber of commerce continues to sponsor numerous events that draw more than 500,000 total visitors a year.

Neighborhood block parties and porch-decorating contests encourage pride in the community. Bike trails are being expanded, Oil City Stadium is home to competitive baseball teams, and the Lost Marsh golf course provides a great place to hit the links. Whiting-Robertsdale has long been a full-service community packed with stores, services, businesses, and recreational activities, and it continues to get better with age.

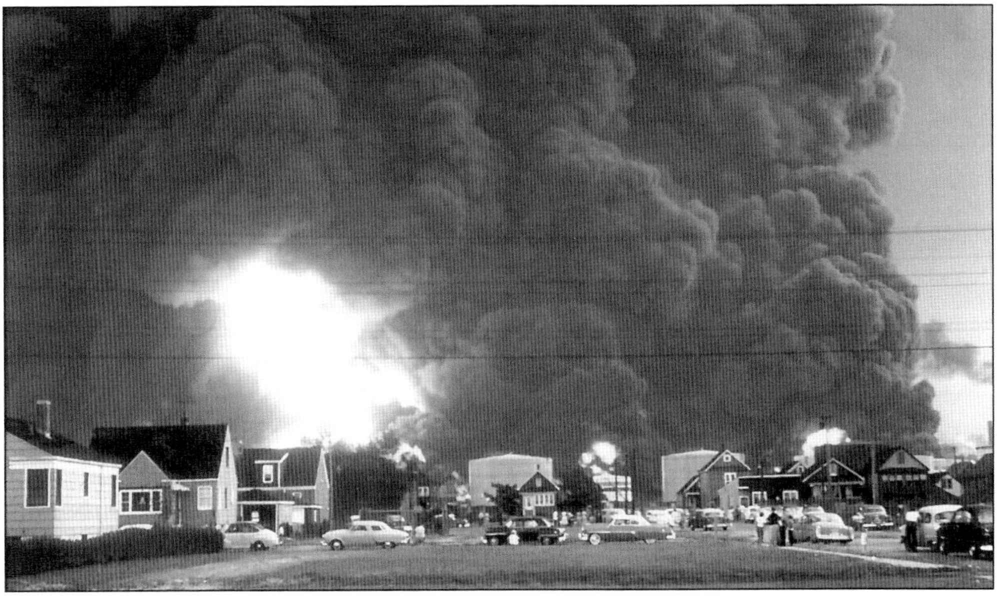

On August 27, 1955, an event long feared by Whiting residents became a reality when an explosion rocked the Standard Oil refinery. Gases and vapors had combined to form a volatile situation in a 252-foot-tall hydroformer. A series of explosions occurred, tearing apart the unit and sending dangerous fragments in all directions. A young child asleep in his bed was killed when a large piece of debris sliced into his bedroom, also severing the leg of his brother. The other casualty was a worker who died of a heart attack. Three homes were completely destroyed, 80 more were heavily damaged, and more than 450 families were evacuated. (Above, Whiting Historical Society; below, Whiting Public Library.)

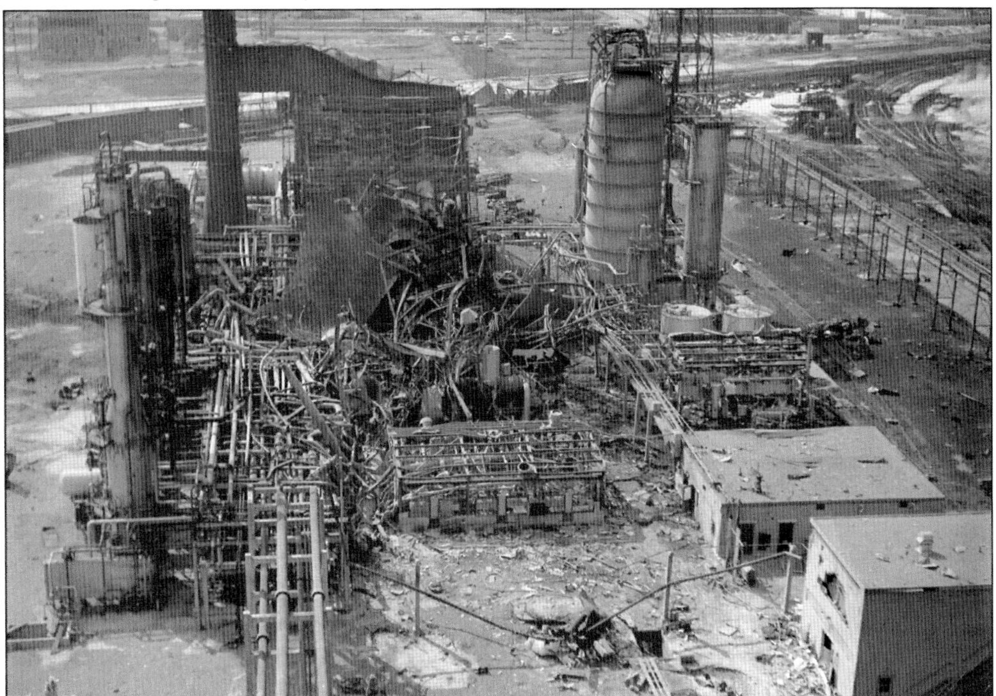

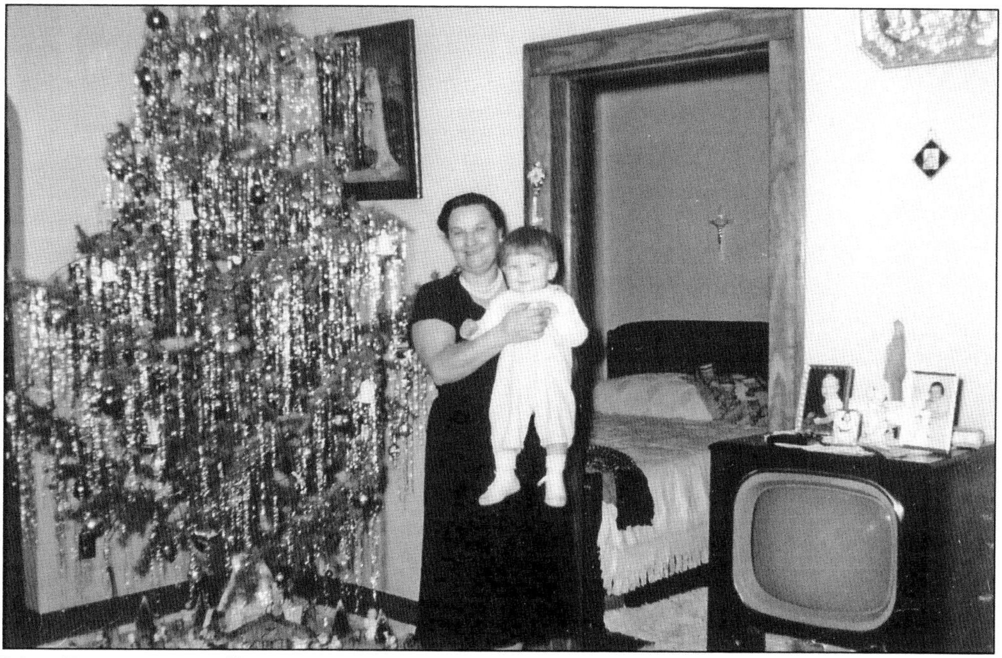

Mary Domasica proudly holds up her grandson, Greg Domasica, as they pose next to a tinsel-laden Christmas tree in the 1950s. (Domasica family.)

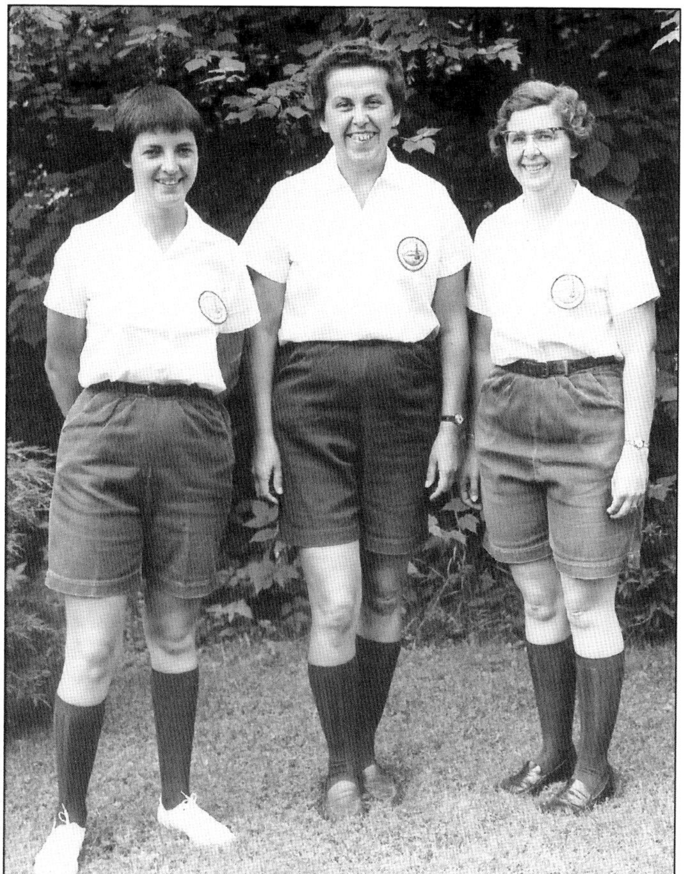

Robertsdale native Elaine Gehring spent 66 years in the Girl Scouts, starting as a Scout in 1936 and becoming a troop leader in 1945. She likes to boast that Whiting was the first city in Indiana to have a chartered Girl Scout council. Gehring is seen here on the right with other Whiting Girl Scout leaders Elaine Routh (left) and Ann Anthony (center). (Elaine Gehring.)

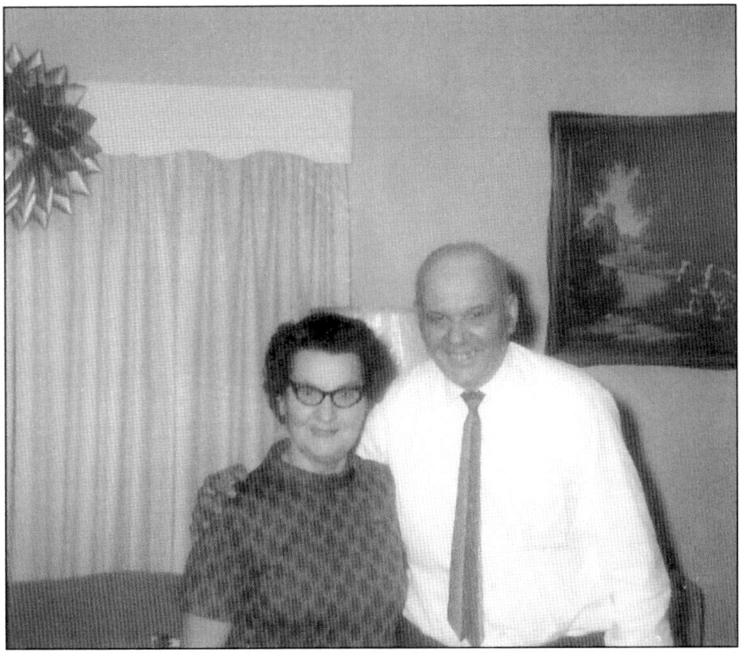

Mary and Mike Domasica brought their young family to the United States from Slovakia in the 1920s. Except when he was in his work gear at Standard Oil, Mike was known for always wearing a tie. (Domasica family.)

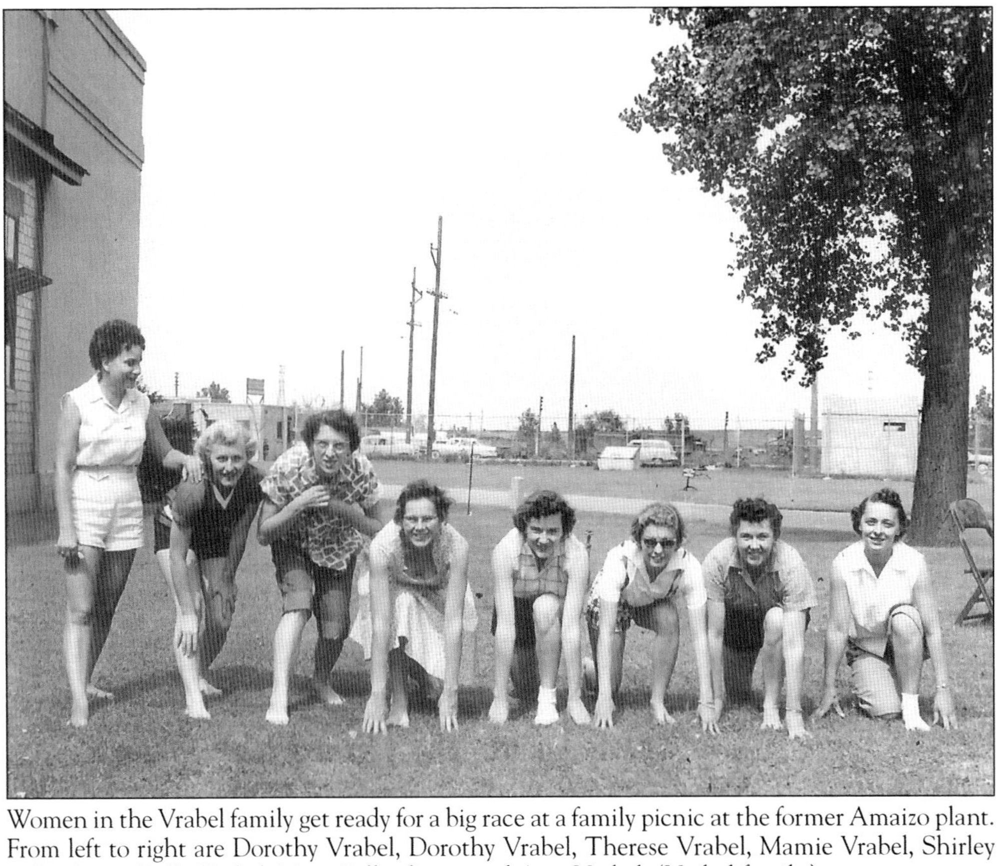

Women in the Vrabel family get ready for a big race at a family picnic at the former Amaizo plant. From left to right are Dorothy Vrabel, Dorothy Vrabel, Therese Vrabel, Mamie Vrabel, Shirley Polkinhorn, Della Vrabel, Mary Polkinhorn, and Ann Vrabel. (Vrabel family.)

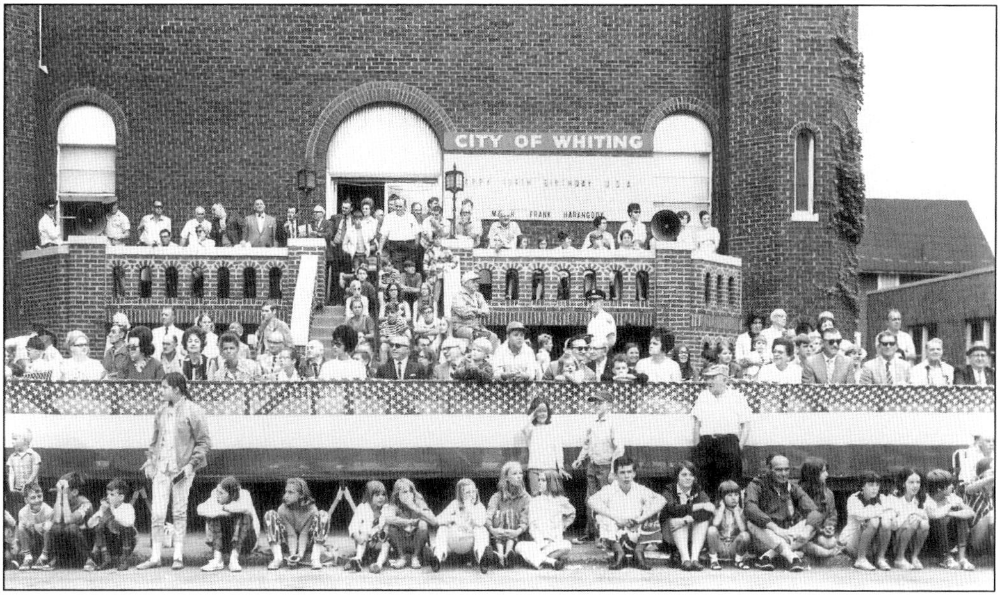

Whiting's city hall on 119th Street was once home to the Plymouth Congregational Church and was built in 1894. In 1927, the Indiana National Guard purchased it and converted it into an armory. In addition to being the hub of city government, it also serves as a great vantage point for watching Whiting parades. (Whiting Historical Society.)

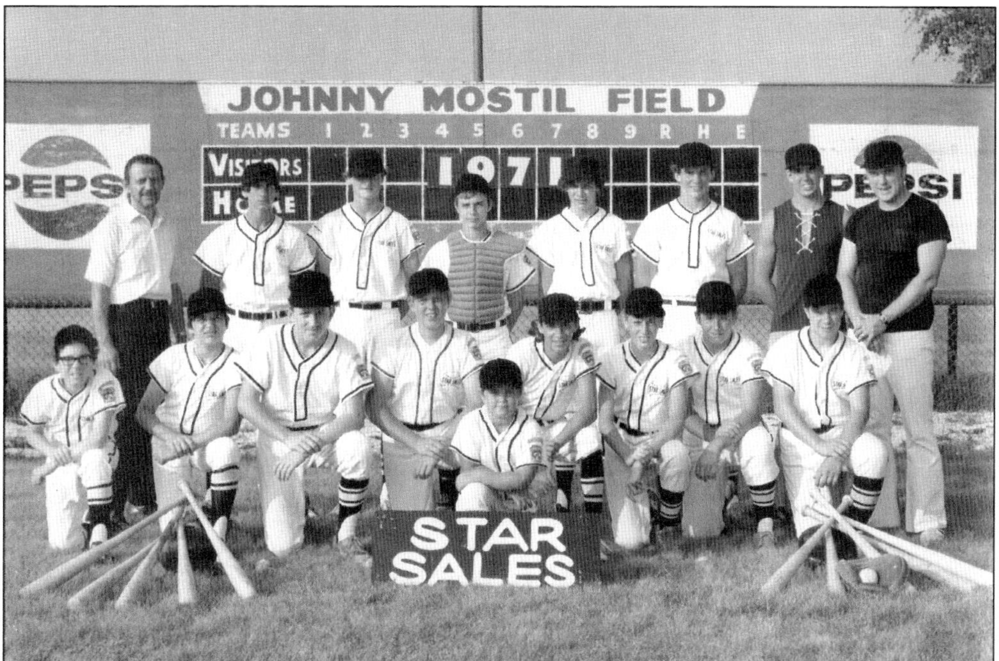

Whiting and Robertsdale have produced hundreds of young baseball players over the years. This group of players, sponsored by local business Star Sales, got a constant reminder of the possibility of making it big playing at Johnny Mostil Field. Mostil is a hometown boy who played for the Chicago White Sox and holds the distinct record of being the only center fielder to catch a foul ball in Major League Baseball history. (Mores family.)

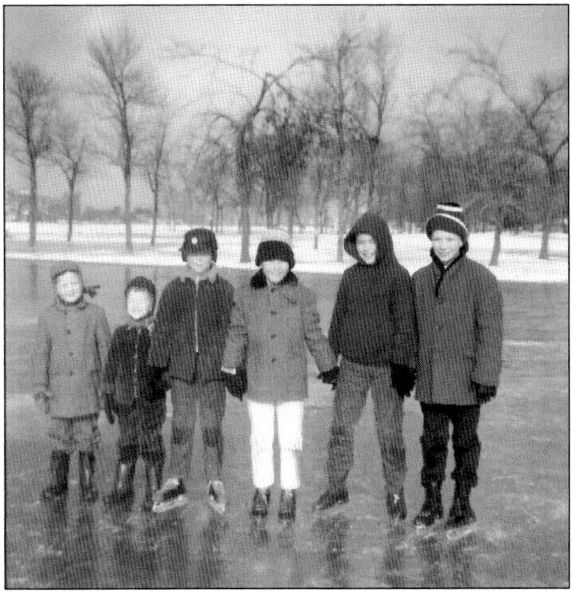

This group of young men are ready for a day on the ice at Wolf Lake in Forsythe Park. From left to right are Greg Mores, Tom Mores, David Mores, Greg Geffert, an unidentified boy, and Donald Novak. (Mores family.)

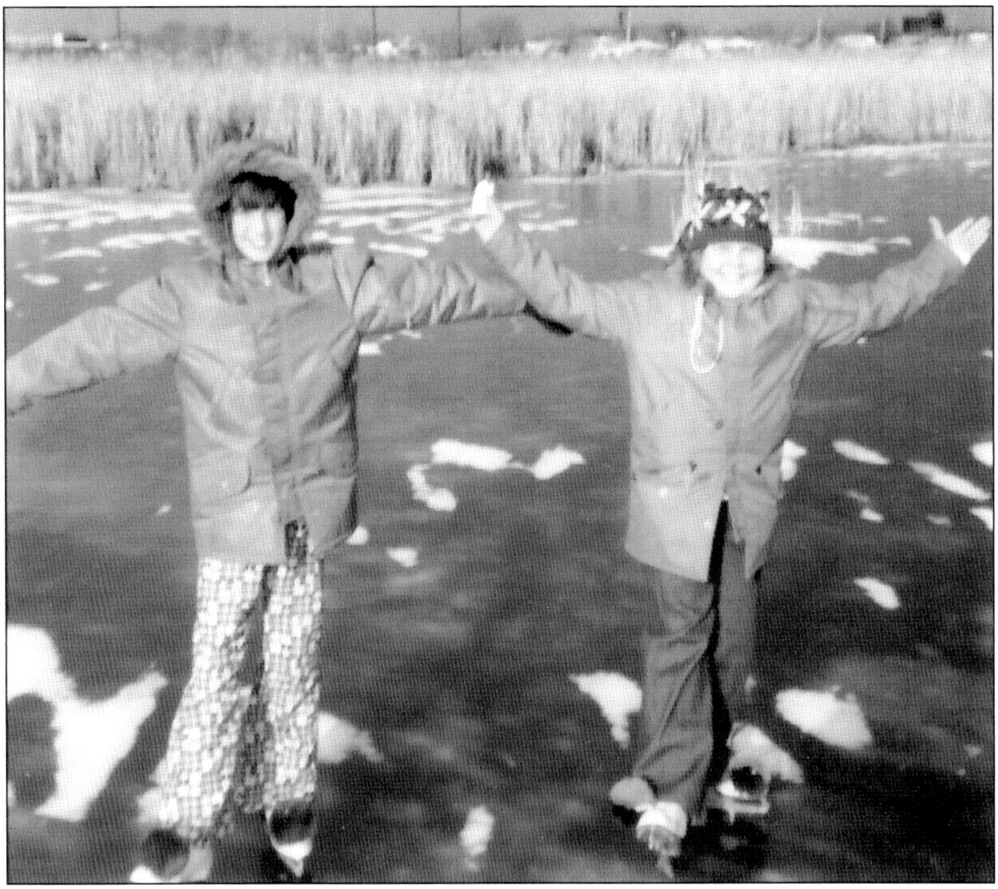

Karen Saliga (left) and Jennifer Domasica pose on George Lake. Remnants of the area's marshes can be seen in the background as well as part of the oil refinery. (Domasica family.)

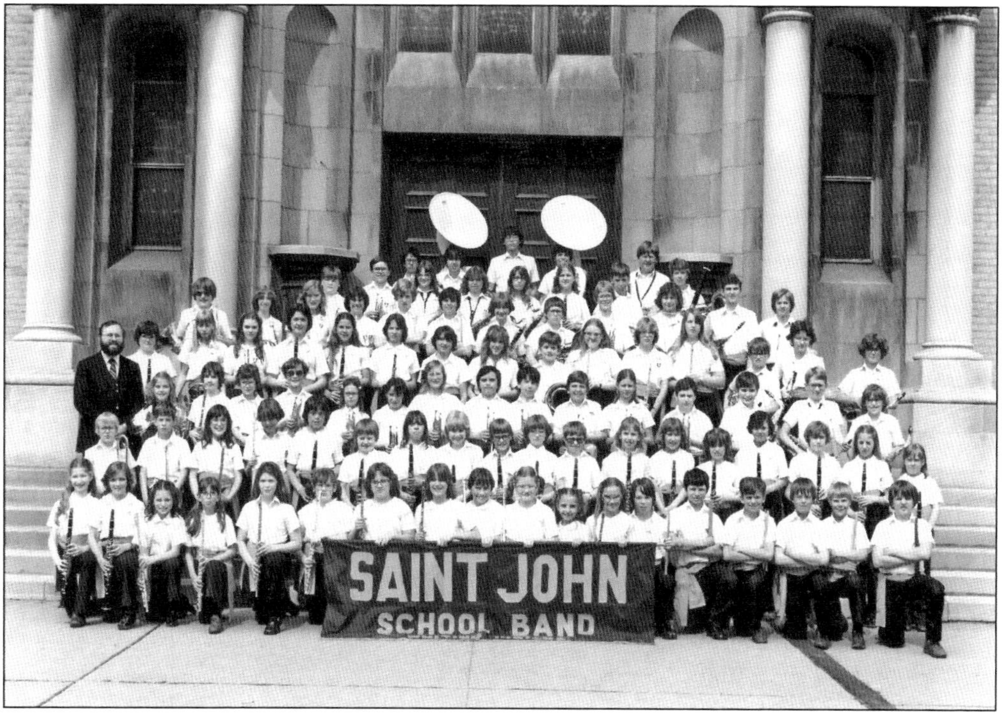

Nearly every organization in Whiting had its own band at one point. School bands were particularly popular, and as the size of the community grew, so did the size of the bands. Pictured here is St. John's school band in the 1970s. (Domasica family.)

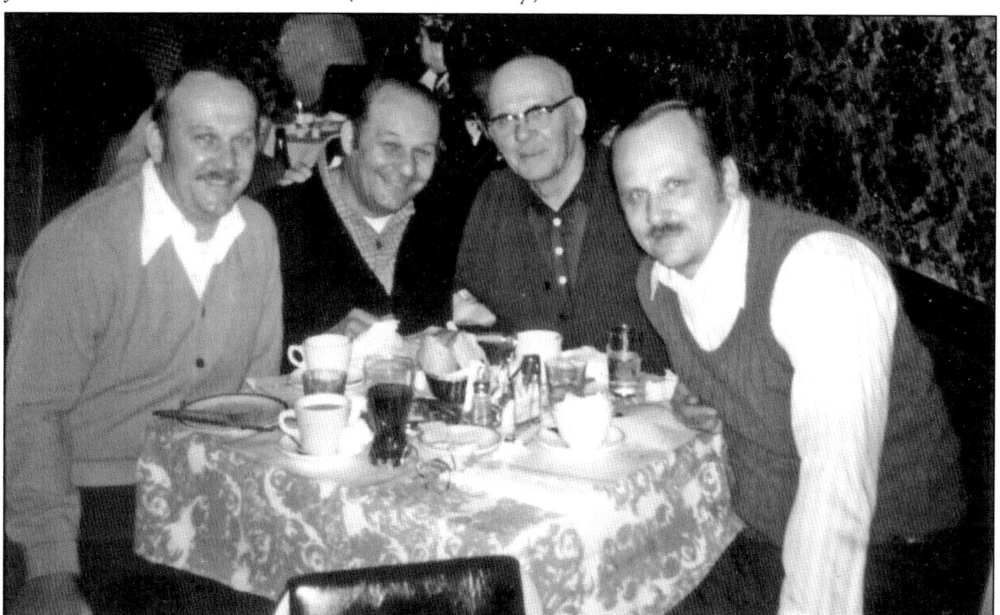

Seen here from left to right are longtime Whiting-Robertsdale residents Joe, Mike, Mike Sr., and Ed Domasica enjoying each other's company at a local restaurant. Mike Sr. brought his young family to the United States from Slovakia and worked for many years at Standard Oil. (Domasica family.)

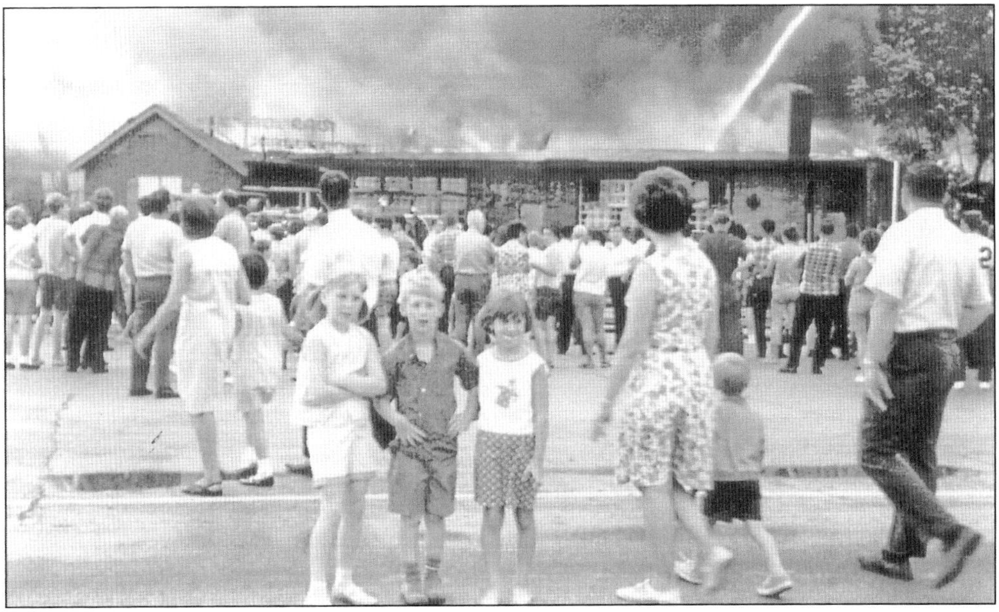

It was a sad day for the Madura family and the entire Whiting-Robertsdale community when Madura's Danceland was destroyed by fire on July 23, 1967. The venue offered live music four nights a week all year long, and many remember dancing the night away on its famous maple wood floor. The loss of Madura marked the end of a memorable era. (Vrabel family.)

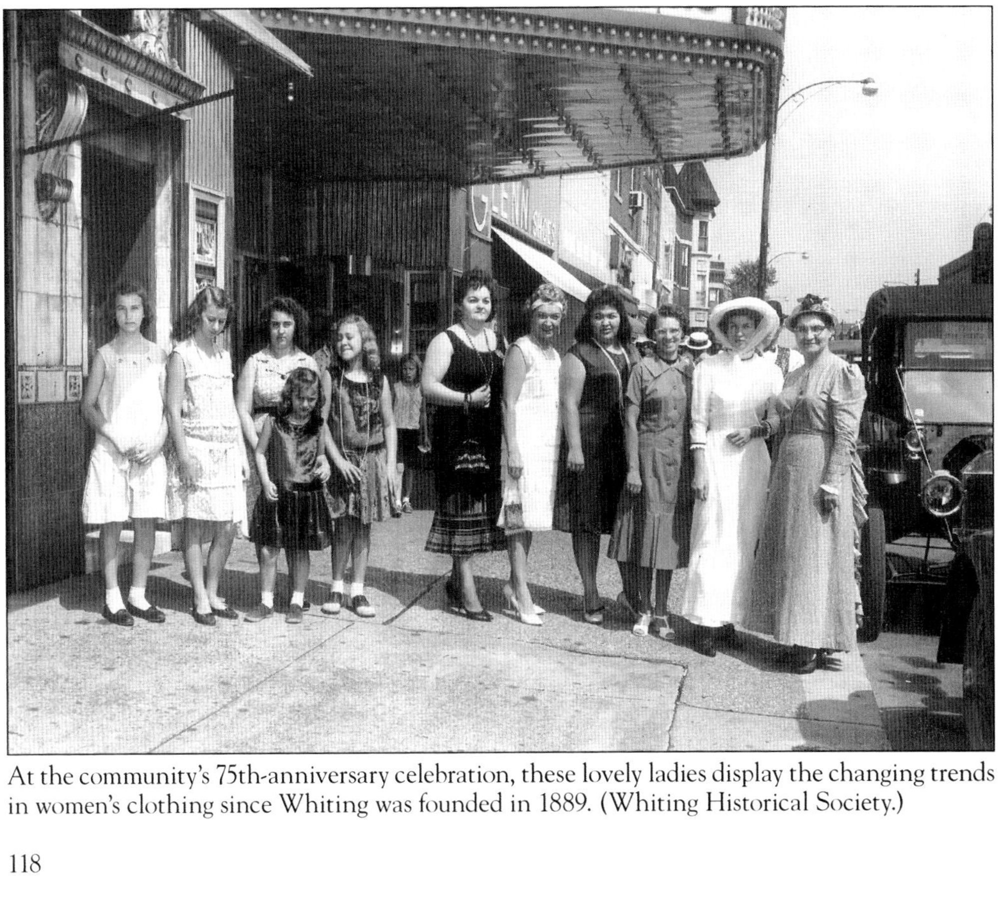

At the community's 75th-anniversary celebration, these lovely ladies display the changing trends in women's clothing since Whiting was founded in 1889. (Whiting Historical Society.)

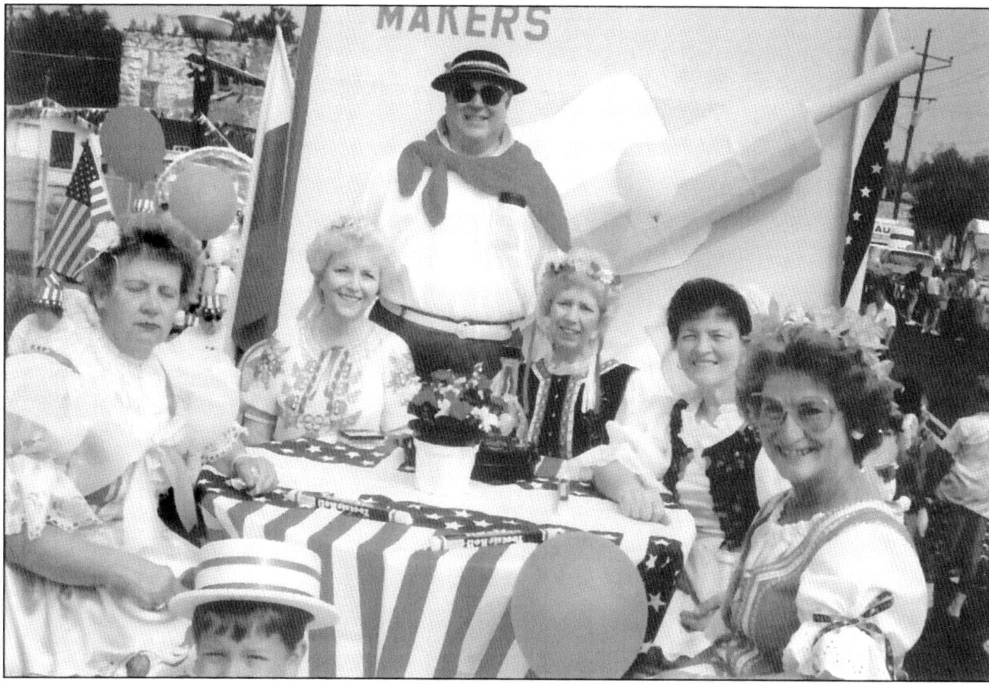

For many years, a group of St. John the Baptist parishioners gathered to make pirohis to sell at fundraisers. Pirohis, a true Slovak treat, are triangular-shaped pillows of dough with savory fillings such as potatoes and cheese that are smothered in butter. This contemporary group of pirohi makers gathered for Whiting's 100th-anniversary celebration. (Saliga family.)

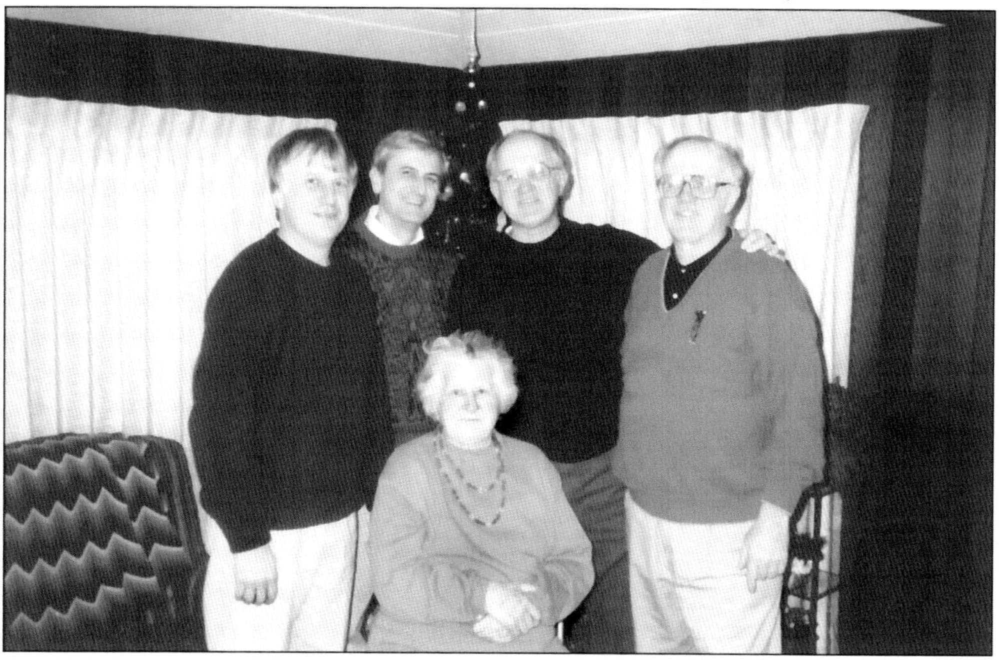

The Vrabel brothers and their mother, Ann, have seen many changes come and go in Whiting and Robertsdale during their many years there, but the values of family and togetherness have remained steadfast. From left to right are Ronald, George, Donald, and James. (Vrabel family.)

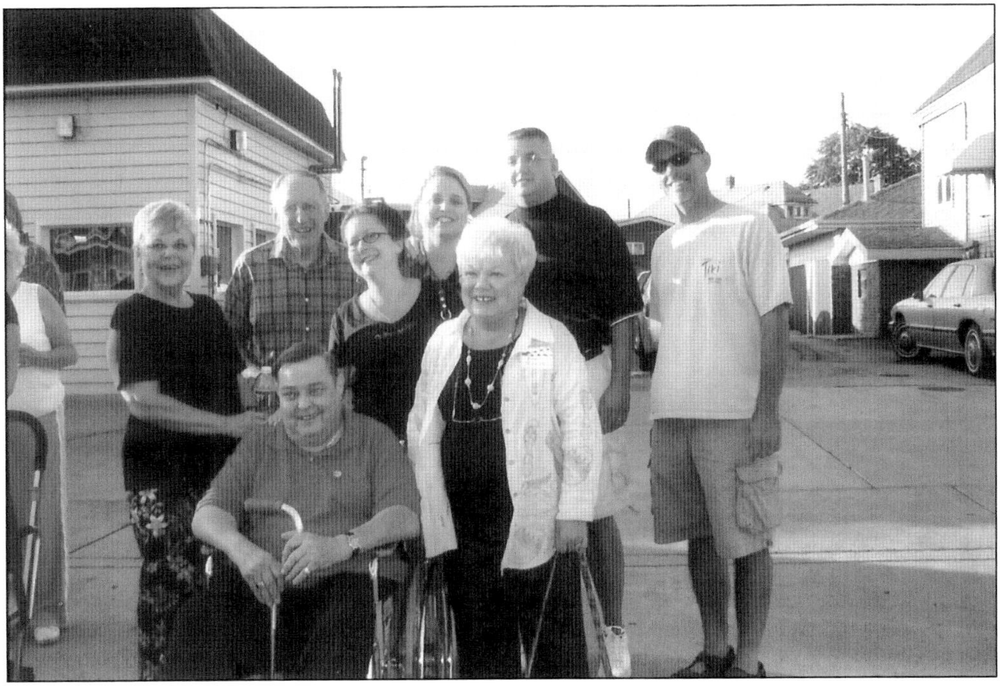

Former residents return every year for the summer festivities such as the Fourth of July parade and Pierogi Fest. Here, the Tatarek, Lentvorsky, Kutcka, and Eck families gather in front of their favorite spot by Poppen's Service Station to watch the Polka Parade, which kicks off the annual Pierogi Fest on the last weekend in July. (Eck family.)

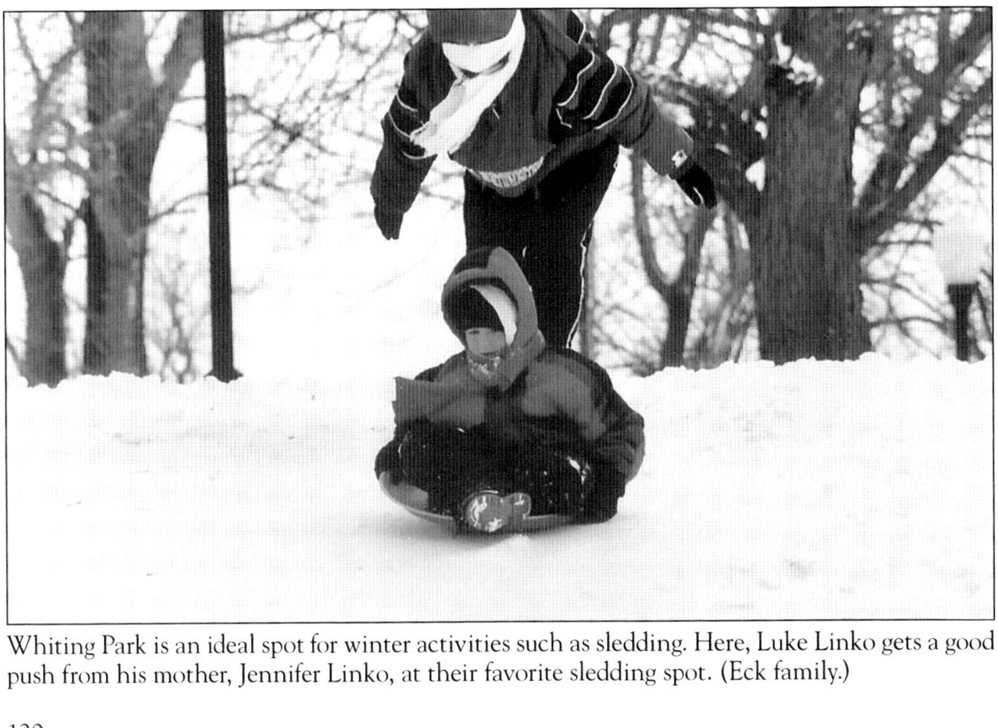

Whiting Park is an ideal spot for winter activities such as sledding. Here, Luke Linko gets a good push from his mother, Jennifer Linko, at their favorite sledding spot. (Eck family.)

Nine

Claims to Fame

One of Whiting-Robertsdale's greatest claims to fame has been the oil refinery that shaped the community and the numerous discoveries that have taken place there. In 2001, a memorial was unveiled at the BP Whiting Business Unit to commemorate the refinery's role in the founding and growth of the former Standard Oil Company of Indiana. The memorial is made of bricks from the wax refinery building and features the original company logo, the Amoco torch and oval logo, and an engraved plaque that reads, "In commemoration of the 112 years of operation of the Whiting Refinery, represented by the emblems shown here, as the Flagship Refinery of The Standard Oil Company of Indiana." Officials at the dedication acknowledged that the success of the Whiting refinery can be attributed to the generations of employees, their families, and local residents, who were loyal and dedicated to the facility and the products it made.

Whiting-Robertsdale is also well known for the many fine dining facilities that have operated there, particularly those at the Five Points intersection, where one could enjoy delicious cuisine at Vogel's, Levent's, Lundgren's, Margaret's Geneva House, the Hammond Beach Inn, and Phil Smidt's. The restaurants' specialties of fish, frog legs, and prime-cut steaks attracted many from Chicago as well as local residents. Famous diners included James Cagney, Babe Ruth, Bob Hope, Al Capone, and John Dillinger.

One of the community's newest claims to fame is the annual Pierogi Fest, a three-day festival that celebrates the ethnic heritage of the community. Starting out as a small street festival taking up a few blocks, it has expanded to an event that impacts the entire community and runs along several blocks of 119th Street, attracting more than 250,000 people each year.

Whiting-Robertsdale's proximity to Chicago, its natural and man-made assets, and its strong ethnic roots have positioned it well for the future. The community remains committed to preserving its past while embarking on major projects to prepare it for the future. There are definitely more great things to come in the "Little City by the Lake."

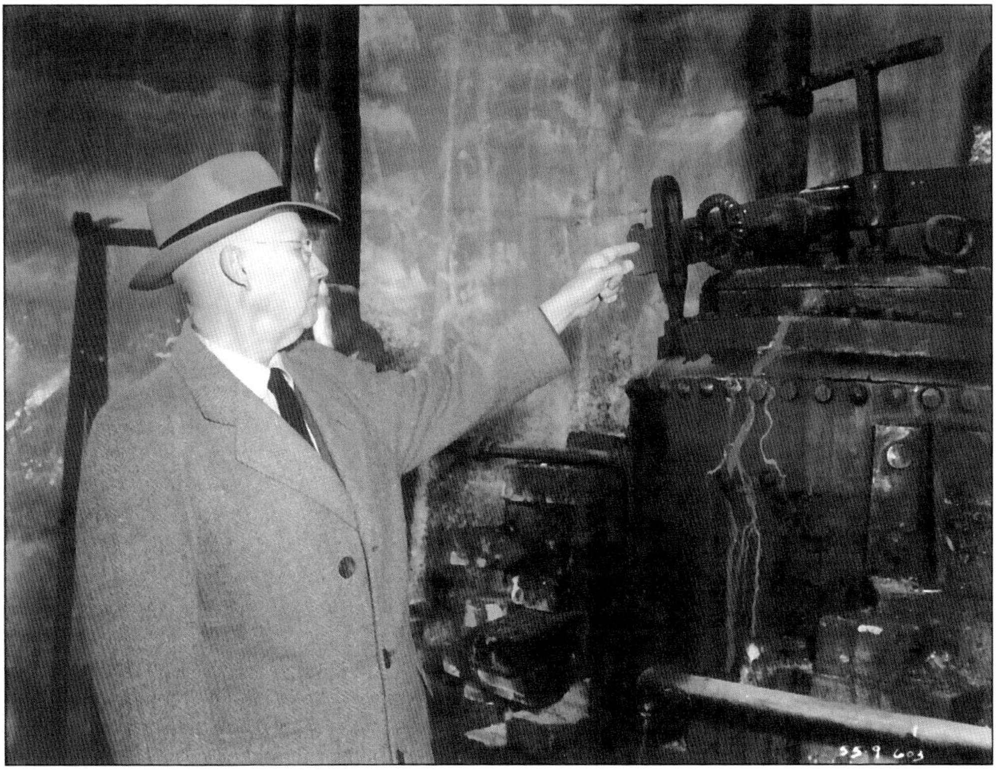

At a time when the automobile industry was growing rapidly and the demand for gasoline was increasing, Dr. Robert E. Humphreys, a chemist at Standard Oil's Whiting refinery, revolutionized the petroleum industry. After years of experimenting, he discovered the thermal cracking process, which made it possible to obtain a higher yield of gasoline from crude oil. (Whiting Public Library.)

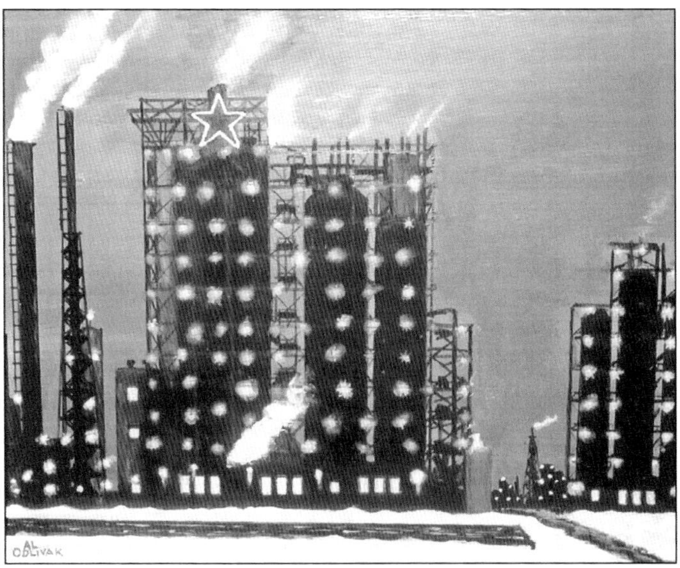

Those who grew up in the 1950s remember being loaded up into cars and driven through the industrial areas at Christmastime to see all the lights and decorations. One of the most famous was the star that hung from the "cat cracker" at the Standard Oil refinery. This painting of the star by Whiting resident Al Odlivak conjures warm and pleasant memories of a simpler time when companies could celebrate Christmas without controversy. (Odlivak family.)

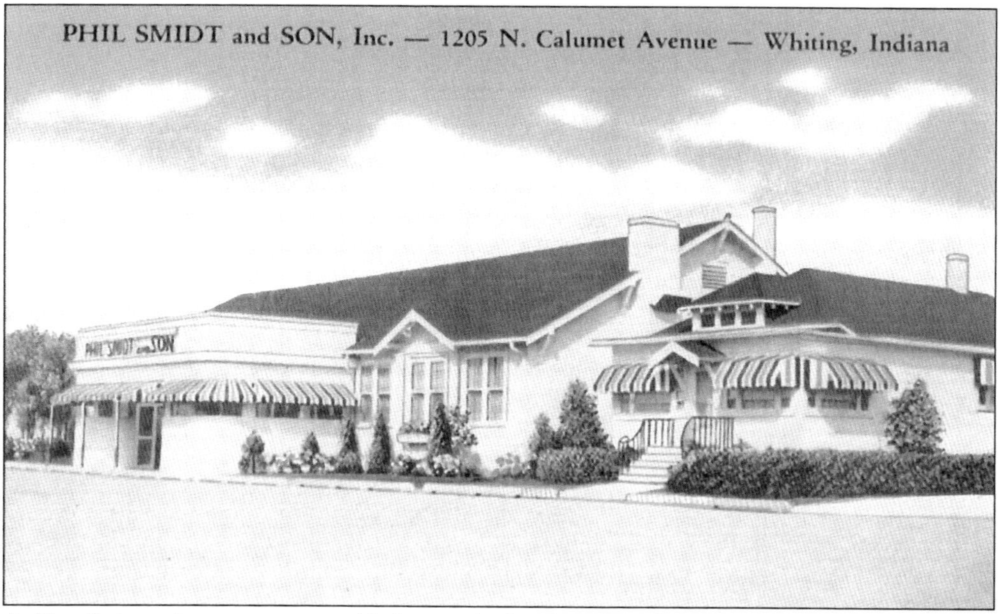

At Five Points, the intersection of Indianapolis Boulevard, Calumet Avenue, and 114th Street, several wonderful restaurants served specialties like lake perch and frog legs. Phil Smidt's was the longest-lasting restaurant, serving the area for 97 years before closing in 2007. In 1939, for $1.25, patrons could feast on all-you-can-eat perch, swimming in butter. (Specker Library, Calumet College of St. Joseph.)

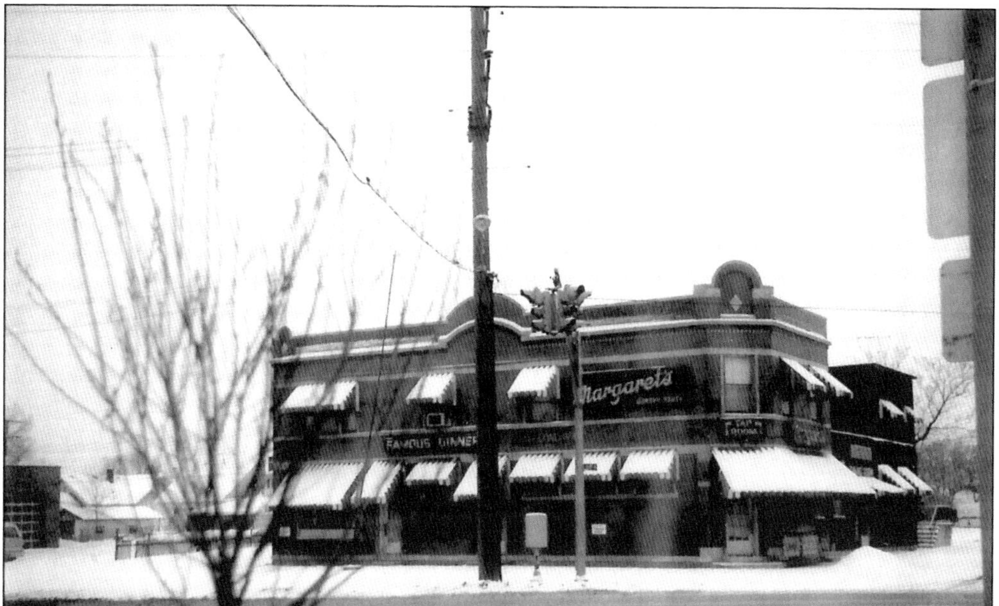

Margaret's Geneva House was another popular restaurant at the Five Points intersection. Margaret Winkelried Carroll, the proprietor, did much of the cooking herself. Her parents opened the Geneva House in 1913, bringing new touches not yet seen in other local fish houses, such as a real floor, white tablecloths, and European-style service. Much of Margaret's business came from Chicago. (Whiting Public Library.)

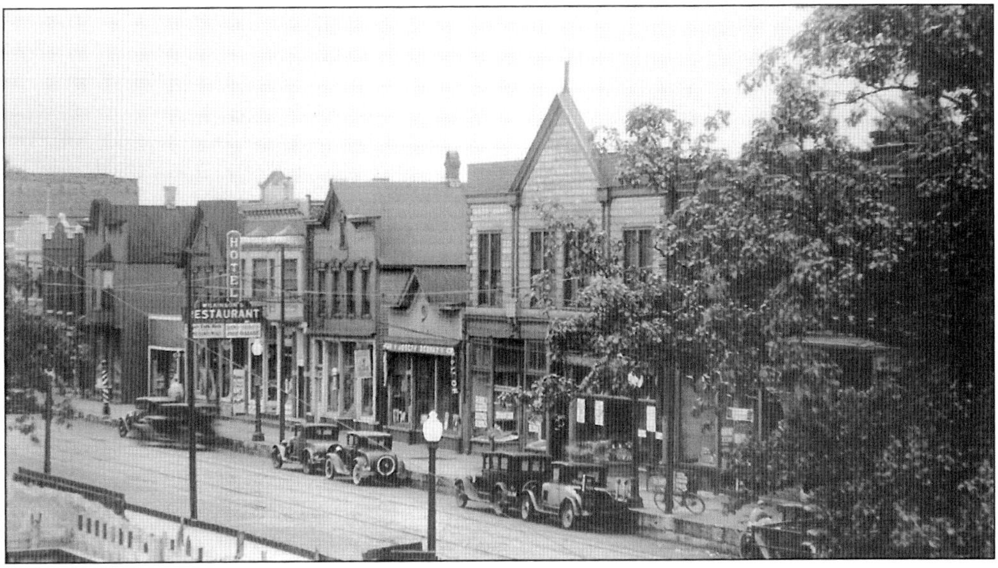

Whiting and Robertsdale have three main thoroughfares: Indianapolis Boulevard, which takes travelers to and from Chicago; Calumet Avenue, running north and south; and 119th Street, the main street housing the community's business district. The names of shops and businesses have changed many times through the years, but 119th Street still serves as the heart of the community and remains a charming and quaint place to dine, shop, and visit. (Sandrick family.)

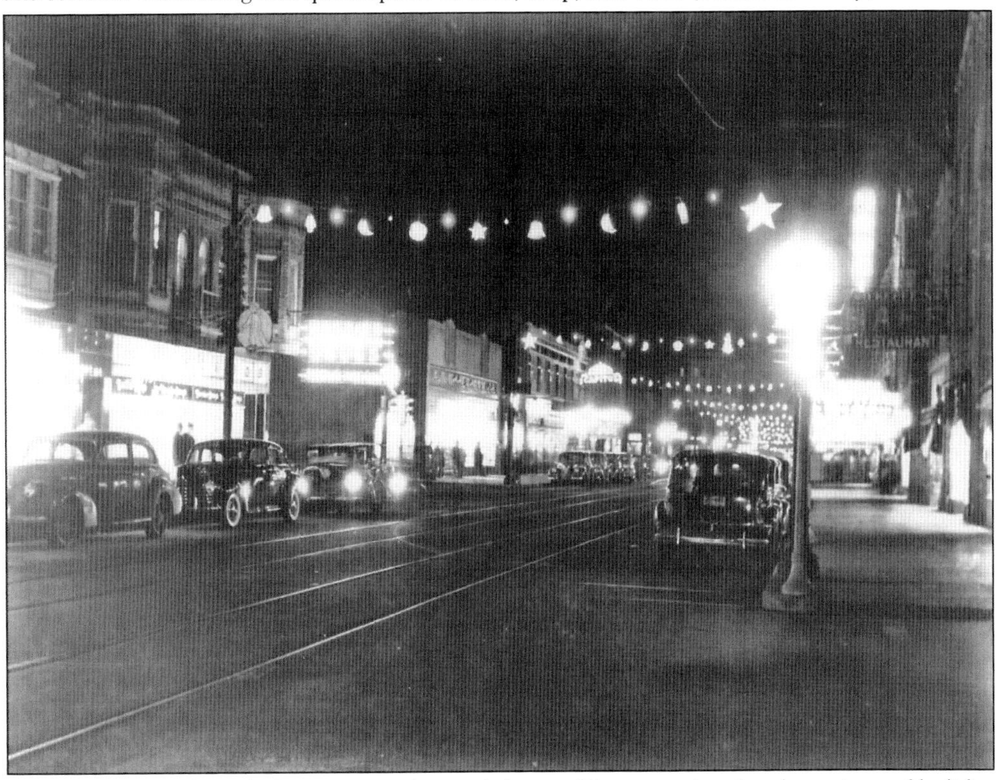

The quaintness of 119th Street was enhanced during Christmastime by the strings of holiday lights that were traditionally strung across it. (Karen Holmes.)

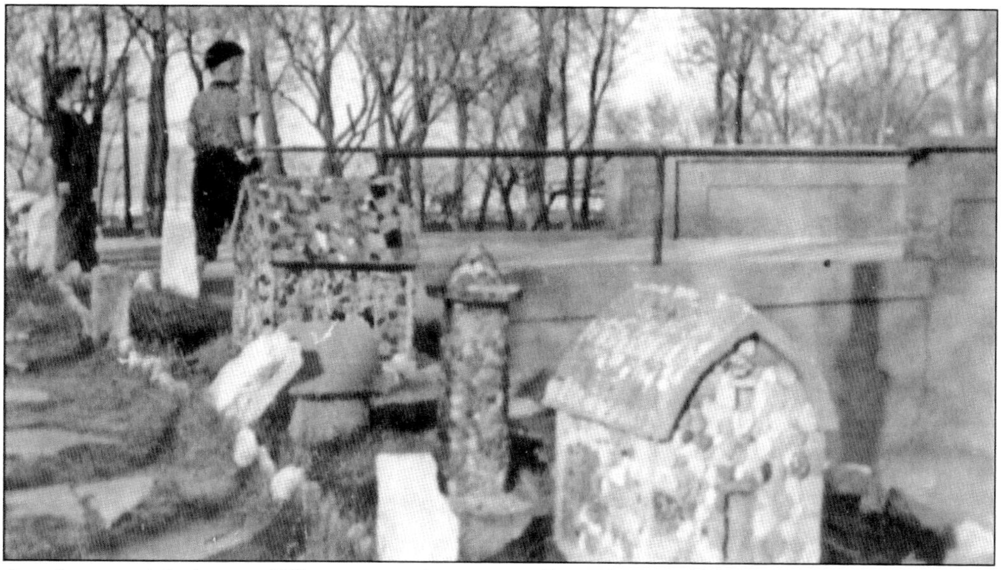

Another special place in Whiting was the stone village that could be found on the hillside at Whiting Park. There is a bit of mystery surrounding its origins, but many believe it was built to resemble a typical Slovak village. It consisted of several concrete houses decorated with stones and smooth pieces of glass, as well as a barn, a silo, and a lighthouse. Visiting the houses was an after-church event for many families on Sunday. The houses have since disappeared, but remnants of their foundations are still scattered on the park's hillside. (Sandrick family.)

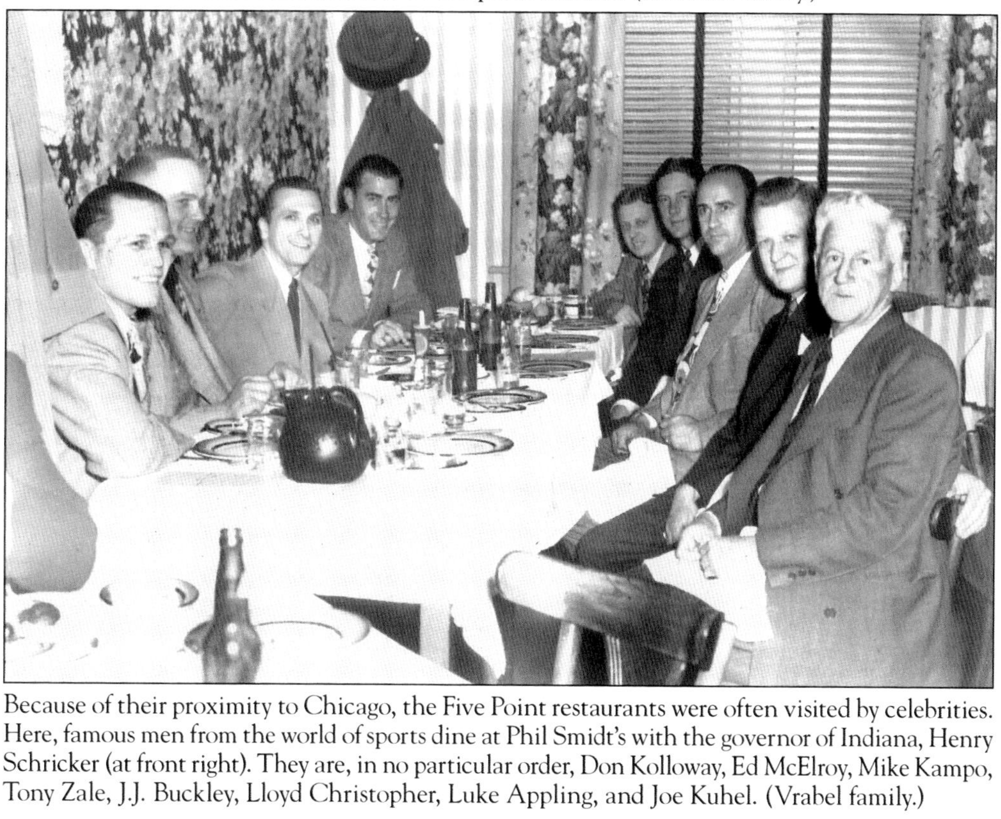

Because of their proximity to Chicago, the Five Point restaurants were often visited by celebrities. Here, famous men from the world of sports dine at Phil Smidt's with the governor of Indiana, Henry Schricker (at front right). They are, in no particular order, Don Kolloway, Ed McElroy, Mike Kampo, Tony Zale, J.J. Buckley, Lloyd Christopher, Luke Appling, and Joe Kuhel. (Vrabel family.)

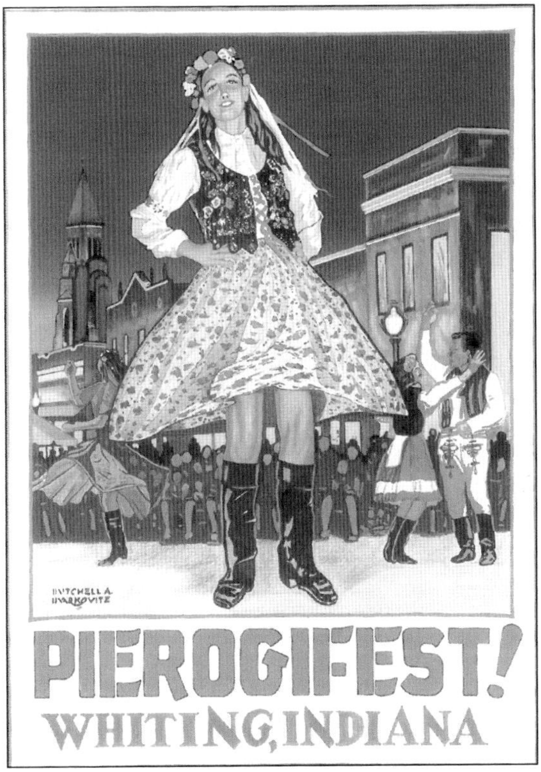

Every year on the last weekend in July, the Whiting-Robertsdale Chamber of Commerce presents Pierogi Fest, a three-day celebration of the community's Slavic heritage. Pierogi Fest has grown from a small community festival into one that draws more than 250,000 visitors each year and offers events such as folk dancing, Eastern Bloc Jeopardy, and pierogi-eating contests. Local artist Mitch Markovitz created this rendering of a Slovak dancer in costume in honor of the event. (Whiting-Robertsdale Chamber of Commerce.)

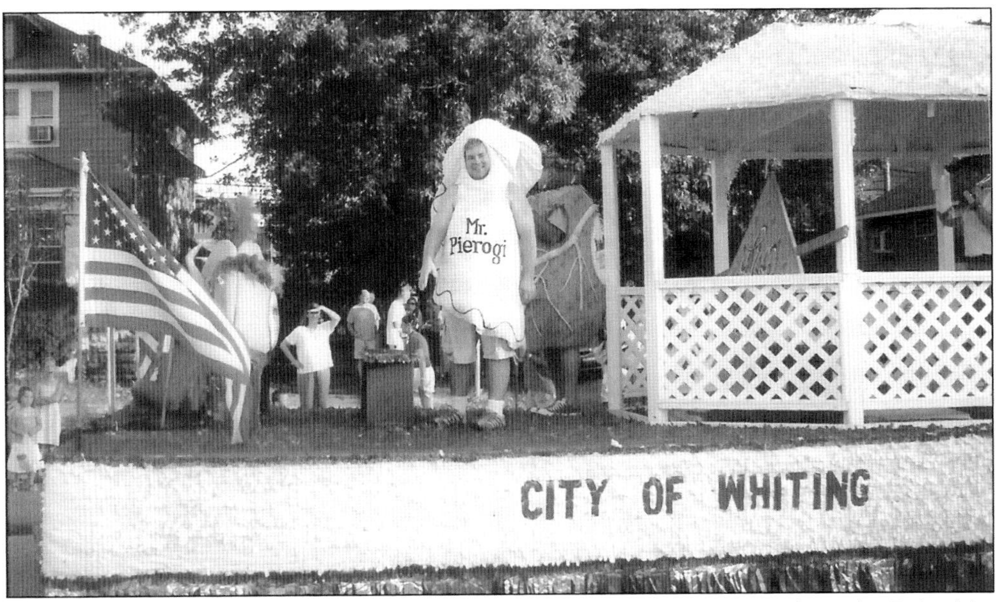

The fun-filled Polka Parade kicks off Pierogi Fest and features entries such as the Babushka Brigade, the Precision Lawnmower Drill Team, the Buscias, and, of course, Mr. Pierogi, the master of ceremonies. Thousands of pierogies are served over the course of the three-day weekend, along with a wide variety of other Eastern European cuisine, such as *halupki*, Polish sausage, and *pazckis*. The festival has received national and international coverage for its crazy antics and delicious ethnic cuisine. (Eck family.)

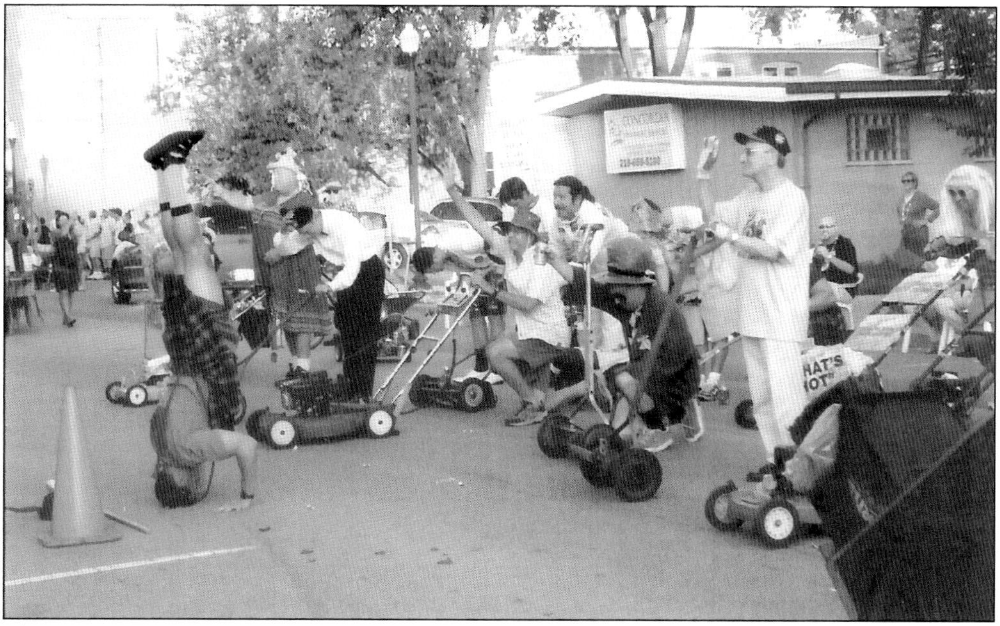

The Precision Lawnmower Drill Team is one of the most popular and fun-filled entries in the parade. They are seen here in all their glory as they stop to send a special greeting to their longtime friend Donald Poppen that includes an impressive headstand and kilt unveiling. (Eck family.)

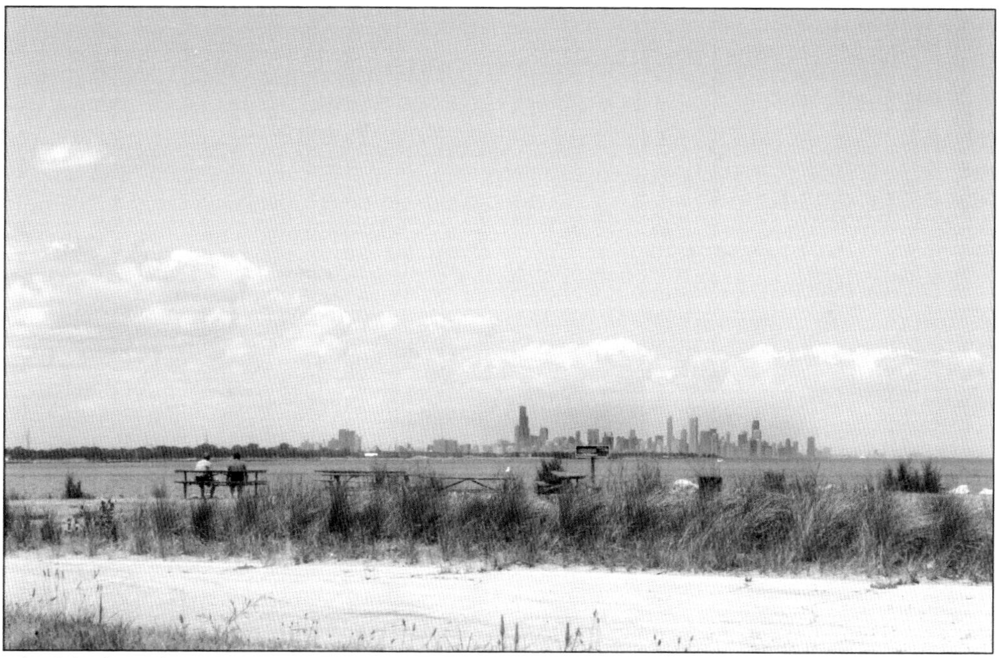

The lakefront location is what attracted Standard Oil to the Whiting-Robertsdale area more than 100 years ago, and it is still one of the community's most valuable assets. Looking toward the future, the community has embarked on a multiphase enhancement project that includes new housing near the lake and revitalization of the park and the lakefront. Future plans include a two-tiered boardwalk along the lakeshore, a new nature area, boat harbor renovations, and a Whiting-Robertsdale Historical Museum. (Eck family.)